POWERS OF THE MIND

POWERS OF THE MIND

John and Anne Spencer

New York

Publisher's Cataloging-in-Publication Data
Spencer, John, 1954–
    Powers of the mind / John and Anne Spencer. — 1st ed.
      p. cm. — (True life encounters)
      Includes bibliographical references.
    ISBN: 1–57500–028-8
    1. Parapsychology.   2. Psychokenesis.   I. Spencer, Anne, 1956–
II. Title.
    BF1031.S74 1999   133.8
                                QBI99-216

TV Books, L.L.C.
1619 Broadway, Ninth Floor
New York, NY 10019
www.tvbooks.com

Interior designed by Rachel Reiss
Manufactured in Canada

Contents

On that day when science begins to investigate non-physical phenomena, it will make greater progress in a decade than in all the centuries it has existed.

—Nikola Tesla, physicist

Introduction

In 1972 a company based in London was proudly demonstrating its latest computer. It weighed one ton and took twenty-one tons of cooling equipment to keep it functioning. It could play chess and learn from its mistakes against particular players. The computer was attracting public attention with a state-of-the-art graphics screen. This was the time of the Apollo Moon landings, so the black and white screen displayed a small picture of the Lunar Module, moving left to right across the screen. With the press of a button, the Lunar Module would begin descending. If the operator hit the button at the right moment, the Module landed safely; if not, it crashed.

Now, only twenty-six years later, that sort of computing power can be purchased for just a few pounds. The graphics capabilities on "game computers" are approaching the clarity of television images. The computing and storage power of modern computers, which are a fraction the size and cost of the 1972 model, is phenomenal. The development rate of computers is so rapid that machines are virtually obsolete even as they are installed in offices, shops and homes.

Yet, despite their technological sophistication and computing power, the most efficient and advanced machines, at the present time at least, are moronic compared to the human brain.

The human brain can store massive amounts of data in a huge and easily accessible memory. This storage is selective; information can be retrieved when needed but does not clutter up everyday thinking when not needed. The brain learns and grows from its learning. It can do complex calculations, access the environment and make selective decisions. It can appreciate arts and sciences. To some degree it is self-repairing, and in some cases is capable of initiating back-ups or new areas of operation if certain areas are damaged.

But those are only the brain functions we currently understand. We know the brain can do these things, and, to some degree, understand how it does them. Yet there are some brain processes whose mechanism or depth of complexity we have yet to comprehend. The most obvious example is dreaming.

Occasionally a brain-damaged person exhibits extraordinary talents; "calendar counters," for example, can make instant calculations and name the day of the week for any given date over a several thousand year span. There are many other unusual feats that the human brain seems capable of. There have been claims of extrasensory perception (ESP), telepathy, premonition, dowsing, mediumship and much more. The processes of the mind seem to be able to heal the body, or damage it and even destroy it, just by sheer force of will. Their manifestation is often spontaneous and therefore difficult to study. But reports from all around the world of these strange phenomena seem to indicate that these special powers are an innate aspect of human thinking.

Some unexplained phenomena, such as ghosts, poltergeists, the ability to move objects without physical contact by sheer force of mind power, may also originate in the human mind. This extraordinary range of mind powers is the subject of this book; these faculties, generally encompassed by the term "paranormal," are the territory we shall explore.

If there is one change in public perception that has characterised the 1990s it is the increasing acceptance of the paranormal. Subjects such as alien abductions and mind powers have been given wide public exposure in television documentaries and presentations of a more "entertaining" nature, in the press and in a plethora of books. The paranormal has been the subject of films such as *Phenomenon* and TV programmes such as *The X Files*. Today there are serious discussions of the paranormal in offices, shops and factories; a decade ago such topics would probably have met with derision.

There are several reasons for this growing interest in paranormal phenomena. For some people paranormal powers offer hope for the future, an improved humankind. For others, they offer an alternative to conventional religions, which are not apparently meeting their needs. For still others, they represent a challenge to science, which in spite of its stunning successes still fails to explain the meaning of life. As a new millennium approaches, people wonder what promise the next thousand years hold for the future of humanity.

In 1998 the *Daily Mail* newspaper undertook a wide-ranging survey of the paranormal. It interviewed 1,092 people and the findings were fascinating. They revealed a general belief in "hidden" abilities within the mind, and the belief that these abilities may have a particular "place" in the brain. The survey also revealed differences between men and women, suggesting that it is the so-called feminine traits that house these abilities. This does not mean that men and women are necessarily different, though they may be, but that because the world we live in tends to force men and women down different roads, each sex tends to use different areas of the brain.

In the survey sixty-four per cent of those questioned believed that some people had "powers" that could not be explained by science. This opinion was almost equally split between men and women. A similar number, reasonably enough, believed that there were things science could not explain that could be encompassed within the term "paranormal." In this book, however, we suggest that more paranormal phenomena, such as extrasensory perception and psychokinesis (PK), should be attributed to the powers of the mind than is generally acknowledged.

The *Daily Mail* survey also showed that a similar number believed in God. This is hardly surprising given that God fits more easily within the term "paranormal" than "scientific." God does not act according to the rules of science, but certainly fulfils many of the criteria for the paranormal, i.e. beyond scientific analysis or replication, spontaneous or at least with cause and effect unknown to people, and intuitively felt within people rather than "provable."

In general, women believed in many more individual components of the paranormal than did men. For instance, women were more likely to believe in survival of spirit, communication with the dead, telepathy, psychokinesis, clairvoyance and fortune-telling, healing and reincarnation. They were also more likely to believe in ghosts. Generally, more women than men reported having had direct experiences within these areas. It is believed that it is in the so-called "feminine qualities" that these phenomena reside; for example, it is "easier" to see ghosts if you are using the intuitive aspects of the mind.

On the other hand, men were more likely than women to believe in extraterrestrials and alien visitation to Earth. It seemed that men found it easier to believe in what are thought to be external phenomena; i.e. those that are objectively real and would be seen by anyone as clearly as cars are seen on the roads.

The survey also showed that optimism was high. Few people believed that alien life forms would prove to be hostile, and far more people believed in heaven than hell. (About equal numbers believed in the devil as in angels, however.)

Predictably, given the focus of recent media attention, more young people believed in the paranormal than older people, though not in all individual aspects of the paranormal. Belief was also higher amongst "professional" classes than "working" classes, though not significantly so.

Some Church leaders, and quite a few scientists, expressed concern about these beliefs. But The Reverend Dr. Brian Castle, a vice-principal at Oxford University, showed a very healthy and open-minded reaction to the survey in commenting: "The Church needs to be more alert and more open to paranormal ideas. We must look at these things and see what we can take on board." He added: "If more people are reaching out to have their spiritual needs met then we need to make sure we're there to respond."

More people are reaching out than ever before. And one area of research that will eventually provide answers to many unexplained phenomena is the study of the human mind. This book looks at the powers of the human mind and tries to explain how and why they might have evolved and their implications for the future of humanity.

Many of the mind's abilities are not fully understood by present-day science. But they are not supernatural. They are not beyond understanding. However, their existence poses questions that must be answered. J. Allen Hynek, an American astronomer, wrote: "There is a tendency in twentieth-century science to forget that there will be a twenty-first-century science, and indeed, a thirtieth-century science, from which vantage points our knowledge of the universe may appear quite different."

I

Processes of the Mind

1

The Extraordinary Mind

To understand the mysteries and powers of the mind we must first examine the brain and its relationship to the mind, and look at some known and scientifically accepted abilities of the brain/mind combination. What the brain can achieve is remarkable in itself, and the similarities and possible connections between the power of the mind and the paranormal will become apparent. Even dreaming offers a fascinating picture of the mind's processes, and there are links between the brain and such phenomena as out-of-body experience and channelling.

In this section we shall also examine the fascinating evidence of what happens when the brain malfunctions: the savant syndrome, Multiple Personality Disorder and a relatively new phenomenon, alien abduction syndrome. We begin by looking at the brain/mind connection.

The Link between Brain and Mind

The link between the mind and the brain has been the subject of much controversy, certainly for the past 350 years and arguably back to the fourth century BC when Plato stated that the physical body was inhabited by a non-physical soul. In 1641 the French mathematician and philosopher René Descartes formalised the so-called mind/brain debate with the concept of "dualism." He declared that the mind (the *res cogitans*, or "thinking thing") was separate and distinct from the brain. According to Descartes, the physical matter of the brain, constrained by the laws of physics and forced to act like a machine, was incapable of producing the wide range of activity encompassed by thought, which he believed was generated by a non-physical phenomenon.

A link of sorts was established in the eighteenth century when a French doctor, François Gigot de La Peyronie, was treating a patient with a deep cut in his head that had split the skull. When he washed the wound with water the patient fainted; when the water was drawn off, the patient revived. In his paper to colleagues, de La Peyronie argued that this incident showed that basic consciousness and the physical brain were related.

In recent decades the attempt to answer the essential question posed by Descartes has resulted in the collaboration of two disciplines: cognitive psychology (of the mind) and neurobiology (of the brain and nervous system). Science has largely rejected dualism: Daniel Dennett, professer of Tufts University in Massachusetts and director of the Center for Cognitive Studies, stated: "What the dualist does is invent a magical space and inhabit it with some new substance, the mind. . . . But that couldn't solve the problem—that is just giving up. It leaves all the truly interesting questions of how the mind works not only unanswered but unanswerable." Neurologist Richard Restak put it more succinctly: "Mind is what the brain does."

But whether or not the mind and the brain are linked is not the main focus of this book, which is concerned with examining abilities available to humans. Whether those abilities derive from the physical brain or a non-physical soul is, for the purposes of this book, an unnecessary distinction. Having set out the essence of what may well be an important debate about "mind functions" for the future, we will, for convenience of terminology, assume that the mind and brain are linked.

The concept of "functional localisation" was first given serious attention with the work of Franz Joseph Gall, a doctor working in Paris and Vienna between 1785 and 1828. Gall worked out that certain areas of the brain seemed to be responsible for certain functions: memory, artistic talent and so on. His work was based on observation; he matched bumps on the head with observed talents or characteristics: bumps in front of the ear indicated attentiveness, and so on. It gave rise to the Victorian studies of phrenology—reading the skulls of people by the bumps present. His observations were naïve and failed to take into account, for example, that the brain's actual contours adjust according to the activity of the moment; but the idea that the brain was geographically divided into certain areas was a valuable contribution to understanding the brain. Others who followed examined the brain more scientifically with this view in mind, most famously probably the French doctor Paul Broca who identified the area of the brain that deals with elements of speech.

For convenience it is also worth describing the physical development of the brain in relation to abilities. These physical areas provide a "geography" of the territory that is relevant to the discussions in this book.

In the 1970s a scientist at the Laboratory of Neurophysiology at the National Institute of Mental Health in Washington DC, Paul MacLean, suggested that the brain was an evolved organ that could be divided broadly into three areas, each having developments separated by huge chunks of time:

- The first area, the brainstem, operated the basic motor functions that sustain life, such as breathing, heart activity and so on. MacLean believed that this area of the brain controlled "instinctive" responses such as the body language that signals an individual's response and is difficult, if not impossible, to suppress.
- The second area, the old brain, or old mammalian brain, encompasses the hippocampus, the thalmus, the amygdala and controls the emotions and basic needs, such as desire for food, the need to reproduce and so on.

- The third area of the evolutionary brain, the "neocortex," or "new covering," governs abstract concepts such as language, the ability to model and predict the future, to reason logically, to calculate and to consider.

MacLean's model of the brain generated great controversy because it implied that the human being was governed by a brain that was two parts irrational and instinctive, and only one part logical and reasoning. This seemed to debase humankind to the level of the animals. Our own argument is somewhat the opposite: the development of the human neocortex—rationality, reasoning, etc—may have suppressed or replaced some of the instinctive animal abilities. And perhaps some of those instinctive abilities, still present in many animals, are the key to phenomena such as extrasensory perceptions (ESP).

Another crucial aspect of the human brain that was more recently identified is its two-fold "evolution" during the life of its "owner":

- First, it is thought that the basic physical structure exists at birth and dies off during life. The brain works by a process of electrical sparking across gaps not unlike the spark plug in a car. The physical matter of the spark plug are the neurons, or nerve cells, of which we have somewhere between ten and a hundred billion. The gaps are called synapses and there may be approximately twenty quadrillion (20,000,000,000,000,000) of them. All, or most, of the neurons exist when the human is born; neurons do not reproduce themselves and they begin to die off early in life. This dying off would appear to be a natural feature of the brain's individual development. The brain seems to put its resources into maintaining the most important and efficient connections and allows unused connections to wither. The old adage "if you don't use it, you'll lose it" would seem to apply.
- The second feature of an individual's brain development is

that learning causes actual physical changes in the brain. Work in this area was pioneered by Eric Kandel at Columbia University in New York during the 1960s. He started his work with the marine snail, which has only around 20,000 nerve cells. By giving the snail electric shocks he found it produced changes to the brain's synapses. New dendrites ("arms" of the neurons) grew, creating new synaptic "connections." The brain was physically growing according to its experiences. The implication is that the same process is possible for humans: those areas of the brain that we use can generate new connections.

· The reconciliation between these two aspects of brain development was the surprising discovery that even though the brain cells, once dead, did not seem to be able to regenerate, if the individual sought to learn new skills, or if certain areas of the brain were damaged, there would be a development of a "back-up" area in some other location of the brain.

It is worth noting that for all this concentration on the physical brain, scientists are not yet agreed on even the nature of the connection between brain and mind. In 1963 Sir John Eccles, a highly respected physiologist, received the Nobel prize in medicine for work on the chemistry of nerve action. Yet he rejects the idea that physical cells that are not self-aware can create consciousness and concludes that a non-material force flows into the brain. Dualism lives on.

Whatever the connection there is sufficient evidence to show that the mind works within the brain. Between the 1930s and the 1950s neurosurgeon Wilder Penfield found that stimulating the physical matter of the brain with probes could both stimulate activity—such as making muscles twitch—and memory. In one patient he touched an area of the brain and triggered a detailed memory that replayed as if it were happening then and there.

Modern technology has allowed for non-intrusive studies of the living brain while it functions. Positron Emission Tomography (PET), Computed Tomography (CT) and Magnetic Resonance Imaging (MRI) scans allow researchers to watch the brain in action. PET scans, for example, have shown that brain activity moves from one area of the brain to another depending on whether the individual is reading or listening to the spoken word.

Right and Left Brain

The functioning of the brain is localised and specialised. Throughout this book we shall refer to the division between so-called right-brain functions and so-called left-brain functions. It must be remembered that for normal everyday living both hemispheres have to function and indeed relate to each other. Some researchers have suggested that "right mind" and "left mind" might be more appropriate. However, we shall use the more conventional right brain/left brain distinction.

The left brain is the logical brain. It deals with number skills, with language skills, with logical reasoning, with scientific skills. It deals with rationality.

The right brain is the artistic brain. It is not logical: it is the centre of intuition and insight, of imagination and creativity.

In modern day we are forced to live in a "left-brain" world. We are expected to be rational, to be logical, to base decisions not on instinct but on reasoning. In school we are taught left-brain skills with more enthusiasm than right-brain skills (reading, writing, arithmetic). But it is likely that the abilities to perceive or trigger the functions we call paranormal are housed in the "right brain"; the evidence for this we shall examine in the various sections of the book.

For study of the paranormal, right-brain skills are tested and challenged by science using left-brain logic; and right-brain skills do not seem to respond to that approach. Science therefore argues that these abilities are "unreal," that they are a result of wishful thinking and fantasy rather than reality. We disagree, believing the evidence strongly supports the reality of many phenomena referred to as paranormal. But proving it in a right-brain way to the satisfaction of left-brain thinking is not yet possible. Indeed, as this book argues, when people who have demonstrated paranormal abilities are put under stressful challenge they often cannot reproduce their skills; perhaps because they are being forced to use their left brain, their right-brain abilities suffer. When dowsers who had successfully found water in test conditions were faced with disagreeable and aggressive experimental situations they failed miserably, to their own surprise (see pages 96–106). In contrast, when metal bending was tested by a scientist who empathised with the subjects and supported them and believed in them, they did well (see page 287).

Memory and Retrieval

Probably the most fundamental power of the brain is memory and retrieval; the ability to learn from, and draw from, experience is arguably our most valuable attribute. A two-tier system of memory is probably a most efficient system for "everyday" use. If we find ourselves threatened, it is useful to have at our disposal every piece of information and to be able to recall every situation we have ever found ourselves in. This knowledge gives us the greatest chance of finding the most expedient course of action. But there would be severe drawbacks if all that information were constantly available in conscious memory. When you cross the road you would be swamped by the images of every road you had ever crossed. When you ate a meal you would recall the taste of every meal you had ever eaten. This kind of total recall would be a hindrance in the normal course of things. It seems that forgetting is not a failure of mind, but one of its essential characteristics. The mind holds information that it needs or is likely to need for "instant recall," while at the same time it holds other data in the subconscious (or whatever name we choose to call the other compartment of memory). When under stress—or in certain emotional or exceptional situations—the memory begins to draw from these other "subconscious" resources, which perhaps explains such things as channelling and mediumship, an argument we put forward in this book. We do not suggest that this explains every paranormal ability; but it seems to be one of the possibilities. Similarly, other paranormal capabilities—psychokinesis, telepathy, healing and so on—could well be the mind tapping its unused attributes. The challenge is to learn how to draw consciously and effectively on these latent talents.

Part of our understanding of what the mind might be capable of "when stretched" comes from studying what the mind can do when it is not working "normally." In fact, the so-called dysfunctional mind often reveals some intriguing human potentials. We look first at the phenomenon of savant syndrome.

Savant Syndrome

Savants are people who seem to view the world and process information in quite different ways to those of the general population. Savants are regarded as mentally impaired, suffering from a mental deficiency of sorts. Savant syndrome affects only a small number of people, specifically autistic individuals, schizophrenics and others with mental impairment. There are some savants whose abilities are spectacular only because they are being viewed in relation to their general mental abilities, but a smaller sub-set of savants have talents that are spectacular against any benchmark, and even when viewed in relation to "normal" individuals. Some savants do not have the necessary skills to interact socially with others on a "normal" basis, some do not even have the wherewithall to maintain their own personal needs without assistance, yet they have some very special qualities. These individuals and their special qualities may offer insight into the workings of not only defective minds but also the unused potential of normal minds.

The gap between the apparent skills of the savant and the application of these skills was evident to Dr. J. Langdon Down, who was working as a psychiatrist in 1887, and was superintendent of Earlswood Asylum for thirty years. One of his patients could "read an entire book and ever more remember it." But in reading the *Rise and Fall of the Roman Empire* the boy missed one line. Realising his mistake he went back and read it. Thereafter, when reciting the book he would follow the same pattern; he would recite the book with the line missing, then go back and correct the error.

Dr. Alfred F. Tredgold, who published *Mental Deficiency* in 1914, which contains an authoritative chapter on savant syndrome, observed that most savants are "fond of music." There are many cases of savants who can play thousands of pieces after hearing them just once, or play several instruments without formal training, yet who have almost no vocabulary and few other obvious skills. This type of exceptional musical ability was apparent in the case of "S," who had contracted epidemic encephalitis just after birth, resulting in brain damage. By the age of thirty-eight, when his case was written up, he exhibited a dependency on rigid schedules; for example, when a man arrived to see him fifteen minutes early he made him wait outside his "personal room" (his music room) until exactly the right time. He would talk to mirrors, make faces for no obvious reason and balance objects on his head, acting in a very child-like manner. His lack of social graces was evident; he would belch in public, push people out of his way and act very boorishly. His IQ was measured at sixty-seven, a mental age of ten. His talents lay in both music and memory. He could reproduce from memory up to two pages of script at a time after a single reading. He had a flawless memory of family events and a vast store of historical knowledge of, for example, European composers. He played the piano, either from sight or by ear, and was regarded by leading musicians as outstanding. He played for several leading orchestras. It seems that S had some understanding of music theory, though he was unable to explain any of it. He never used his knowledge for compositions of his own.

The question of savants' ability to create their own compositions is of interest because it seems that composition requires
more than mere memory of the rules of music; it requires intelligent manipulation of those rules. Several savants have shown an
ability to improvise on standard compositions, which is an indication of composition. In 1986 this question was put to the test at
the University of London Institute of Education. The five male
savants in the test were aged from eighteen to fifty-eight with
IQs ranging from fifty to sixty-nine. All had displayed musical
talent. One, for example, at age eight, had taken his teacher's
place at the piano and played everything he had just listened to.
A control group of children was also set up, aged between nine
and seventeen; all were proficient on the piano and some on
other instruments. The two groups were tested and compared on
their ability to perform the following tasks:

- to continue an unknown song where it was left off
- to play or sing a new composition
- to play an accompaniment to the examiner
- to produce both melody and accompaniment
- to improvise over a sequence

They were also examined for general music competence in terms
of timing, rhythm and complexity. The savant group was clearly
more advanced than the non-savant group. The conclusion was
that "the savant can invent as well as reproduce music that con-
forms to those familiar structural patterns."

How they do it is still a mystery, but some savants have
thrown a little light on the matter by their descriptions of the
process as they see it. They describe the rules of music in mathematical terms, a series of counting. It appears that, memory
apart, which may be the mechanism rather than the feat itself,
savants seem to excel in both music and mathematics.

It may be that savants are using right-brain skills rather than
left-brain skills. By this we mean that the natural, intuitive skills

may be coming to the fore in these savants rather than the calculating, rational abilities "normal" people use. But normal people may be the worse for it. As we shall see throughout this book, the ability to access areas of the brain more efficiently, or differently, may be the key to so-called paranormal abilities. So have these savants found a way to treat music as a form of science? Or have they found a way to treat mathematics as a form of art? Is their use of the rules of both mathematics and music an artistic application of the processes? While the answers to these questions are not clear, the speed of accessing memory—especially among "mathematical" savants—suggests that savants are using some alternative processing mechanism to that used by non-savants.

Consider the following cases of mathematical ability, and speed of calculation.

Charlie and George were autistic identical twin brothers (produced from the same egg), born prematurely. From an early age it seems they were mentally impaired; they habitually fought, banged their heads and bit themselves. They would often rock backwards and forwards. Their IQs were between forty and seventy. They could read only very simple words and count—conventionally—up to thirty. Their general memory was not very good: for example, they could not remember the names of the US Presidents. But the twins had a special talent as "calendar counters" and were perhaps the most extraordinary of that type of savant. Asked on what day of the week the fourteenth of May will fall in the year 22,098, they could calculate it instanteously. Indeed, they could give the answer to any date over an 80,000-year span. They were first presented to the American Psychiatric Association in Los Angeles in 1964 by a team of psychiatrists.

Studies showed that the twins were not relying solely on memory. Although such a memory feat is possible for some savants, there was evidence that Charlie and George were actually calculating at a lightning speed that would put a computer into a sweat. This was made apparent by the fact that they could not understand the change-over from the Julian to the Gregorian calendars; their answers had to be adjusted by ten days whenever they calculated back beyond AD 1582, the date of the change to the Gregorian calender.

One of the researchers, Dr. William Horwitz, suggested that the twins had learned by rote the complete 400-year calendar cycles and then subtracted blocks of 400 to arrive at the present date-range where they would search for the answer. Dora Hamblin suggested, when they were her patients at the New York State Psychiatric Institute, that the twins were probably using memory as well, because of their ability to know when Easter would fall. This is not a simple calculation. The rules that determine when Easter falls were decided in AD 325 by the First Council of Nicaea. It falls on the first Sunday following the first full moon after the vernal equinox (21 March). This can place Easter anywhere between 22 March and 25 April.

The twins obviously had mathematical abilities. They "swapped" twenty-digit prime numbers with each other for their own amusement and could factor numbers easily. But neither could work out the change from a ten-dollar bill if they purchased something for six dollars.

No one really knows how savants like Charlie and George do what they do. George himself threw little light on the debate: "It's in my head and I can do it," is all he offers.

S. Jungreis, studied by Dr. Abraham A. Brill in the 1920s, was a non-savant who displayed savant-like abilities, which then disappeared. This shows that non-savants, i.e. those not mentally deficient, can acquire savant-like abilities. Jungreis was a lightning calculator. Brill examined him at the age of six when his skills were apparent. Jungreis had an average IQ. Although apparently unable to distinguish one numeral from another he could add "formidable" columns of figures. He could add six-digit numbers with the ease with which "ordinary" people can add single-digit numbers. His talents were spotted by accident. Two older brothers were doing their homework when Jungreis was in the room. The brothers were sharing their work with each other out loud, and they heard the infant Jungreis shouting out what seemed to be random numbers. Although he was unable to read or write at the time, the older brothers were astonished to discover that the numbers he was shouting were the correct answers to their problems. But at the age of nine, his unusual talent disappeared, and from that time onwards his mathematical abilities were average at best and remained so into adulthood. This case study may offer a clue as to the forces that can shape these skills. Brill thought that Jungreis' abilities might have developed as a result of the deaths of his mother and sister; his abilities disappeared following the death of his father, when Jungreis was aged nine. This may or may not be relevant but it is interesting that many people who have paranormal experiences—healing, clairvoyance, mediumship, etc.—have also had trauma in their lives, or suffered considerable ill health. It may be that when the individual is stretched by these difficulties, the mind seeks to activate its otherwise unused powers.

Brill's analysis of these mathematical savant abilities is pertinent to our study of "mind power" and where these powers might be located in the brain. He reasoned that these abilities required a remarkable memory, but he described it as "memory without consciousness." He believed that savants solved problems in the way that the brain does when we are asleep, drawing on memory in an unconscious manner. Perhaps this ability, rather than being special to savants, is actually a normal function of our intuitive brain but we "unlearn" the ability as we learn to use our logical, reasoning, brain.

Perhaps even more fascinating is the account of Benj Langdon who studied with the savant twins Charlie and George. Langdon wanted to see if a non-savant, with non-savant abilities, could learn to do what they did. Was calendar counting just a feat of learning? No matter how hard he tried he could not match the twins' achievements, until suddenly one day he did. He seems to have memorised the mathematical table Charlie and George used for their calculation and, once memorised, he could access it with similar prowess. He did not seem to have to calculate, at least with his conscious mind. The problem was, he could not explain what he had done and in fact could add nothing to the explanation of the process. In effect, he ended up with no more contribution to that answer than George's "It's in my head and I can do it." Like so many things we learn—driving a car, riding a bike, tying a shoelace—it takes a lot of learning but then becomes almost automatic. Dr. Bernard Rimland in *Psychology Today* (August 1978) states his belief that Langdon switched from using his left-brain functions to using his right-brain functions.

Indeed, most analysis of savant syndrome seems to hinge on something akin to this. Most savants are poor in verbal and language skills, which are housed in the left brain; most savants are skilled in music, which is right-brain dominant. As Darrold A. Treffert, a leading expert on savant syndrome, comments: "Savant Syndrome, in general, tends to be associated with non-analytic strategies...." Of course savants are also often skilled with numbers, which is, at face value, a left-brain activity; but Langdon's experience indicates that there are at least "two ways" to process the numbers. Perhaps savants use an "artistic," right-brain approach, which Langdon found so hard to emulate.

Treffert relates in his book *Extraordinary People* the story of a woman who, unfortunately, managed to switch "the other way." She had been a "natural" musician who could play by ear any song she heard and decided to pursue a musical career. But when she took piano lessons, her natural talents left her, never to return.

The conclusion seems to be that while savants have disabilities that impair their full functioning in our modern society, their exceptional abilities may not be a "malfunction" at all but rather an ability to access a normal and intuitive process that is the brain working at its most efficient. But something has prevented the vast majority of people from accessing that process. Perhaps what is holding us back are teaching methods of the past hundred or so years, or our dependency on the rational and the calculating functions of the brain, or our dependence on modern technology.

Savants may be offering us an insight into the unused potential of the brain; they may even be showing us how to accelerate learning and develop memory-use. Perhaps this means learning to switch from the left brain to the right brain.

Synaesthesia

Synaesthesia is another condition that clearly demonstrates the mind's ability to operate in unusual ways. The rare person who has this condition seems to "mix up" their senses. They taste shapes, they smell colours, they feel sounds. It appears that synaesthetics do not have the natural barriers that classify sense perceptions into distinct and separate experiences.

The condition has been recognised for nearly 300 years. In 1690 philosopher John Locke described a blind man who understood the colour scarlet to be the sound of a trumpet. In 1710 Thomas Woolhouse, an ophthalmologist, described the case of a person who was blind but who reported coloured visions triggered by sounds. There have been famous synaesthetics. Alexander Scriabin, the Russian composer, used his symphony *Prometheus, the Poem of Fire*, written in 1910, to express his own condition: a silent keyboard played forms of lights and shapes. Artist Vasily Kandinsky expressed his condition through an opera called *The Yellow Sound*.

One person suffering from synaesthesia described tasting by shape. When cooking food he knew it was tasty if it had shapes. When he tasted food it would be like a feeling that would flow into his hands and arms and feel just as if he was holding something. Another synaesthetic would hear music and see objects as her form of "listening"; balls, lines and fluid movements floated in front of her eyes.

Artist Elizabeth Pulford had heard words and sounds in colour all her life. She was tested by London University's Institute of Psychiatry. She was asked to describe the colour of 100 different words. "Moscow" for example was grey, green and blue; "Maria" was dark violet-blue, etc. When asked again a year later, her answers did not vary at all. Her consistency suggested a real and, for her, a quite "natural" condition.

A study of a family in which father and daughters were all synaesthetic showed that days of the week were understood as colours or shapes between family members. One of the authors of this book, John Spencer, has a perception that might be akin to synaesthesia, or at least shows how memory can trigger slightly offbeat feelings:

> As a child I enjoyed the television series called *Watch with Mother*, a pre-school series of programmes that was broadcast each day. Monday was *Picture Book*, Tuesday was *Andy Pandy*, Wednesday was *The Flowerpot Men*, Thursday was *Rag, Tag and Bobtail*, and Friday was *The Woodentops*. I enjoyed *The Flowerpot Men* more than any others, and have little memory of *Picture Book*. But each programme and day are inextricably linked in my memory by feelings: Wednesday is a "good" day, it feels hard and somehow round. Monday is very vague—little feeling at all, but in a sense positively shapeless. Friday is a sunny day—I think the Woodentops lived on a farm and most of the "action" was outdoors; perhaps that is the origin of the feeling. And so on. Even now, as a forty-something adult, whenever I use my diary these "feelings" are attached in some way to each day. It is certainly useful for remembering appointments because when I scan the diary of the week ahead each appointment has a feeling according to its day, which makes it easy to remember what is coming up each day ahead.
>
> Having said that, there are two problems with the above narrative. Firstly it sounds too "up front" whereas it is nothing I consciously think about and only had to start trying to analyse it when writing about it. It is very much a natural background feeling, and my main appreciation of my diary is rational. But secondly is the recognition that the descriptions above are wholly

inadequate though I cannot express them more clearly. Wednesday, for example, has a "mood" about it but "good," "hard" and "round" are really my inadequate attempts to express it. I sit here now feeling that "Wednesday" feeling quite clearly and I feel as if I could almost visualise it, but somehow it is truly intangible. There simply are not words to express it. It is nonetheless a very real and quite easily remembered feeling.

Blood flow around the brain is providing a clue as to the mechanics of synaesthesia. Volunteers with synaesthesia were shown to have increased blood flow in the visual cortex when they heard sounds, whereas those with "normal" senses did not. While this shows that the condition is related to activities of the physical brain, it does not, of course, explain its origin or purpose.

Interestingly, some experts studying the subject are unsure how the state we call "normal" arises. It has been suggested that the synaesthetic state is how we are born, and that over time we develop the barriers that put each sense into an appropriate "box." Simon Baron-Cohen, clinical psychologist at London University's Institute of Psychiatry, suggests: "Synaesthesia may be showing what happens when this modularity is not achieved."

We have yet to be certain if sense barriers are an advantage or a disadvantage. In a world created by those with discrete sensing, the condition of synaesthesia is a clear disadvantage if only because it makes it difficult to describe the consensus reality world. But if everyone had synaesthesia and could appreciate all aspects of the world through all five senses simultaneously, senses might be heightened, understanding and appreciation all the more exquisite. Perhaps our appreciation of opportunities and dangers would also be clearer because they would be "measured" by all senses together. In short, synaesthesia could be an aid to survival by providing a more alert analysis of the environment. It is perhaps a condition that we humans have largely lost, to our detriment.

But is synaesthesia "paranormal"? The condition as described above seems normal enough, but there are claims that stretch into the paranormal: the case of the Seeress of Prevorst, for example.

The Seeress of Prevorst was the title of a book published in the nineteenth century, written by a doctor, Justinus Kerner. The subject of the book, the "Seeress," was a peasant woman, Friederike Hauffe. In childhood she experienced strange visions and spoke to spirit companions. In late teenage, following the birth of a child, she suffered extreme post-natal depression. She went into a trance and saw the spirits of the dead. Kerner was asked to treat her.

Apart from clairvoyance and mediumship of sorts, she demonstrated to the doctor an ability that, if not a form of synaesthesia, is a close cousin. She could read through her stomach. She would lie on a couch or bed with her stomach bare, and her eyes closed, and an opened book would be placed face down on it. She would read the book with the same ease with which others could using their eyes. This condition alone convinced the doctor that he should take seriously her many other extraordinary claims.

Sheila Ostrander and Lynn Schroeder in their book *Psychic Discoveries: The Iron Curtain Lifted* outline the case of Rosa Kuleshova who had "eyeless sight." Tested by her doctor, Iosif M. Goldberg, the blindfolded Rosa could "see" with her fingers. She would run her fingers across a page and could call out the colours on the page. She could read text and describe a photograph accurately, all blindfolded and using only her fingers. The resultant "fad" that arose when her talents became widely known is reminiscent of the Victorian enthusiasm for seances and physical mediumship. At one point it seemed that everyone wanted to study Rosa, and that everyone wanted to learn to "see" with the fingertips. Surprisingly, many people discovered they could learn to do it. Psychologist Dr. Abram Novomeisky tested eighty students and found that after about half an hour of practice approximately one-sixth of them could distinguish between two colours blindfolded. That something akin to synaesthesia was part of the process was suggested by comments from one student, Boris M. He described the red as "a clinging, pulling, viscid sensation" as he passed his fingers over the colour. There was a general consensus that colours were divided into the smooth (light blue), the sticky (red and green) and the rough (orange). As they progressed, students could learn to differentiate between the colours without touching them; they merely passed their hands above the colours on the paper.

Multiple Personality Syndrome (MPD)

A good description of Multiple Personality Syndrome comes from *The Filthy Lie* by Hellmut Karle:

> Two or more separate personalities seem to inhabit the same body; the person seems to have periods of time, which may last minutes, hours, days, or even weeks, for which they later have no memory at all, and during which time they behave in ways that are totally different from their normal ways. During these episodes, they call themselves by a different name, live quite a different life, and altogether appear to be a different person.

In such cases the primary personality has no knowledge of the existence, let alone the character, of the other personality or personalities. A secondary personality will know of the primary and may or may not know of other secondary personalities. Only one personality at a time can be dominant.

Multiple Personality Disorder (MPD), or Dissociation of the Personality, may be a factor in some, not all, claims of certain paranormal manifestations, such as channelling, alien abduction (particularly in relation to "missing time") and especially possession.

One curious feature noted by Dr. Deepak Chopra, in *Quantum Healing: Exploring the Frontiers of Mind/Body Medicine*, is that "when a person with multiple personalities shifts from one to the other, his body shifts too." He gives the example of a situation in which one personality has diabetes but the others do not. The body registers insulin-deficient if the diabetic personality is dominant, but has normal blood sugar levels when other personalities are dominant.

Chopra also discusses the case of a patient of psychologist Daniel Goleman. "Timmy," as the patient is known, has nearly a dozen personalities. One of them is allergic to orange juice, and if Timmy drinks it while that personality is dominant then Timmy's body breaks out in a rash. If the primary personality is dominant and Timmy drinks orange juice, there is no allergic reaction, but if the allergic sub-personality takes over while the juice is being digested, there is an immediate reaction. Furthermore, if the primary personality returns while the rash is itching, it immediately stops and the blisters subside. The implications of this are far-reaching for the medical profession, as they are for this study. For instance, could such personalities account for some possession claims? Presumably MPD could also account for what are thought to be apports, disapports and the poltergeist-related displacement of objects. If a sub-personality within one individual in a household is removing items from the house or bringing them in without the knowledge of the main personality, the appearances and disappearances of these items would seem mysterious.

It may be simplistic to assume that MPD is an "illness" or disorder in the strict sense. It may be that a mind under extreme stress manifests these sub-personalities as a form of protection, a defence mechanism to protect the individual from information overload, mental trauma and so on. It is even possible that the so-called disorder is perfectly normal and inherent in everybody, but manifests only at times of perceived stress. Many people without any mental disorder, other than perhaps stress at the moment or illness-related fever, have occasionally reported hearing a voice that seems to come from their head. If the brain has complex ways of communicating with areas of itself, then an inherent sub-personality might occasionally be a route taken for that communication. This could account for some claims of channelling.

It is only when "unhealthy" personalities begin to dominate or prevent normal everyday functioning that there is cause for concern. If a sub-personality, for instance, incited behaviour that was extremely anti-social, such as murder, or self-destructive, such as suicide, then in those extreme situations, the person would be in dire need of help. The phenomenon of multiple personality might explain some paranormal claims, and it may also provide insight into the workings of the mind. Certainly it shows the mind can operate quite differently than is normally assumed.

2

The Dreaming Mind

One area of human functioning guaranteed to generate conflicting opinions is the process we call dreaming. There is debate about its purpose, or lack of it, and about the meanings that might be ascribed to particular dreams.

It seems that most early cultures believed that dreaming was a mechanism that allowed humans to enter the realm of the gods, and allowed the gods to communicate with humans. Dreams have been valued as glimpses into the spiritual world, prophecies of the future, divination as to inner meanings, and travel to other "astral" levels.

Ancient Greeks believed dreams were a pathway to healing. Their cult of Aesculapius—the god of healing—was popular from around 400 BC. The shrines to Aesculapius were an early form of health resort comprising temple, gymnasium, hospital and library. Patients could stay there for months, and in some cases even years. They would sleep in the temple and their dreams or visions would hopefully lead to cures. Records of patient cures were kept at Epidaurus—the "Lourdes of Greece." One recorded case told of a woman, blind in one eye, who dreamt that the god cut her eye open and poured ointment into it; she recovered her sight. Another man paralysed in the hand dreamt that the god jumped on his palm, straightening his fingers and curing him. There were several recorded "miracle" cures, not unlike those reported for Lourdes.

Perhaps the earliest written material on dreams is the "Chester Beatty" Egyptian papyrus dating from approximately 2000 BC. It analyses the possible meanings of dreams and discusses the concept of "contraries," i.e. the dreamer experiences in actual life the opposite of what he or she dreamt.

Artemidorus, in the second century AD, argued that dreams reflected the previous day's activities. He believed that dreaming was a product of the dreamer's age, sex and social status. The psychoanalyst Sigmund Freud similarly believed that dreams are created by unconscious wishes and reveal the conflicts and neuroses of the dreamer. Both Freud and Artemidorus related dreams to the everyday real world and to the individual character of the dreamer.

In the twentieth century, psychological analysis of dreams was pioneered by Sigmund Freud and Carl Jung. Freud believed that dreams were the pathway into the dreamer's unconscious mind. He saw dreams as the mind's way of working through unfulfilled desires. His interpretation was strongly biased towards sexual interpretations. Jung took the slightly tangential view that dreams were the mind's way of learning about itself; they helped the dreamer come to a better understanding of his or her own needs and wants. Jung divided dreams into two categories: those that were "personal" to the dreamer and those that reflected the "collective unconscious." The "psychological" interpretation of dreams stresses that dreams are uncensored by social rules and taboos and they allow more direct access to the mind. Jung's belief was that our own psyche seeks to commune with us in a number of increasingly dramatic ways. It would first try to communicate through dreams, but if desires and guidance were ignored, the mind would communicate through "creating accidents" to draw imbalance to our attention. If still ignored, the mind would create both physical and mental disorder and illness to get attention. By following the guidance of dreams, the more harmful calls for attention could be avoided.

The mechanism of dreaming was studied scientifically at the

University of Chicago in 1951. A student, Eugene Aserinsky, studied sleeping infant children and noticed that twitching body movements occurred at the same time as movements of the eyes. By linking the dreaming subjects up to an electroencephalograph (EEG) he could study the relationship between dreaming and electrical activity in the brain. This was the first recognition of rapid eye movement (REM) sleep. In particular Aserinsky observed that as the sleeper dropped into deeper and deeper sleep, the eye movements did not, as might have been expected, lessen, but rather continued in furious bursts. Aserinsky, working with his professor, Nathaniel Kleitman, observed the same pattern in adults. The difference was that children reached the state of REM sleep more quickly and remained in it for longer periods than adults.

Changes in the brain's activities are measured by monitoring the brainwaves present at certain times. There are four waves:

- alpha waves, present during sleeping states or periods of relaxation with the eyes closed
- beta waves, present during fully alert times
- theta waves, associated with drowsiness or sleep
- delta waves, associated with deeper sleep.

In the period of descending into sleep the alpha waves of relaxation gradually shift to theta and then delta waves. REM sleep shows more similarity to wakefulness than to sleepfulness according to the brainwaves in evidence. The alpha waves of relaxation and the point of "switching" from one wave to another are often evident during the type of specialist mind functions we examine in this book, especially premonitions, pain resistance, psychokinesis and that special form of concentration athletes refer to as "the zone."

"The zone" is a state of mind that is almost trance-like in its concentration, and without it athletes could not, it is believed, be top performers. Scientific testing has proven that people at the extreme—in this case athletes—do indeed experience something "normal" people usually do not. Sally Gunnell said on breaking the 400-metres hurdles world record in the 1993 World Championships: "I don't even remember coming off the last hurdle. As I crossed the line, it felt as though my life had been on hold. . . . I didn't know that I'd actually won." It was a rare state of mind even for an accomplished athlete such as her. She went on to say: "Everyone just thought I was being very calm. But I had no idea. I don't remember any of it. This has probably only happened to me once or twice in my career."

It seems that when an athlete is in "the zone," rational, thinking processes are set aside in favour of instinctive, unconscious action. As top tennis player Greg Rusedski put it: "It's not always the brightest people who get to the top in sport. It's the ones that are able to focus on one thing at a time."

Scientific analysis of the zone proves that it is a very real state, a measurable state of brain and mind. There is a direct physiological link between meditation and the zone, which becomes a place where the most focused abilities of the unconscious mind come into play, overriding the conscious mind. Athletes are saying much the same thing as mediums who claim they have to give up intellect and let their feelings rule.

Studies show that alpha waves are the clue to the zone; alpha waves increase when athletes are in this state of mind, which suggests that actual thinking processes are at a minimum. The alpha rhythm is usually associated with a meditative, quiescent state. Furthermore, alpha waves are "blocked" in most people when they open their eyes; they shift immediately to the beta waves of alertness. But highly trained and highly focused athletes remain in the alpha state with their eyes open, a clue to the state of mind that they are producing.

In the late 1960s, when identifying movements in the alpha waves, Peter Fairley, the ITN science correspondent, said: "If there is such a thing as premonition I reckon it's in some way connected with the alpha rhythm part of the brain." (See the section on

premonitions; pages 106-15.) In what looks like promising laboratory research into a type of psychokinesis phenomena, the mind
switch (see the section on PK, pages 283–89) is similarly measured
as the brain moves from alpha waves to theta waves. These shifts
in brainwaves are also speculated to be the points at which other
paranormal abilities or perceptions may be activated.

The brainwaves are merely the barometer showing what is
happening. And there are hopeful signs that reseach may in the
future discover other barometers that will prove many aspects of
the paranormal.

In dream research, tests to see if there was a direct connection
between REM and dreaming seemed at first to show that there
was. Indeed, this was the conventional wisdom for many years.
Test subjects would be woken up during REM activity and they
would recall dreams, which would then "fade from memory" in
about ten minutes or so. The conclusion seemed to be that REM
was the body's activity when dreaming. Those who were awakened during non-REM sleep did not have such vivid recall of
their dreams. Some experimenters assumed that this was because the dreaming was over and the memory, when awoken,
was already fading. (As we shall see, it was later discovered that
there may be dreaming in non-REM sleep as well.)

The differences between REM state and non-REM state may
be important in understanding the purpose of dreaming.

When a person first falls asleep he or she gradually relaxes for
around three-quarters of an hour, descending into deeper states
of sleep, then, as time progresses, the process seems to reverse
itself but veers off into REM sleep. During REM sleep the brain
activity is similar to that of an awake, active person. The eye
muscles are very active, the tips of fingers and toes twitch, snor-
ing stops. The rest of the body is at rest however, seemingly
paralysed. It is assumed that the body more or less paralyses itself to prevent movements that could be dangerous during
dreams. Experiments on cats, where REM sleep had also been
observed, not only suggested this was the case but indicated that

this function was controlled from an area of the brain called the "pons." Experimenters destroyed the pons area in test animals, and although their sleep pattern was unchanged and they entered REM sleep, they would then move around, sit up, and even attack what has been interpreted as "imaginary prey."

There are differences in the amount of REM sleep among different age groups. Children spend around fifty per cent of their sleep time in REM state, and babies of premature birth up to eighty per cent. Children also spend more time asleep overall. Adults spend around thirty-five per cent of their sleep time in REM state, and the elderly around seventeen per cent.

But why dream at all? The first clue perhaps comes from what happens when we do not dream. Dream-deprivation experiments were conducted in the late 1950s by William Dement at the University of Chicago. He woke test subjects up whenever they exhibited signs of entering the REM state. In fact, each night during the experiments it became increasingly hard to wake them, suggesting that the brain was working hard to get into that state, a sure sign of a need that should be met. As REM state was denied to the subjects, they became anxious, stressed, ill at ease and apathetic. There were reports of hallucinations. Once the experiment ended the sleepers immediately went into longer than usual periods of REM—the expression "catching up on much needed sleep" is apparently no figure of speech. But an obvious need for REM sleep does not explain its purpose; nevertheless, there have been no shortage of theories put forward.

One theory is that dreaming allows the body to rest but keeps the mind alert to potential danger and threat, and in a state where full wakefulness is easily achieved so that the person is ready to defend or flee. Another widely held theory is that dreams allow us to sort out and "reject" the garbage that collects in our minds throughout the day, expressing their release as self-generated fantasies. Still another theory is that dreaming is rather like an appendix, a remnant of something that was useful once but is no longer a part of the human need.

However, people deprived of dreams do suffer, so it would seem dreaming serves some function.

The most satisfying theory is that dreaming is connected to learning. There are several observations that seem to justify this view. In the 1960s Howard Roffwarg at Columbia University, New York, suggested that dreams stimulated the brain and allowed for the development of neural connections, believed to be the basis of memory and thought. In the 1970s this work was continued by psychiatrists Ramon Greenberg and Chester Pearlman. Their experiments with rats in mazes indicated that deprivation of REM sleep, and presumably dreams, while not greatly affecting the rats' abilities to deal with known tasks, made it difficult for the animals to learn new tasks, or to carry out the more complex of their routines. People exhibited much the same problems. This seems to tie up with the observation that children, who are more adept than adults at learning new skills, have the most REM sleep, which gradually diminishes as time progresses. If true, then the question remains, which was the driving activity? Does learning become more difficult as people get older—as for many it seems to—because there is less REM sleep to assist, or does the lack of perceived need to learn reduce the requirement for REM sleep?

Another question relates to exactly what happens during REM sleep. Many people believe that during REM sleep long-term memory is stored in a retrievable memory. In other words, short-term learning during the day is transferred to and organised in the long-term memory during sleep. We might speculate that perhaps REM sleep is also a time when information is stored from the conscious mind into the subconscious. Our ability to draw from experience is thought to be a major factor in human evolution, and, as argued elsewhere in this book, when pushed "to the edge" the mind finds creative ways to access the subconscious store of "lost" memories.

Support for this theory also comes from the comparative observations of animals such as reptiles that do not seem to experience REM sleep but nonetheless seem to survive very healthily. It has been speculated that the lifestyle of these animals simply does not need "learning," because their survival is based on primitive conditioning. But what about mammals that generally seem to exhibit complexity but still do not exhibit REM sleep, such as dolphins and spiny anteaters? Neuroscientist Jonathan Winson, at The Rockefeller University, New York, noted that the anteater has the largest prefrontal cortex of all mammals (relative to size). This is the area of the brain where short-term decision-making takes place. Although, as a mammal, the needs of the anteater are complex, it is believed that its huge prefrontal area replaces the need for REM because it has sufficient capacity to "update" the long-term memory in waking time during the day. The REM could be likened to computerised "off-line" backup that takes place at night so as not to interfere with the operation of daytime computer applications. It is assumed that the anteater's brain has such a huge store of "on-line" memory that it can set aside some of this memory for "backing up," without interfering with the animal's day-to-day needs.

This seems a reasonable speculation. The brain must organise its learning, and during sleep seems as good a time to do it as any. Dreams, on this basis, could be the fragments of memory being "moved around" during storage, which is why they might seem rather haphazard.

But the connection between REM sleep and dreams is not as solid as was once thought. David Foulkes at the University of Wyoming was perhaps the first to challenge the assumed connection between REM and dreams. He found that people seemed to be doing plenty of dreaming when they were not in REM state. During experiments to see when dreaming began he woke up test subjects before they had entered REM state. Many reported dreams that they must have been having just prior to being woken up. In fact, he concluded from further observations that although REM state reduces with age, dreaming increases. Foulkes believed that dreams followed the progression of "self-awareness." Children under five—who perhaps accepted their existence as "given"—did not report many dreams. Slightly older children reported "disconnected" dreams "like snapshots." Animated, complex dreams came with age. This evidence suggested that dreams are a reflection of the complexity of the mind having them, which puts dreams back into the area of psychology.

It is generally accepted that there is a connection between the chemical and electrical activity in the brain and dreaming. But there is still debate as to whether dreams are the by-product of that brain activity or simply the method the brain uses to undertake this vital function.

But can we throw any light on this debate by studying dream material itself? It seems likely that we can. Studies of dreamers indicate basic patterns. We have already considered the age pattern: simple dreams at a younger age becoming more complex with maturity. But other studies have shown that dreams seem to reflect the lifestyles and cultures of the dreamers. Perhaps this is not surprising, but it challenges the assumption of dreaming as a purely random collection of "brain sparks." One study compared the dreams of children in the USA with those of children in India. Although they were all well-fed test subjects, the Indian children dreamt more about food than their American counterparts. No obvious reason comes to mind, but perhaps it reflects the "importance" with which food and eating are viewed in each culture.

Another study showed that aggressive dreams were rarely reported amongst Cuna Indians whose lifestyle involves very little violence. Children in the USA reported a good many aggressive dreams, perhaps because American children are fed a more aggressive diet of images through television.

These studies suggest that dreaming relates specifically to the mind of the dreamer. We have a model, then, of dreaming as a useful function: the brain uses dreams to organise itself, to allow the person to develop, and to "test run" future situations. We can see that dreaming might well be a path to the subconscious, allowing dreamers to learn a good deal about hidden parts of themselves if they take the trouble to analyse their dreams. Desires, fears, fantasies can all be analysed and even tried out in dreams, to the benefit of the dreamer.

It is possible that the mind houses a memory of every experience that the "owner" has had. To obtain access to such a huge pool of information would be invaluable in times of uncertainty. And dreaming may provide the access to the store of knowledge that cannot be readily recalled by the conscious mind.

One aspect of dreams that seems beyond dispute is their ability to provide inspiration and solutions to problems. Probably most people have had the experience of struggling unsuccessfully with a particularly knotty problem. After trying long into the night to find a solution, they wake up the following morning finding themselves equipped with a solution and even wondering why it was ever a problem the night before. As Albert Szent-Gyorgyi, a Nobel prize winning chemist, said: "I wake up, sometimes in the middle the night, with answers to questions that have been puzzling me." If the solution is not actually the product of dreaming, then some other process during sleep seems to work through problems in a way not readily available to the wakeful mind. But specific cases that do relate to dreaming can be cited. Elias Howe is said to have discovered the design for a sewing machine—a problem that had eluded him for years—in a dream. In 1865 the German chemist Frederich August Kekule von Stradonitz, working in Vienna, was trying to solve the problem of how the Benzene compound of six atoms was designed. He dreamt of six snakes, all biting each other's tails, and in the morning he had the solution to his problem: the atoms were arranged in a circle.

The American psychotherapist Dr. Carol Warner attributed a career change to dreaming. Discontented with the path she was on, she asked herself "what next?" before going to sleep. She dreamt of the church she had attended when younger and the following morning called the church to find that there was a vacancy for a job they had not yet advertised. It was, Dr. Warner said, the "perfect job for me." Indeed, she commented: "I've asked my dreams for guidance at major junctions throughout my life and they've infallibly led me in the right direction." We would argue that perhaps Dr. Warner had infallibly led herself in the right direction, using her dreams to access her best resources. Dreams seem to access the intuitive, artistic aspects of the mind, which may be more reliable for subjective decisions such as career choices than the rational, intellectual side of the mind.

Many people who are psychic have made comments similar to the perceptive one offered many years ago by psychic Lois Bourne, whom we have spoken to at great length about her experiences. She said: "One of the greatest barriers to mediumship is the intellect, and the most serious problem I had to learn in my early psychic career was the suspension of my intellect. If, during the practice of extrasensory perception, I allowed logic to prevail, and permitted myself to rationalise the impressions I received, and the things I said, I would be hopelessly lost within a conflict. It is necessary that I totally bypass my conscious mind." People who are entrapped in the rational, logical way of thinking that the world tends to force most of us into do not get as much practice as Lois at "bypassing the conscious mind"; but perhaps we all do when we dream. Dreams seem to access the mind in quite different ways to logical thought. Learning more about our own responses to dreams may open paths to greater mental faculties. But Dr. Gotthilf Isler, a teacher at the Jung Institute in Switzerland, made an interesting point. "It's a good idea to ask for answers from your dreams, but I'm not sure the answer you get will be the one you expected. Your unconscious mind may know that you've got a bigger problem than the one you're asking about, and which needs to be addressed much more urgently."

Interpreting dreams can be difficult, though many people with hindsight admit that the answer was intuitively known to them. Examples of interpreting dream mirages are manyfold. Take the case of Robert van de Castle. He dreamt he saw a man in the street who looked "like a concentration camp survivor."

In his dream he sought to put the man "out of his misery" and looked for a doctor to help him. When the withered individual was laid on a marble slab, brown tobacco juice flowed out of his body. Van de Castle never smoked again! This dream probably did not tell the dreamer anything he did not already know about the harmfulness of tobacco, but the dream appears to have found a way to get a very compelling message to the dreamer, presumably for his benefit.

But can dreaming take us into that world we label "paranormal"? Some dreams appear to offer glimpses of the future, which is clearly useful from a survivalist point of view. Take this example of the dream of four-year-old Jake Delph. On 13 January 1988 the *Daily Mail* reported the case of the "Boy whose lottery dream came true." Jake had two dreams, on successive nights, that his family would get rich because of the "balls on TV." Jake told his father about these dreams, and when he was buying his National Lottery tickets he remembered what his son said and purchased extra "lines" of numbers. He won £177,356. Easy to dismiss as coincidence, or to argue that in any family that plays the lottery there will be incidences of thinking about winning. Easy even to argue about the many cases of such "premonitions" that do not come true. And these are valid arguments. But when precognitive dreams are closely examined, the arguments against do not always stand up.

Psychologist Keith Hearne is at the forefront of dream research in the UK. He conducted a test with one subject who experienced precognitive dreams, collecting one year's worth of such dreams. Three years later he asked independent judges to compare the dreams with actual news events in the papers for up to one month after the date of the dreams. As a control he asked them to check the dreams against an identical month of another year; he did not tell the judges which year corresponded to the precognitive dreams. The conclusion was that the dreams more accurately tallied with the events of the "right" year, though the matches were not accurate enough to be conclusive.

Sceptics of this kind of study argue that the sample is biased, that if every dream reported was included the statistics would not differ from those expected by chance. But that does not take into account the fact that those who experience precognitive dreams insist that there is "something" different—and more compelling—about these dreams.

There were precognitive dreams about the ill-fated maiden voyage of the Titanic in 1912. There were well over a hundred reported premonitions about this ship's only voyage and people changed their course of action as a result. Only a few of these premonitions overtly involved dreams, but a good many referred to people who "had bad feelings," and it is unclear if dreaming formed a part of their "feelings." In one dream-related case an emigrant's mother apparently dreamed on three successive nights that the ship would sink. She persuaded her son to cancel his voyage. Mrs. Shepherd of Nebraska had a dream prior to her husband's voyage in which she saw the ship sink; her husband changed his reservation to another ship. Just after boarding the *Titanic*, Isaac Frauenthal told his family that he had earlier had a dream in which "it seemed to me that I was on a big steam ship which suddenly crashed into something and began to go down. I saw in the dream as vividly as I could see with open eyes the gradual settling of the ship, and I heard the cries and shouts of frightened passengers." He and his family survived. Two would-be crew members, Thomas and Alfred Slade, missed the ship after delaying their own arrival at port because one of them had a dream that made them feel uneasy about the ship.

Setting aside the argument about the validity of premonitions, it may be inappropriate to consider premonitions as an aspect of dreaming; dreaming may merely be the mechanism by which some premonitions make themselves known rather than a function of dreaming *per se*. The question of premonitions, and their obvious contribution to survival, is discussed elsewhere in this book (see pages 106–15).

The most fertile ground for the survivalist mind in this section is where the dream, far from showing us our inner selves or the world around us, can be controlled by the dreamer. These dreams seem to give the dreamer the opportunity to "model" situations which he or she either has experienced in the past or expects to confront in the future. A person who feels "put down" by others may need to be more assertive in everyday life, and dreaming of situations where he or she is more assertive may provide helpful insight into the benefits of a new approach to life. Many non-assertive people confuse assertion with aggression; dreaming allows the mind to "try out" techniques so that the dream has a better chance of changing positively. We know of people who have been motivated to make changes recommended by books they have read, or courses they have attended, because they have dreamt of the positive outcomes that might come their way.

Similar modelling processes are possible using imagination and conscious thinking. But the drawback of these conscious models is that the conscious mind censors what it will allow the individual to "model"; dreaming is uncensored and allows the creative mind more latitude to "play" with possibilities.

But how far can the modelling be in the control of the dreamer? According to the evidence, quite considerably. This is known as lucid dreaming.

Lucid Dreaming

Lucid dreaming—though not then known by this modern name—was written about at the turn of the century by psychologist High Calloway under the pseudonym of Oliver Fox. His most famous example was of a dream where he was in his bedroom but the view outside was of undeveloped fields instead of the houses he knew were really there. This indicated to his mind that he was dreaming. His wife, in the dream, insisted he was awake, but he reasoned that the lack of houses meant that he had to be dreaming. So, in the dream, he jumped out of the window and floated gently to the ground. On touching the ground he woke from the dream. He had known that he was dreaming, and he had some control over his dream.

Lucid dreaming amounts to being aware in the dream state and to some extent controlling the direction of the dream. It is thought that there are two ways to enter a lucid dream state. The first method is known as Dream Initiated Lucid Dreaming (DILD). The dreamer is aware of having a dream and begins to control its shape and its outcome. It is said to work best if dreamers "programme" themselves before going to sleep with the intention to wake up inside the dream and control it. With practice many people claim to be able to achieve lucid dreaming with some frequency.

The second method is called Wake Initiated Lucid Dreaming (WILD). The dreamer is very briefly woken, for just a second or two, immediately before entering REM state. This can happen naturally, but for experimental purposes sensors can be set up to detect the onset of REM state and cause a slight awakening. Those who advocate this method of inducing lucid dreaming suggest that the best way to capitalise on the moment of slight awakening is to focus on the hypnogogic images—hallucination-like flashes—that arise in the transition between wakefulness and sleep. Other techniques include reciting the alphabet or counting during the pre-sleep period and trying to carry the sequence on into the dream.

A typical "use" of the lucid dream is to fly, which many people find breathtaking and awesome. Most people have such dreams; some find it better to design them and control them if possible.

The lucid dreamer is then able to gain the most benefit from "modelling" situations before trying them in real life. As a technique, lucid dreaming is bound to increase the accessibility of the dreamer's own mind, and presumably can make the person more "rounded" because it allows for the development of both the rational and the creative, intuitive mind.

We have reached a point in our discussion of the dreaming mind where we begin to see an overlap with the phenomenon known as out-of-body experience (OOBE). The section on OOBEs is found on pages 125–37. For the moment we shall continue to look at another dream-like state—hypnosis.

Hypnosis

Hypnosis is sometimes still referred to as mesmerism, a reference to the revolutionary findings of Franz (or Friedrich) Anton Mesmer. His original work was the basis of not only hypnosis but also many other processes we now label "psychological."

Mesmer was born in 1734. Drawn to the spiritual, he went to a Jesuit university but veered towards philosophy. He also showed a deep fascination with science. By the time he was just over thirty years old, he had acquired a degree in medicine, had studied law and had shown an interest in science and philosophy. His medical thesis was entitled "On the Influence of the Planets," a title that was to echo down the years to modern times.

Mesmer believed that the human body, as an integral part of the broader universe, was affected by universal energies such as magnetism and gravity. When a person was in tune with those energies, he or she was healthy: when not in tune, ill health—mental or physical—followed. Anyone with even a rudimentary knowledge of yoga and the chakras will recognise the underlying truth of this assertion. Spiritual energy or life force is said to travel through the body along various pathways connected by seven chakra points. Meditation and yoga are designed to open up the chakras to allow for the free flow of this spiritual energy. This universal life force is referred to as *chi* by the Chinese and *ki* by the Japanese.

To "unblock" the energies Mesmer recommended the use of magnetism. By passing magnets over the body he felt that he could clear the pathways and thereby cure illnesses. In 1773, following similar work by his friend Father Maximillian Hehl (a Jesuit priest who was astrologer to Empress Maria Theresa), Mesmer attempted the technique on a young woman, Franziska

Oesterlein. He passed magnets down her body towards her feet. The young lady reported feeling energies passing around her body, and she told Mesmer she felt much better for the treatment. After a period of treatment she was pronounced well again.

But during a more "conventional" medical treatment—"bleeding a patient"—Mesmer saw that blood flowed more quickly whenever he moved nearer the patient. When he passed his hands over a patient's body he received similar comments and results as he had when using magnets. In this respect, he was practising a form of "psychic healing," although Mesmer actually touched his patients whereas "healers" tend to work close to the body without touching. Some healers contend that they are working on the body's aura, which they say extends out from the physical body. Mesmer had originally concluded that it was the magnetism of the Earth or the magnets themselves that was causing the patient's reactions. But the fact that he could have the same effect using his hands led him to conclude that it was what he called "animal magnetism," a "magnetism" inherent in the living person, that was responsible. Predictably there was an outcry from the medical profession who immediately denounced Mesmer as a fraud. They argued that he was healing only with the power of suggestion. It is highly likely that to some extent that is exactly what he was doing. But the medical establishment failed to see the value and the advantages of activating the body's ability to heal itself. In 1778 Mesmer moved to Paris to escape the bile of his colleagues, but unfortunately his fame was so widespread that criticism followed him even there. His flamboyant manner and his wizard robes and magnetic wands did nothing to endear him to the generally staid medical profession.

However, in Paris he came to the attention of King Louis XVI, who was so impressed with Mesmer's cures that he was on the point of supporting him and his researches. But Mesmer somehow managed to clutch defeat from the jaws of victory. He upset the king by refusing an offer of a pension and demanding a sum for research, which the king refused. The king, not one to be slighted, demanded an investigation into Mesmer's claims by a team that included Benjamin Franklin (who was firmly opposed to Mesmer) and, somewhat ominously, Dr. Guillotin, inventor of the execution device.

The investigation team did not even interview Mesmer, and their procedures lacked thoroughness, to say the least. The whole matter looked like an official whitewash with a predetermined conclusion. The "official" conclusion was that Mesmer's claims were in error at best, the product of an overworked imagination. He was in effect driven out of France and his work discredited for the remainder of his lifetime.

One legacy Mesmer left was the training he had given a protégé, Armand Marie-Jacques de Chastenet, the Marquis de Puysegur. De Chastenet used the "magnetism" techniques on his domestic servants. One servant in particular, named Victor Race, seemed to fall asleep during the experiment while he was tied to a tree. De Chastenet then instructed him to wake up and untie himself, which Victor did with his eyes still shut. Victor was in a trance, the first recognised hypnotic trance. De Chastenet christened the technique "mesmerism." (The term hypnosis, coined by the surgeon James Braid in 1842, comes from Hypnos, the Greek god of sleep.)

But because Mesmer had been discredited—and there was probably no more certain way of getting discredited in the late 1700s than to be the victim of opposition from a powerful French king—mesmerism was derided from the start. It was claimed to be fraudulent, or the product of imagination. Indeed, in France mesmerism was outlawed. The medical profession made it a priority to reject and destroy the claims of mesmerism. If it were not for this false start perhaps the whole history of hypnotism would be less "music hall" and more medical. But, as with most officially rejected claims, some first-rate minds took Mesmer's theories "underground" and experimented with them privately.

In the 1800s hypnotism began to recover a measure of acceptance. Dr. Jean-Martin Charcot at the Salpêtrière Hospital in Paris discovered that he could induce strange conditions in patients. He was examining the phenomenon of hysteria where strong belief creates a physical effect. For example, if someone believes he or she is blind then that person may be unable to see, even though there is nothing physically wrong with the structure of the eye or optic nerves. Charcot found that by using hypnosis he could induce these hysterical conditions in subjects. He believed that hypnotism was a form of hysteria; since hysteria was a recognised medical condition, hypnotism became medically respectable. Certainly the two are close cousins, and some have argued that hysteria is just a specialist form of self-hypnosis.

From the very beginning, hypnosis seemed to be a useful tool. Since hypnotised patients felt no pain during operations, hypnosis was regularly used as an anaesthetic until the introduction of chloroform in 1848, after which interest in hypnotism as an anaesthetic tapered off.

However, in recent years there has been a resurgence of interest in hypnosis as an anaesthetic. The British Medical Association endorsed the use of hypnosis in 1953 for the purpose of controlling pain; similar endorsement was given in the USA in 1958. In the 1990s hypnotism has come to the fore with a few celebrated cases, the most publicised being the vasectomy operation of Andy Bryant. Using self-hypnosis he not only blocked pain and was able to be operated on without anaesthetic but he also reduced the flow of blood during the operation.

In 1998 Kathleen Duff was operated on in what is thought to have been the first surgical operation done through the National Health Service where hypnosis was used to control pain. The forty-minute operation removed two metal pins from her hand while she was fully conscious, but hypnotised. No anaesthetic was used. "I knew it would work," she said. "It was just a matter of convincing other people. . . . It is perfectly safe and painless." She had been put into a trance by a qualified clinical hypnotherapist, Margaret Kendrick. Mrs. Duff has used hypnosis to cure her husband of phobias and to relieve the debilitations of multiple sclerosis of which she suffers. "A year ago I was in a wheelchair. Now, I'm not. I go into this deep relaxed state and just tell my body it is better. It just works. Almost anybody can achieve the deep relaxation that I do."

The use of hypnosis in operations may be making news today, but it is not new. James Esdaile while working in India performed more than 300 major surgical operations using hypnosis as an anaesthetic. These operations included limb amputations and the removal of large tumours. Esdaile believed that hypnosis was a far more effective anaesthetic than chloroform and remained of that opinion until his death in 1859.

Although the medical use of hypnosis was gaining acceptance, what was not so well accepted was that hypnotic subjects also showed signs of heightened psychic abilities, often to extraordinary degrees. Dr. Charles D'Eslon, who attended King Louis XVI's brother and was one of Mesmer's original supporters, noted one example of a hypnotised subject who could play cards with his eyes shut. The subject Victor Race, referred to earlier (see page 55), also demonstrated enhanced qualities during hypnosis: he would respond to de Chastenet's mental commands even though they had not been voiced out loud, and he picked up a song that de Chastenet was mentally holding in his head. De Chastenet also noted that Victor's intelligence seemed on a much higher scale when hypnotised.

Another characteristic of the hypnotic state is heightened suggestibility, which can be used to cure disorders, break habits such as smoking, relieve insomnia and enhance learning.

Regression hypnosis enables a person to be "taken back" in the mind to a previous time in order to relive an experience and perhaps discover more about it. The two most common forms of regression hypnosis within the field of the paranormal are past-life regression and alien abduction research.

Suggestibility can be a drawback in the use of hypnosis. If a hypnotist is searching for a "lost" memory, there is a tendency to keep questioning and re-questioning under hypnosis; this

can have the side-effect of introducing imagery into the hypnotised subject's mind. To add to this problem, the hypnotist generally has a rapport with the subject, and one effect of hypnosis
is that the subject seeks to please the hypnotist. So if the hypnotist is a well-known past-life regressionist, for example, there
is a subconscious pressure on the subject to produce a pleasing
story of a past life for the hypnotist.

Some years ago we conducted a series of experiments to determine the effectiveness of hypnotic recall, which are mentioned in John Spencer's book *Gifts of the Gods?* The hypnotist,
Lucien Morgan, undertook a series of tests with volunteers. One
subject named Tony "learned" the script of a prefabricated story
of abduction by alien beings from Jupiter; he would be regressed
to this script during our session. Under hypnosis he created a
great deal of imaginary detail that was not in the script. It was
also obvious that he was picking up information from within the
room as well; he suddenly described the aliens as wearing cow-
boy boots when a person wearing such boots walked into the
room. (Tony's eyes were shut at the time.) Another subject had
learned the details of a particularly nasty, violently intrusive abduction, but with the slightest prompting towards the spiritual
and the use of subliminal spiritual terms (e.g. "cathedral-like" to
mean big) her recall became one of benign, friendly aliens. Morgan concluded: "We've shown how easy it is to lead the witnesses. And how easy it is for the witness to lie under hypnosis."

But what if there were no language used at all? Could a
person's memory be distorted by the hypnotist under such conditions? It appears that the answer is yes. There are two explanations for this: one "normal" and one "paranormal."

The normal explanation rests on the analysis of how we gain
our understanding during human communication. It is thought
that we communicate about twenty per cent of the information
others pick up through our words and vocal tones: a staggering
eighty per cent is transmitted through eye contact, body language and so on. It is worth remembering that many hypnotised

subjects do not have their eyes closed and can take in their surroundings quite effectively, and with enhanced concentration.

According to the "paranormal" explanation, if hypnosis does enhance psychic abilities such as telepathy, then inevitably the subject will be influenced by the hypnotist's unspoken desires and beliefs.

In regression hypnosis there is the clear danger that the memories brought to the fore are false, inspired by fear and the desire to please the hypnotist, enhanced by suggestibility and reinforced by repeated concentration on certain memory areas. It may be that the alien abduction syndrome is a false one, a modern belief system being imposed by faulty research the world over. Past-life regression may also be false, but there are some clear examples where this type of hypnosis is at least a good therapy. In one case a woman with an unexplained pain in her arm causing her great suffering was regressed back to an alleged past life when she was supposedly shot in the arm by an arrow during a battle. The hypnotist talked through a cure during the session and when the woman awoke the pain was gone. But was she really shot in the arm in a past life? Probably not; the mind could have created a past-life theatre that allowed a cure to work, enhanced by hypnosis.

Regression hypnosis has been a major factor in the relatively new phenomenon of reported alien abductions, which has received considerable public attention in recent years. This phenomenon is examined in the next chapter.

3

The Developing Mind

When the mind seeks to really "stretch itself" it creates "theatres" for itself in which it plays out psychodramas and learns to communicate with aspects of itself. Arguably some religious experiences would fall into this category, for example some insights we call revelations. The near-death experience may be similar. The shamanic journey undertaken by shamans of non-technological tribes can also be viewed as a deliberate attempt to activate the mind in this way. In the latter half of the twentieth century is seems that we are able to study a new and developing "theatre" in the subject we call "alien abductions," which grew out of the broader subject of UFOs. These, as reported, seem to be spontaneous images, often arising as a surprise to the experiencer. As we shall see, they also bear a striking resemblance to religious experiences, near-death experiences as well as the sought-for journeys of the shaman.

Alien Abduction Syndrome

The latter half of the twentieth century has been marked by an upsurge of "UFO" sightings and claims that extraterrestrial beings have visited planet Earth. Since the early 1960s, and to a greater degree since the 1980s, an intriguing new twist has been the alien abduction phenomenon.

The explanation for the many claims of alien abduction

might actually be quite simple: aliens from another planet, or another dimension, or another time, are visiting Earth to study people as part of a long-term programme to learn or acquire something. To dismiss this theory out of hand would be reckless, but there are many reasons why it falls short of a coherent explanation for alien abduction.

It maybe that the abduction syndrome is a complex theatre of the mind created to work through mental experiences. Alien abductions have a lot in commom with—may even originate from the same stem as—the near-death experience and the shamanic journey. Such an analysis makes more sense than the idea of alien visitation in the context of the nature of the reports received. Each alien abduction report, while superficially similar to other reports, is also characterised by its uniquely personal component, which suggests a significant amount of personal input to the experience. At the present time the claims of alien abduction are treated with little more than contempt by the medical and scientific professions as a whole, but it may be in time that alien abduction syndrome will be recognised as a modern mental process, be it positive or negative.

The abduction reports started in the early 1960s with the claims of Betty and Barney Hill, from New Hampshire. In September 1961 when the couple were returning home from holidaying in Canada, they first encountered a bright light in the sky, which they thought at one point was pacing their car, and over time it gradually seemed to come close enough for them to see a structured object in the air. While Betty stayed in the car, Barney went across a field carrying his binoculars and examined the object while it hovered at tree-top height. He could see windows and could make out human-like figures on board. He became frightened and he fled across the field back to the car. So agitated was he that he snapped the leather strap that had been holding the binoculars around his neck. He told Betty that he thought they were going to be captured. They drove off and were conscious of hearing a sequence of "beeping" sounds; sometime later they heard the sounds again as they became more clearly aware of their surroundings. They had suffered a period of confusion or memory loss and were now some miles away from the scene of the UFO sighting; they drove on towards home. Quite some time later researchers examining the case suggested to the couple that the time taken to complete the trip was too long, that they seemed unable to account for a two-hour period. Thus was planted the seed of the idea that there were hidden memories waiting to be uncovered; something must have happened in that two-hour period. This became the subject of the book, written by journalist and UFO researcher John G. Fuller, *The Interrupted Journey: Two Lost Hours Aboard a Flying Saucer*. The book, published in 1966, became an international bestseller and ushered in a new phase of the flying saucer interest that had been captivating America and Europe for around twenty years.

Fuller's book was based on research into the claims of the couple and the reported after-effects of their ordeal. Betty suffered nightmares during which she dreamt that aliens had in effect taken control of her and Barney, made them steer off the main road into a small side road (which they could never find on subsequent excursions) and had brought their car to a halt near the landed flying saucer. Betty became deeply interested in the UFO phenomenon, passionately reading all the then current literature. In particular she was drawn to the writings of Major Donald Keyhoe, at the time a leading author on the subject with a strong bent towards the extraterrestrial hypothesis. Over time the couple became concerned that Betty's nightmares in fact reflected reality, that their car had actually been under alien control and they had been abducted. The experience left them with stresses and concerns, and they sought out someone who could use hypnosis to release possible hidden memories. The nightmares, even by today's standard, provide a good working model of a "typical" abduction.

Betty dreamt that when the car had come to a halt in the clearing it was approached by small humanoid aliens who separately led both Betty and Barney out of the car and onto the flying saucer. There they were taken into separate compartments, stripped and forced to lie on medical examination tables where they were subjected to various tests and examinations with a particular bias towards the reproductive organs. Under hypnotic regression by Dr. Benjamin Simon, a Boston psychiatrist, these same dreams emerged as memories. Betty certainly was convinced that her memories were accurate, that she and her husband had in fact been in contact with aliens.

When Fuller's book came out in 1966, the subject of regression hypnosis in "mystery" cases had already captured the public imagination. In 1956 a book called *The Search for Bridey Murphy* by psychologist Morey Bernstein was published telling the story of the regression of a young American woman—Virginia Burns Tighe—who was regressed back to her former life as a poor woman in Ireland. Alan J. Lerner wrote a very successful Broadway musical called *On A Clear Day You Can See Forever*. It was a fictional story with many parallels to the Bridey Murphy case. The show was sold out for six months in advance when it opened at the Mark Hellinger Theater.

The release of the Betty and Barney story in the book by such a respected journalist as Fuller did much to pave the way for acceptance of humanoid-encounter reports, especially since it involved the same hypnotic processes that had already been popularised by the Bridey Murphy case. Until then UFO researchers had either drawn away from such claims or had kept them "self-censored" in their own files rather than bring the UFO subject into ridicule. In the few cases that were made public, the contactees spoke of benign and caring, and very special, relationships with aliens. As might be expected, their claims were soundly ridiculed by the media, the public and many UFO researchers. But whatever the public thought, there were many researchers now following in the footsteps of Fuller, seeking out and researching the abduction claims that were beginning to surface.

But it would be the 1970s before the abduction phenomenon really took off. In addition to the reports of current abductions there were many claims of past abductions, some even predating the Hills' case. For a while it seemed as if everyone had a hidden abduction waiting to be revealed.

Two of the most famous abduction stories at that time were the Pascagoula case of 1973 and the Travis Walton case of 1975.

On 11 October 1973, Charles Hickson and Calvin Parker, fishing at Pascagoula in Mississippi, heard a "zipping" sound and saw, around twenty yards away, an egg-shaped object come down and hover nearby. They had been fishing off the end of a pier and the object had now cut off their return to their car. It was around ten yards in length, three yards or so high, and had a small dome on top, with a revolving blue light.

Before the pair had the opportunity to discuss or plan an escape route, an opening appeared and three bizarre entities floated out. Hickson said: "My flesh crawls now when I think about the three things that appeared through the opening." More or less humanoid, they appeared to be covered in wrinkled cloth, had protrusions around the "head," though these did not match the shape of "normal" facial features, and claws for hands. It was not clear if they were biped with their legs together, or had only one "leg." The aliens grabbed Hickson and Parker as hapless victims and "floated" them into the craft. Parker passed out at this time; he was later badly traumatised by the event. But Hickson remained alert throughout; he felt he might have been tranquillised at the start of the encounter.

Aboard the object Hickson was scanned by a mechanical eye-like object and then removed from the craft. Parker, Hickson noticed, was transfixed in terror. From the dock where they now found themselves they watched the object take off at astonishing speed, leaving them alone. Unsure what to do they drove around for a while and then told their story to the local sheriff. The case was investigated within days by law enforcement officers, medical people and UFO researchers. Rarely has such an important case been studied so close to the time of the event. This meant there was little time after the event for the pair to "contaminate" each other with their own feelings about the experience. The general conclusions of those involved were that the men were sincere and genuinely traumatised by the events. Parker had nervous breakdowns in subsequent years, which were thought a consequence of the encounter.

Hickson came to believe that this was the first of many contacts, and he later perceived mental impressions that he believed came from the alien entities. In effect, he went from abductee to contactee quite quickly.

And that is not a rare claim. Many abductees claimed they were subsequently either blessed or plagued (depending on their point of view) by further experiences. It has to be said that for most "repeater" witnesses the subsequent experiences are more mental in nature, such as voices and perceived telepathic communications, rather than UFO sightings. Betty Hill, for example, has, in the thirty-plus years since the experience reported many other sightings and contacts. In one documentary she revealed that she could drive to isolated places and use a "code" with her headlights that would communicate with the aliens.

Another abduction, the Travis Walton case, was extraordinary because there were several witnesses to the UFO encounter, which culminated in one of the longest abduction periods on record. On 5 November 1975, a team of seven woodcutters working late in the Apache-Sitgreaves National Park, in Arizona, saw a fairly classical flying-saucer-shape hovering in the air near their truck. Travis Walton left the truck and approached the object, but was struck down by a beam of light. The event so frightened the rest of the team, which included Walton's brother Duane, that they drove off to the nearby town and reported the incident to the local police. The police and some members of the team returned to look for Walton—the rest of the team were too shaken to go back into the woods that night—but could not find any sign of him. Sheriff Ellison, who led the search, pointed out that "one of the men was weeping. If they were lying, then they were damn good actors."

Walton did not turn up that night or indeed for the next five nights, during which time the team had come under suspicion of murdering him. When Walton reappeared he claimed to have been abducted by aliens and taken aboard the flying saucer, even possibly taken on a flight; he has recollections of seeing images of flying in space through the windows. Lie detector tests were taken. One psychiatrist, Dr. Gene Rosenbaum, said of these tests: "This young man is not lying... He really believed these things." The abduction phenomenon started to pick up a momentum of its own in 1980 following the publication of *Missing Time* by New York artist and regression hypnotist Budd Hopkins. This book related several accounts in some detail of people who had undergone abduction, usually revealed through regression hypnosis and usually following the clue of periods of "missing time," similar to those suggested to Betty and Barney Hill. *Missing Time* was very successful, mostly in the USA, and led to a resurgence of abduction claims.

Hopkins worked with witness support groups in the USA and was involved from the very beginning in the case of writer Whitley Strieber, which was to give further impetus to alien abduction phenomenon. In 1987 Strieber published the first of a series of books relating to his personal experiences; its title was *Communion*. It was a well-written account of a fairly typical abduction that involved, as many did, earlier experiences that only came to the fore while he was exploring his memories. Over time Strieber published other books looking deeper into his encounters with what he termed "the visitors," leaving open the question of their origin. The successive books, *Transformation, Breakthrough* and *Secret School*, have had a widespread following and have undoubtedly helped to shape the modern view of the abduction phenomenon.

In 1997 Budd Hopkins produced his latest book on abductions, which contained more revolutionary information. *Witnessed* describes what the author refers to as "what seems to be an alien display of an abduction for the benefit of an important political figure who was a witness to this." The figure was allegedly the then-Secretary General of the UN, Javier Perez de Cuellar.

The subject of the abduction, Linda Cortile, was abducted in the early hours of the morning of 30 November 1989 by being levitated out of her twelfth-floor window and drawn up into a hovering UFO. Several witnesses who were positioned on the nearby Brooklyn Bridge allegedly came forward. They claimed to have seen the UFO and even the figures floating in the beam. The witnesses included two security guards said to be accompanying de Cuellar. Although this case has the appearance of being multi-witnessed, in fact the information is channelled through very narrow sources, largely through the abductee. Although the case hinges on the two security guards for many important aspects, Hopkins has never met them; their information is passed through letters and tapes.

The problem with these abduction stories is their evolution. In the Betty and Barney Hill case, the basic template was established—possibly derived from Betty's dreams. Subsequent cases have relied a great deal on hypnosis, which, as we discuss elsewhere, is not an effective tool for research. And the later cases, mainly those investigated by Hopkins and those reported by Strieber, advance the subject in an almost linear fashion. The main abduction stories seem to break at points of great public interest in the subject. There is a peak of interest every ten years, around the anniversary of the first reported UFO sighting, in 1947, by Kenneth Arnold. Hopkin's book *Witnessed* met a need; there had been much criticism of the fact that over a fifty-year history of UFOs there had never been a reliably witnessed abduction where the witnesses were not closely associated with the abductees or shared the experience with them. This is not to suggest that any one individual is deliberately prefabricating stories; however, if someone did intend to deceive—to fool a UFO researcher, for example—the best time would be when the publicity is making the subject popular. And, if the abduction scenario is a mental construct of some sort, then it could well be triggered by the surge of other similar reports. At times of media interest in UFOs and abductions it seems plausible that someone who has been looking for a meaning for some strange experience could be drawn to the alien abduction theory as a possible explanation. There is no doubt that the media interest has an effect. After the release of the film *Close Encounters of the Third Kind*, for example, UFO groups were inundated with enquiries and their membership increased. Many people came forward with abduction stories that had apparently lain dormant; the witnesses were waiting for a reason to come forward and someone to come forward to.

Another interesting aspect of alien abduction is the progression of the claims. The abduction phenomenon has evolved over time; the aliens have become "more alien"; their activities have become more sinister; and so on. It is almost unique in the annals of the paranormal to find such a rapid and measurable evolution. Ghosts today are much the same as they were reported in Roman times. Poltergeists have been banging on for 2,000 years. They may use modern and local materials—appearing on film and video, for example—but these apparitions seem to be essentially of the same character. This would indicate that, whatever they are, ghosts and poltergeists represent a genuine set of data being observed and reported. The progression in abduction reports is just a bit too "satisfactory" to be entirely true. But this should not lead the reader to think the abductions are a fabrication. Far from it; but it is highly likely that the popular interpretation—aliens in their flying saucers—is a construct. But what then are the real abductions?

One possibility we put forward is that alien abductions are the modern equivalent of shamanic journeys. In many non-technological cultures, shamans experience psychic journeys, during which they gain wisdom and insights to become spiritual leaders. Both UFO-related abductions and the shamanic journeys seem to be close cousins of the near-death experience. Indeed, they may be components of one of the most important, developmental experiences humans undergo.

The fact that we have clothed the UFO abductions in technology relects our science-fiction bias in our technologically dominated society, just as ghosts and spirits reflect the mystical bias of less technological cultures. The Western world is searching for new meanings to religion, indeed searching for new religions, and the UFO phenomenon seems to be meeting that need. To expand on this hypothesis is not appropriate for this book, but the subject is examined in another book in this series, *Alien Contact*. The arguments as to why the abduction reports do not produce a coherent story of alien intervention, and why researchers need some alternative hypothesis, are also covered in *Alien Contact*. What we are examining here is how this experience might be developing the individual human mind.

Close encounter and abduction experiences may be helping to develop the mind in three ways: as a shamanic, learning journey; as a trigger for opening up and accessing the right brain; and as a focus for psychic development. Such mind development might be operating at a personal level only, but there are those who believe that it represents a stage in human evolution itself. The nineteenth-century philosopher Friedrich Nietzsche believed that humankind was not an end product but a bridge, and that once humanity crossed the bridge it would be ready for the first stage of enlightenment. The belief that humanity is undergoing "enlightenment" through the phenomenon of "alien contact" is strong, although it is often attributed to the "cultist" elements within the field of UFO research.

The Shamanic Journey

The essence of the shamanic journey is purification of the inner self. The more the individual understands about him- or herself, the more is understood about the outer world. In the simplest model of the shamanic journey, the person travels to an alternative world, perhaps deeply underground, and is accompanied by a "power animal" that can guide and assist in the journey. The journey itself is one of sensory development, feeling the sensations, smelling the flowers and so on. When the "power animal" is asked a question, it provides an answer. Different shamanic leaders would interpret this in various ways, but we might assume that the journey is one of spiritual development and that the power animal represents an "embodiment" of the areas of the mind that cannot ordinarily be accessed. During a shamanic journey, the person is in effect talking to other areas of the mind. The journey allows for thoughts to be offered without censorship, so the spiritual traveller is reaching into the "real" person without the constraints of society, taboos and so on.

In alien contact, the alien may also be a projection of the mind; it may be that the person is talking to him- or herself. One experiencer whose contacts included alien entities would be asked questions, and if she got the right answers she would be allowed to ask questions of her own. This seems a very direct form of self-education, assuming the "other entities" were embodiments of her own mind. Betty Hill, and many others that followed, were taken on tours of the spaceships onto which they had been abducted. Indeed, this is so commonly reported that it has become a motif of the experience. It is difficult to see the reason for the tours if the aliens are simply using people for genetic experimentation. We do not take our laboratory rats on a tour of the facilities. But it is a common theme in fiction, and there are many overlaps between the imagery of the abduction and the imagery of fiction, which suggests that both are being drawn from the same creative areas of the mind. James Bond, for example, is usually given a first-class guided tour of the enemy's base and then wined and dined before being tortured. If the abduction is a learning process, then clearly these tours are the travels of the mind, and the visions of space that Travis Walton saw, or the images of frightening devastation on Earth that some abductees have been treated to as a warning, are manifestations of uncensored fears and wishes.

Budd Hopkins (who, we should point out, believes that these experiences are objectively real and connected to extraterrestrial visitation) has suggested that the aliens seek to understand our emotional make-up. They put humans through tests to see how they would react in given moral or emotional circumstances. For example, one subject, during regression hypnosis to work through his abduction story, remembered being asked to kill another human and the aliens watched his responses closely. At one point the human saw that his intended victim was another alien, which was part of the test. The subject learned something about himself that day. Perhaps that was the intention, and perhaps the scenario was self-generated.

The existence of a common source for the imagery that feeds into fiction and into the abduction lore is clear and operates at both the individual and the group level. We have in other books examined the connection between the strongly favoured "hybrid" motif promoted mostly in the USA (that aliens are seeking to create human/alien hybrids) and the current American vogue for introspection that is based on their own hybridisation. Non-native Americans are a hybrid of something because they are new-generation: Irish Americans, Polish Americans and so on. But all this might suggest that abduction experiences are totally internal; mental constructions designed by the experiencer for his or her own purpose. So they may be, but that does not have to be the answer, or at least the whole answer. There could be influences external to humanity that affect our development. These might be natural—aspects of the Earth and the universe that we have yet to understand. They might be intelligent, even extraterrestrial, but not in the sense of alien astronauts, but something closer to the concept we call God. If these influences exist, then the modern interpretation of the alien abduction phenomenon may be a technological way of trying to understand them. To ignore the process—whatever it is—would be detrimental to the understanding and long-term development of humankind.

Accessing the Right Brain

There is clear evidence that people who experience close encounters and abductions change in many ways. *Gifts of the*

Gods?, by John Spencer, examines the case histories of many such experiencers who developed artistic talents that they did not previously have, or at least did not exploit. Not only did they develop an interest in art, but they acquired talent as well.

Peter Holding is a gardener who had UFO sightings and "entity" experiences and who was drawn to artistic expression as a result. His photographs and paintings sell for many hundreds of pounds and his career is changing towards this area. "Bryan" has had experiences since a young age with entities similar to those described by Whitley Strieber and is now working as a commercial artist after a blossoming of artistic talents. Other experiencers we interviewed developed talents in sculpture, music, poetry and other writings.

Some experiencers have also changed their lifestyles, becoming more ecologically aware, more in touch with their intuitive responses, and have become vegetarian. Some became concerned for their general health and made positive changes such as giving up smoking or taking up a healthy regime of exercise. Following the Aveley abduction in England in 1977 the witnesses—a whole family—underwent changes. Both the husband and wife reported feeling much more confident. The husband was "working for himself creating things" and had "written many poems about life." One of their sons suddenly accelerated academically. Four members of the family gave up eating meat. The parents almost completely stopped drinking alcohol, and the father suddenly gave up his sixty to seventy a day smoking habit. Both parents became concerned for the environment.

It does not seem possible to us that aliens come to Earth with a mission to create artists and musicians or to encourage vegetarianism. Either the aliens are not involved or, if they are, these changes are a positive side-effect.

We suggest that the so-called abduction experience is essentially an unknown one for those who go through it, and because of that the mind's natural survival instincts come into play. The first thing the mind will do is liken the unknown to something known in order to gauge the potential threat. Given the nature of our current culture, the mind might well pick science-fiction imagery against which to measure the experiences, hence an "alien" overtone. Then the mind will call on its full databank of resources to help it deal with the perceived threat or opportunity. To access the data, the mind probably engages all its abilities, using the more efficient, intuitive and instinctive right side of the brain (as discussed in the section on savants; see pages 24–31). When the right brain is thus triggered we suggest that other artistic learnings and feelings that reside in this area of the mind are also triggered, and once engaged they are so satisfying that the person holds on to them and develops them. One experiencer (who believed that he was in contact with extraterrestrials with a mission to develop humanity) told us in interview: "If you don't follow these contacts and develop them you will lose them." While we might not agree with his interpretation of the source of his feelings and information, we agree with the idea that if the right brain, when triggered, is ignored and left-brain thinking allowed to dominate then the "contacts" will be lost.

Psychic Development

Some people develop psychic abilities rather than artistic talents after close encounters. We suggest that the process of change is the same for both areas of development.

Several experiencers have found themselves moving into mediumship, into dowsing and commonly into spiritual healing. Such is the case of Betty Andreasson Luca who has had visions of angel-like imagery and out-of-body experiences, and has been subjected to alien abduction. It seems that often it is the close sighting of a UFO or a perceived abduction by aliens that triggers an interest in these spiritual matters.

In summary we believe that the alien abduction scenario is no different to other spiritual phenomena, such as shamanic journeys, near-death experiences, out-of-body experiences, angel encounters and so on, which have existed throughout human history. But because of the particular needs of modern people in a technological society, these experiences have been reinterpreted within the framework of the UFO phenomenon. Because the subject of UFOs is much ridiculed by science, the media and even by parapsychology, these cases could be lost and their import ignored. But they are significant and should be studied and their lessons learned.

Development of Creative/Artistic Abilities from other Mind-Changing Events

UFO abductions are not the only paranormal experiences that have triggered significant changes in individuals. For instance, stigmata have been known to do so (see pages 228–44). The following is a story of personal transformation after a ghost-type experience.

Accrington in Lancashire is an area rich in local hauntings and legend. In 1957, a young boy, Stephen Wood, living in a council house in Great Harwood, just north of Accrington, woke up during the night and saw a vision of five silhouetted figures moving in his room. The five figures were moving forward towards a sixth figure floating in the air but in a seated posture. As each of the walking figures reached the seated figure they would present something, perhaps a gift, to the other. Stephen thought it was shaped like a jug. The seated figure was wearing something like a papal mitre according to Stephen's description. The vision faded and Stephen drifted into sleep. One interesting aftermath of the experience is that Stephen has become a painter and usually paints in silhouettes. He asks himself: "All my pictures seem to be of silhouettes against the sunset...I wonder if my early experience has anything to do with the way I paint?"

Even something as simple as an accident is perhaps relevant. We shall see later in this book how accidents and injury have triggered psychic development, as in the case of "psychic detective" Peter Hurkos. The following story demonstrates the result of a simple accident.

In December 1995, ten-year-old schoolgirl Vicky Wilmore was cured—by accident—of a strange and literal "change around" in her life. A year earlier she had suddenly started "mirror writing"—reversed writing, back to front and upside down, that can only be read by holding the script up to a mirror.

To do such a thing deliberately takes enormous concentration and is rarely perfect. But some mirror writers are as fluent in mirror writing as "normal" people are in conventional writing. Clearly the brain is accessing itself in an unusual way and although mirror writing might be regarded as a disability, it demonstrates that the mind is capable of more creative "thinking" than logical, rational processing would seem to suggest.

The only clues to Vicky's condition, if clues they are, is that she had an unhealthy childhood following a premature birth. She had a serious viral attack and measles and suffered convulsions. On the day of her "change" when she began to mirror write, she complained her head hurt when she awoke that morning. Then, a year later, she was watching her favourite football team, Manchester United, lose a match when she banged her head on the coffee table. From that point on she wrote normally again.

This first section of the book has looked at the ways in which the mind can work when pushed to its limits. We have shown that the mind seems capable of more than we often suspect. The following two sections take that discussion further, looking at the evidence for extraordinary mind powers.

II

Mind as Receiver

4

Receiving from the Living?

For the human mind to serve our needs, it must collect information from the outside world, assemble it into a meaningful set of data, and make it available when needed. The five "normal" senses—sight, hearing, touch, taste and smell—are doing that all the time. But there is strong evidence that the so-called sixth sense is also collecting information. But just how far can the mind stretch when searching for information? To other minds? To other locations? To the past? To the future? To the dead and the world beyond death? In this chapter we examine this additional sense, first amongst the living.

Telepathy

Simply put, telepathy amounts to direct communication between two minds without the use of speech, sign language or body language. The word "telepathy" comes from the Greek for "feeling at a distance"; and as this implies, telepathy is more than just a transmission of words or images over a distance, it is a direct transmission of appreciation. Communication specialists would acknowledge the subtle difference. In communication one person, the originator, has to first analyse his or her own appreciation of a situation, then translate it into a code, which is either speech or the written word, and then offer it in that form to the receiver. The receiver, in turn, translates the code according to his or her own set of beliefs, convictions, attitudes and so on. Inevitably, a great deal can get lost in the translation. If we imagine trying to describe the appreciation of a cup of coffee to another individual we might find words to express how we felt about it, and those words might be understood by the receiver, but the receiver would not actually feel the same way. For example, "it tastes sweet" would mean different things to different people depending on their previous experience of "sweet." Quite what transmits in a telepathic communication, however, is unclear. Some people report "hearing" actual words, which would seem a waste of an opportunity to transmit something more subtle; others report feelings, as we shall see below. (Telepathy between those who are synaesthetic, if any cases could be found and studied, would be fascinating indeed, and in one way would represent the purest form of communication.)

Freud believed that telepathy was a natural ability of the mind, but one that had been lost, or at least diminished, with overdependence on the five senses. This seems highly possible, but on the other hand we must acknowledge that humans have always had those five senses. It seems more likely that telepathic ability has diminished as developing humans became dependent on tools and weapons. Perhaps the development of language, which we tend to see as an advantage, also diminished telepathic ability. Language is useful, but perhaps the price paid for it has also been high.

Twins frequently report telepathic communication, or sometimes telepathic rapport. We interviewed twins "Jan" and "Sue" who lived on opposite sides of the world, one in Australia and one in England. They frequently "felt" for the other one, perhaps the most common form of claim between twins. Sue, living in Australia, had a miscarriage which naturally caused her both physical pain and inner distress. Jan, in England, did not know of it as it happened, of course, but suddenly felt great physical pain; she burst into tears, alarming her husband. She knew immediately that it related to her sister and telephoned her to discover what was happening on the other side of the world.

Twins may or may not hold a clue to telepathy; certainly there are many impressive incidents between twins that suggest empathy, at the very least. Twins Michael and John Atkins were both skiing and both broke their legs in the same way at the same moment of time, resulting in identical fractures. But they were miles apart, skiing on different mountains.

A tragic coincidence (or empathy, or telepathy, or other strangeness) occurred to two sisters, not twins, aged four and five. They lived apart, each with one of their separated parents. In 1899, at the same moment, a mile apart and not in obvious contact with each other, the two girls died from what seem to have been cases of spontaneous human combustion. They both burst into flames in their respective houses at the same time; in both cases where no matches or other inflammable substances could be found.

Eric and Tommy were twins separated at birth and did not see each other for thirty-eight years. When they came together both had identical beards, wire-rimmed glasses, and the same trousers and jackets.

If the environment for bringing up children is thought still to be influential—and Eric and Tommy were both brought up in Yorkshire—then what about Oskar and Jack? Their mother brought up Oskar as a Nazi; while their father brought up Jack as a Jew. But when they were reunited they both had many identical characteristics including both "storing" elastic bands on their wrists, flushing the toilet before using it, and reading magazines from back to front.

All these are not isolated incidences: in fact, the list of examples could fill this whole book. Simple arguments like environment and upbringing cannot explain these conditions. But does telepathy?

Take the case of Nancy and Ruth Schneider. Sitting a room apart during their examinations for college, both chose the same topic for an essay and both wrote the same essay—word for word.

Mrs. Spraggett of Coventry wrote to the "Weekend" magazine of the *Daily Mail*, in January 1996, to report a life-saving event that could well include telepathy. She was relaxing when she became compelled to telephone her father. She kept on the phone, letting it ring until eventually her father answered it, though he quickly said he would call back and hung up. When he telephoned later he explained that he had fallen asleep having left a chip pan on; the kitchen had caught fire and the house was filling with smoke. The telephone had awoken him and possibly saved his life.

Colin Wilson in *The Mammoth Book of the Supernatural* suggests that there is evidence that hypnosis creates an environment conducive to telepathy. During early experiments into hypnosis, the Marquis de Puysegur realised he was getting telepathic responses. He found that under hypnosis Victor Race (see the section on hypnosis, pages 53–59) would obey his mental, unspoken commands. Indeed, over time de Puysegur discovered that he could hold entire conversations with Victor; Victor would reply as if he were hearing normal words and responded with normal words. *In Memoirs in Aid of a History of Animal Magnetism*, published in 1809, de Puysegur describes "singing" mentally a song and Victor repeating it. He duplicated these experiments with a girl, Madeleine, in front of audiences. She obeyed his mental commands, and when members of the audience were invited to transmit their own mental orders she obeyed them equally well. A sceptic who thought that de Puysegur might be leading Madeleine with a code, as is used by stage magicians, had the experiment repeated at his own home. During one part of the experiment he made no sounds or movements at all and Madeleine reached into his pocket and took out three screws that he had secreted there for the purpose; he was convinced of the veracity of the claims. Wilson states: "What Puysegur had demonstrated beyond all doubt was that telepathy exists (although the word would not be invented for another century)."

It would be 1934 before Dr. Joseph Banks Rhine conducted his experiments into telepathy at the Parapsychology Department of Duke University, North Carolina. Subjects were asked to identify a playing card by picking up a mental image of it that was being "sent" by the person holding the card. The playing cards were eventually replaced with cards specially made for this purpose by Karl Zener. The Zener cards had distinctive patterns that would be easy to concentrate on and clear to "receive" telepathically. Each pack of twenty-five Zener cards consisted of five groups of five images: circle, square, star, plus sign and three wavy lines. Rhine believed his tests provided evidence for the existence of telepathy, but something more seemed to be uncovered. In checking the scores, there was a suggestion that receivers were "picking up" not the card in question but the next card; they seemed to be predicting rather than reading images. It was a hint that perhaps extrasensory perception contained elements of clairvoyance.

These experiments have been duplicated many times, and refined. Instead of using Zener cards, some tests have consisted of "sending" the image of a picture or a physical object. Mary Craig Sinclair, for example, attempted to draw images "sent" by others. Of 290 images, 65 were held to be "hits" and 155 "partial hits."

This kind of success poses a question: Is the explanation telepathy or some other process? It would be quite possible for the "hits" to be the result of remote viewing, in which the "receivers" "home in" on the images for themselves. But experiments with Uri Geller at Stanford Research Institute seemed to suggest that telepathy was the main factor. If Geller was "reading" images from a pile that the "senders" had not themselves seen, his overall score was lower than if the senders had seen and were presumably transmitting the images.

The question of overlap between telepathy and remote viewing, and indeed precognition, is an interesting one. Remote viewing is more fully described in a later section on out-of-body-experiences (see pages 125–37), but experiments with retired police commissioner Pat Price, conducted by physicist Russell Targ at Stamford Research Institute in California, had fascinating results. For the test, Harold Puthoff and Dr. Bonnar "Bart" Cox would drive to a location and transmit the images they saw there to Price, who was at the Stamford Institute. Price would then de-

scribe the images. However, Puthoff and Cox decided to disobey
the previously agreed rules of the test and drive at random so
that even they would not know where they were going. They
chose, for example, to turn whenever a car in front did so in
order to increase the randomness. The plan was to stop at the appointed time, wherever they were. But Price started giving descriptions of the location before they got there. He said, before
the appointed time: "I can tell you right now where they'll be....
What I'm looking at is a little boat jetty or a little boat dock along
the bay." In fact Puthoff and Cox ended up at Redwood City Ma-
rina. Since Puthoff and Cox did not know where they were
going, it seems as if some form of precognition was taking place.

If telepathy is a power of the mind, what conditions enhance
or promote that power? Although telepathy might be an ability
that has somewhat atrophied through lack of use and dependence on modern techology, there is evidence that when the other
senses are impaired, telepathy might still act as a "back-up."
Children with dysfunctional brains, for example, have high
scores in telepathy tests. One mentally and physically impaired
child, when having his eyesight tested, was found to be able to
"read" the eye chart more accurately whenever his mother was
in the room with him. He seemed to be "reading" the correct letters from his mother rather than directly through his own eyes.

Telepathy seemed to be enhanced during the dream state.
Experiments in the 1970s at the Maimonides Dreamlab in
Brooklyn, New York, tested sleepers' ability to pick up the images transmitted by others. The scores were above that of
chance alone. In other tests, those who were encouraged and
supported faired better than those who were challenged and
disbelieved. This apparent sensitivity to the emotional atmosphere created by the test situation itself turned up in so many
claims of the paranormal that it seems imperative to devise tests
that, while being scientifically objective, also allow for what
seems to be a genuine factor—and one that cannot be ignored.
Just as remote viewers have argued that they need a variety of

fresh images to read or their abilities become stunted, so in telepathy tests it was shown that boredom and tiredness suppressed scores. These findings are, however, in line with "normal" abilities; most people perform better when they are inspired and motivated rather than bored and uninterested. Not surprisingly, this also applies to paranormal abilities.

Psychometry, Psychic Reading and Psychic Detection

The expression "psychometry" is derived from the Greek for "measuring the soul." This reflects the opinion held by many psychometrists that they are "picking up" a remnant of something someone "invested" into an object. Psychometrists generally touch objects, and from the contact receive impressions of the history of that object or of its owners and handlers.

Probably the earliest scientifically based testing of psychometry is the work in the nineteenth century of Joseph Rodes Buchanan, of the Covington Medical Institute in the USA. He found that some people had the ability to tell what chemicals were contained within a glass phial just by holding it. In other tests, Buchanan discovered that some people could press paper containing certain chemicals to their foreheads and identify the chemicals without "obvious" means. The work was replicated by others, such as William Denton, a geologist at the University of Boston, who found similar, impressive results. Buchanan commented: "The past is entombed in the present. . . . The discoveries of psychometry will enable us to explore the history of Man as those of geology help us explore the history of the earth." Buchanan did not consider the possibility of telepathy, though later researchers did.

T. C. Lethbridge, a well-known Cambridge researcher of the paranormal during the 1960s, considered the uses of psychometry for archaeology, though several of his more academic colleagues tried to warn him off such thinking. Lethbridge was famous for using and expressing his own mind and pressed

ahead. He commented: "The answer, however, must surely be
that there is no magic memory stored up in, or around, inanimate
objects." He believed that the psychometrist was in effect using
telepathy; perhaps the psychometrist was picking up information by using the object as a conduit, or inspiration, to "connect"
with the minds of those with the knowledge being sought.

An impressive examination of psychic reading was undertaken by writer Michael Crichton—most famous as the author of
such books as *Jurassic Park* and *Airframe*. His approach was one
of scepticism. As related in his autobiographical book *Travels*—
one of the most important books for those interested in the paranormal—he sought out psychics and then withheld information
from them; he did not feed them "encouraging" leads, so that
they would need to get the information from another source, presumably a paranormal one. He did not tell them who he was, or
the purpose of his visit. He withheld his nationality and was re-
strictive of his body language and gestures so as not to lead the
psychics down certain roads. He discovered that, as in most professions, there were those who were good at the task and those
who were not, some who perhaps had even convinced themselves of an ability they seemed not to have. Nonetheless, some
of the people he approached impressed him. For example, one
psychic made his task of withholding information all the easier
by being aged, virtually blind and somewhat deaf. Just prior to
this visit he had been in the cutting room editing a film he was di-
recting *(The Great Train Robbery)*. She suddenly said to him, obviously startled: "What on earth do you do for work?" But she
quelled any suggestion of "hunting" information: "Don't tell me,
don't tell me. It's just that I can't put it together. I've never seen
anything like this before." She described seeing Crichton working in what looked like a laundry room with large white baskets
with something like black snakes coiling into the baskets. She
heard a strange sound and could see pictures running backwards
and forwards. She also described high hats and old-style fash-
ions. In the editing room, the prints of the film, *The Great Train*

Robbery—set at the turn of the century with actors wearing high hats and old-fashioned clothes—were being examined, the films running backwards and forwards through machinery that made the strange sounds described. The film—the coiled snakes—fell into baskets below the machinery. Crichton commented: "No matter how much she might have feigned blindness as she did a "cold reading" on me, I knew damned well I couldn't have conveyed to her images of what an editing room looked like."

In general, Crichton concluded: "There was indeed something going on . . . these people had access to some information source that ordinary people did not." These words almost perfectly echo the sentiments of a hard-headed, no-nonsense cop, Thomas Lipes, the then-chief of Miami's homicide division. Lipes was referring to Dutch psychic Peter Hurkos who had helped him in two criminal detection cases. Lipes told Assistant Attorney General John S. Bottomly: "He helped us tremendously on two homicides. I know you people are sceptical up in Boston about things like this, but believe me, this man has something you and I haven't got."

In 1941, Hurkos had been injured in an accident, falling thirty-five feet and fracturing his skull. On emerging from a coma after a few days, he allegedly told his doctor: "Doctor, don't go! Something terrible will happen!" The doctor ignored the advice and went on the overseas trip he had been planning; he was killed shortly afterwards. During his stay in hospital Hurkos gained fame, or notoriety, for describing things to other patients that he should not have had knowledge of.

In 1945, Hurkos visited a theatre where a psychic was demonstrating his powers. Hurkos sent a message claiming to be better than the performer; the psychic asked Hurkos to join him on stage and asked of his methods. Hurkos claimed: "I touch things." At this the psychic passed Hurkos his watch but must have regretted this almost immediately when Hurkos told him that the watch contained hair from a woman who was not his wife. "Her name is Greta and you take her from town to town

with you," he said. He even located her in the audience. After
this Hurkos was given work as a performer. This turned out to be
successful and led to work as a psychic detective, using his powers of psychometry. Hurkos could psychometrise holding an
item or clothing, or hair or fingernails, belonging to the victim, or
use his psychic powers to "pick up" from photographs. Sometimes he would keep an object with him while he slept and
would awaken with information.

The first murder case he dealt with was the shooting of a coal
miner in the Limburg provence of The Netherlands. Hurkos held
the victim's coat and told the Limburg police that the murderer
was Bernard van Tossing, stepfather of the victim, and that the
gun that had been used was on the roof of the victim's house. He
was correct; the gun was found, with van Tossing's fingerprints
and van Tossing was convicted. Hurkos later moved to the USA.

When Hurkos accurately described a double murderer to the
Miami police in 1958, Lipes was inspired to make his comment
to the Boston police. Hurkos had held a photograph and sat in a
taxi belonging to the Miami victim. He described a man whose
nickname was "Smitty" who came from Detroit. Hurkos added
that the man had also killed someone in the Key West area. The
police knew of the other murder but had not thought it was connected to the Miami killing. They found that both victims had
been killed by the same gun. A month later Charles Smith, aka
Smitty, was arrested and convicted for the two murders.

In the early 1960s the Boston police were searching for just
about any help they could get to solve the famous murder cases
attributed to the serial killer, known as the "Boston Strangler."
Hurkos' involvement with that case contains many impressive
moments, though he did not actually solve the case (in fact, no
one ever stool trial for the murders).

On 29 January 1964, Detective Sergeant Leo Martin and Assistant Attorney General John S. Bottomly picked up Hurkos
from the airport. The arrangements were secret, at Hurkos' request because he did not want to be pursued by a curious press

and public. When they stopped for coffee Hurkos asked Martin, "Who is Katherine?" Katherine was Martin's mother's name. Hurkos explained: "You tell her, take doctor's advice. I am worried about her legs. Very bad varicose veins—she should do what family says." Martin was impressed; he and his family had for some time been trying to persuade his mother to go to the hospital but she had been refusing. Hurkos also went on to add: "One good thing, Leo. It is good she got those glasses two months ago. That left eye, very bad." Now Martin was seriously impressed. It fitted his mother's details very accurately, and Hurkos went on to describe with equal accuracy Martin's mother's back-pains and a childhood injury. But the sceptic would argue that Hurkos, having been asked to work for the police, could have investigated the officers' lives in detail and been prepared to impress them with his apparently psychic knowledge. Perhaps so, but that could not explain Hurkos' ability to describe Julian Soshnick. Bottomly informed Hurkos that he would be working with Soshnick and offered to describe him so that he would recognise him. Hurkos waved aside the suggestion and described him instead, including very minor details such as his vanity about his hair. This time there could have been no pre-warning. Soshnick was not a member of Bottomly's staff, had not yet been working on the Strangler case, and he was one of forty-five attorneys that could all equally well have been chosen to assist, assuming that anyone was. At the time when Bottomly selected Soshnick for the assignment, Hurkos was already aboard the plane and in the air on his way to Boston.

Hurkos' approach to the stranglings was to touch photographs, or objects connected with the case, to get a sense of the killer. He was presented with more than 300 "scene of crime" photographs but instantly pulled one out and exclaimed: "This phoney baloney. This not belong!" Soshnick had inserted the photograph—from a previously solved strangling case—as a "control." During the time that Hurkos touched photographs and objects his "readings" were impressive. He described the scenes on photographs without looking at them; he described events happening at the scenes of the murders as if he were there, including details that were being withheld from the public.

Hurkos described the man he believed was the Boston Strangler: height of around five feet seven or eight; weight around 130 or 140 pounds; a "spitzy" nose; a scar on the left arm from an industrial injury; damage to his thumb. He added a plethora of other, minor details such as a history of working with diesel engines, and that the murderer slept on a bed with no mattress. Hurkos eventually pinpointed and named someone whom he believed was the strangler. Hurkos arrived at his conclusion while psychometrising a letter written by that person. Curiously, some of Hurkos' descriptions fitted a different suspect that the police were considering: Albert DeSalvo. Eventually the police accepted the confession of Albert DeSalvo who seemed to have detailed information about the crimes, including details not made available to the public. DeSalvo had a "spitzy" nose, a scar on his left arm and worked with diesel engines. For medical reasons, DeSalvo never stood trial but has entered the history books as the Strangler. Hurkos always believed that DeSalvo was not the Strangler.

DeSalvo is now dead and took any secrets to the grave. But we might consider an interesting, and even frightening, possibility that would reconcile these claims. It is well known that some people have a predisposition to confess to crimes they did not commit. The police, as in this case, had withheld details to enable them to assess whether this was happening. They accepted DeSalvo's confession partly because he seemed to have information that was not readily available to the public. But they seem to have overlooked the fact that they were working with a man, Hurkos, who was also gaining information not available through "normal" means. If Hurkos was right and another person was the killer, it is just conceivable that DeSalvo could have been an unfortunate combination: an unbalanced person with a predisposition to confess to crimes he had not committed, and a psychic able to detect the details to make his confession believable. We shall never know for certain, but we do know that Hurkos had an impressive ability, and he rejected DeSalvo's claims.

Psychometrists describe the process of psychometry as one of interpreting impressions, and sometimes they get it wrong. Every impressive psychometrist, including Hurkos, has a score of "misses" alongside the "hits." Another individual with impressive hits amongst the misses was a fellow countryman of Hurkos," the Dutch psychic Gerard Croiset. Croiset was called in by Dutch police on several cases; they seem to have an open mind about psychic abilities.

Croiset was reportedly psychic as a child. His first experience of psychometry arose when he held a ruler belonging to a watchmaker and scenes from the life of the watchmaker came into his head spontaneously. In the 1940s he was investigated for his psychic abilities by Professor Willem Tenhaeff, a parapsychologist. Croiset did not take payment for his work, but he did ask that those he helped should be prepared to send a report to Tenhaeff.

Croiset did not always need to go to a scene, or touch an object. Over the telephone he was able to describe the whereabouts of the body of a murdered four-year-old girl and pinpoint the location of her killer. In another telephone call Croiset comforted Professor Walter E. Sandelius whose daughter had gone missing. Croiset told him that she would be located alive and well in six days, which she was. Descriptions that Croiset had offered the Professor of the girl's movements over the period of time she was missing turned out to be very accurate.

This ability to psychometrise over the telephone raises a question of how it could be done, or what mechanisms might be involved. It suggests that Lethbridge's theory that psychometry amounted to telepathy might just be correct; perhaps Croiset picked up the impressions from the girl herself. Alternatively we must consider the description given to us directly in interview with a well-known British psychometrist, Jenny Bright.

She told us she could psychometrise over the telephone by "touching" the sounds coming out of the telephone. This, too, would fit with Croiset's description.

Sometimes the impressions give sufficient information for the "hit" to be impressive, but still leave unanswered questions. Such was the case of the murder of Scottish teenager Patricia Mary McAdam who went missing in 1967 after accepting a lift from a lorry driver. In 1970 journalist Frank Ryan involved Croiset in his enquiries. Croiset gained some information about McAdam after he touched her Bible, which her parents had sent him. Croiset told Ryan that McAdam was dead and he was able to describe his impressions of her surroundings. His description of where the body would be found included a wrecked car with a wheelbarrow leaning up against it. A location as described was found, and a wheelbarrow was leaning up against the wreck of a car, but the girl's body was never located.

In his book *The Psychic Detectives* Colin Wilson discusses the abilities of Suzanne Padfield. She took on the case of a nine-year-old girl from Moscow who had gone missing. Padfield received a package containing a photograph of the girl and examples of the girl's own writing. Immediately Padfield received impressions of the girl at a skating rink. She somehow knew that the girl had been talking to a thick-set burly man, and she "saw" the girl accompany the man to his home. There, he strangled the girl, wrapped the corpse in "something blue" and took it on a bus to a local river where he dumped it. Padfield gave a description of the killer to Russian parapsychologist Viktor Adamenko. Her description fitted a suspect that had already been questioned by the police. When they confronted him with the detail provided by Padfield he broke down and confessed.

Arguably the most famous British "psychic detective" is Nella Jones. The Metropolitan Police have admitted that they have used Ms. Jones' insights on a number of occasions. She assisted in the discovery of the stolen painting *The Guitar Player* by Vermeer. She was able to say where the discarded frame and alarm mechanism would be found and to sense that the picture would turn up in a cemetery, which it did. Former Detective Inspector Bayes concluded: "There could only be two answers. Either she was involved in the theft, or she was indeed psychic." There was a time when the police were in fact considering questioning her in case she had been involved, but became quite certain she could not possibly have been.

Ms. Jones also counted among her "hits" some identification of the Yorkshire Ripper, Peter Sutcliffe, sixteen months before he was captured. She gave a description of the killer to *Yorkshire Post* reporter Shirley Davenport, who, after Sutcliffe was arrested, looked back in her files to discover the clues had all been there from Ms. Jones. She had described the Ripper as a lorry driver called Peter (which he was); and she saw a name beginning with "C" on the side of his cab ("Clarkes" as it turned out); she described him living in a house in Bradford, No 6 (which he did); she described it raised above the street, having wrought iron gates, and steps up to the front door (which it did). Shirley Davenport stated: "it was the most weird experience. It went far beyond anything coincidence or guesswork could possibly have provided."

Nor was Ms. Jones the only psychic to be tuned in to the Yorkshire Ripper during his reign of terror. Bob Cracknell gained impressions of the Ripper and predicted correctly when he would next strike. He also predicted that he would be caught shortly afterwards, which he was. Cracknell also felt that the Ripper lived in Bradford.

But Cracknell's most impressive case is probably that of Janie Shepherd. Janie was raped and strangled in February 1977; her body was found in April. While being interviewed about his psychic abilities, Cracknell reported "impressions" of the Janie Shepherd case, which included a "vision" of her murder. He mentioned a contraceptive on the back seat of her car. The police dismissed his comments because of the inaccuracy of this detail, until detectives working on the case admitted that such an item had been found but was being withheld from the public. Cracknell became a suspect for the crime until he convinced the police of his innocence, and his psychic impressions. He went on to describe the killer as having a scar on his cheek and said that he had probably already been arrested for another crime. Years later Cracknell found out that he had been correct. The killer, David Lashley, had by then already been jailed for another crime—and he had a scar on his cheek.

Reporter Lesley Gibson reported her own encounter with psychometry in the Yorkshire *Evening Courier* of 21 April 1994. While attending a psychic awareness course, she handed an object to one of the "students" on the course, Linda Covington. Linda said: "You have just got out of the bath. You are clutching a towel around you, a creamy yellow one. You are wishing that someone could come and see you but you know he can't." According to Gibson this was an accurate picture of an incident that had happened a few months before. She had received a phone call from a friend just after getting out of the bath and was wrapped in a faded yellow towel. Her friend and she had been hoping to get together but this had to be called off because her friend had to work to cover an absent colleague who was ill. Gibson commented: "I had met Linda only five minutes before and she knew nothing about me. She didn't look at me or ask questions—we just talked."

As this section shows, the same result—a psychic reading— can arise from psychometry (touching an object) or from a similar process that does not involve touching. The edges are so blurred between these aspects of the phenomena that it is impossible to separate them. Perhaps the use of an object is merely an aid to focus whatever ability is operating. That was the logic behind a seemingly bizarre instruction to US officials, which was intended as a "psi countermeasure." It was suggested that if officials travelling abroad on foreign visits were presented with gifts, the gifts should be housed away from sensitive locations in case enemy psychics could "home in on them" and obtain details of the secret location.

From the psychometrist's point of view, what does the

process feel like? Each person tends to describe it somewhat differently, but the description given to us in interview with psychometrist Jenny Bright offers some idea of the process: "The first thing I do is still my mind. The first thing with psychometry is the impressions you're feeling from the object; warm, dead, or flat, for example. Whether you like the object, or not; whether you feel heavy with it, perhaps tired with it. All logic has to go out of the window; you have to feel your way. Override your conscious mind; once your conscious mind begins to analyse the object, all is lost."

This echoes the description used for many aspects of the paranormal. The rational mind does not seem to be able to deal with these concepts; it is the instinctive, animal processes that come into play.

Jenny continued with her description: "The next thing is I close my eyes and start talking immediately, getting my impressions out. The way I see pictures are like photographic negatives, in black and white. I see pictures, maybe symbols. I usually see the person doing what they were doing at a certain time."

Jenny considered some of the mechanisms that might have been involved in the "laying down" of the impressions she can detect. Firstly, that strong emotion is probably part of the process. Mundane events do not seem to leave lasting impressions. This alone might explain why many psychometrists seem to detect emotional moments, times of death and, in the case of the psychic detections described earlier, murders. Secondly, Jenny believes that an actual energy is involved, that the energy is "invested" in the object and that when "read" some of that energy is drawn off. For that reason she believes that objects that are frequently handled are less easy to read than those that have been locked away or buried for years. At the very least she feels that objects owned by fewer people are easier to psychometrise than those that have been owned by many people.

At Loughborough University, in August 1992, Jenny psychometrised items owned by seventeen people, all of whom she had no knowledge of and had not previously met. She scored 125 correct "hits" out of 160 impressions. Ronald Kay, writing up the experiment for *PSI Researcher* (Winter 1993), commented: "So many of the facts produced were known only to individual members of the group (all responsible people who have explicitly denied any previous contact with Jenny) that collusion or fraud must be ruled out."

Dowsing

Perhaps the most common form of "psychic searching" is dowsing. The majority of people who try dowsing find that—to their surprise—it works, though often, at first, they do not know what they are dowsing for. As a result they get random results until they learn to phrase a clear question in their minds. Dowsers point out the importance of a clear question—it leads to a clear answer.

In 1952, when the British army was setting up its new headquarters in Germany it faced a water-shortage problem. The site would house 9,000 people, who would need approximately 750,000 gallons of water per day. To purchase this from the existing water supply companies would have been very expensive. Colonel Harry Gratton, CBE of the Royal Engineers, dowsed the likely sites, searching for water. He located considerable, and sufficient, water resources at Mönchen Gladbach, and test bores showed that his dowsing results had been accurate. Although the population has since grown, the water supplies that Gratton located still support the area today. His dowsing not only located a source but also accurately mapped out the boundaries of a "soft" water supply in an area of generally "harder" water— boundaries later confirmed by more conventional means.

There have been other high-profile dowsing successes. The Fox Brewing Company of Chicago used the services of A. Gotowski to dowse for oil; he located the largest oil field that had been discovered for many years. Clayton McDowell also located oil, in this case for the Edwards County Senior High School, an oil field that produced over 100 barrels per day.

Armies have used dowsing for detecting more than just water. During the Second World War, and indeed during the Vietnam War, army units used dowsing to locate buried or concealed landmines. The Royal School of Military Engineering at Chatham even ran courses and demonstrations in dowsing. Jim Schnabel in his book *Remote Viewers: The Secret History of America's Psychic Spies* comments: "The Czech Army also used 'dowsers' to search for traps, mines and drinking water." He adds that Hitler employed map dowsers (see below) to "try to detect Allied divisions and air units."

Harry Price, as part of his varied studies of the paranormal, invited the Abbé Gabriel Lambert to demonstrate his abilities by dowsing for water in Kensington Gardens and Hyde Park. It was successful. Price reported:

> The Abbé would purposely swing the bobbin laterally, and when we came over the hidden stream, the bobbin would make a spasmodic movement, change its course and begin spinning furiously, describing a larger and larger circle the longer we stood over the source of activity. When we reached the bank of the subterranean river the bobbin would stop dead—just as if it had been hit by a stone. The cessation of the spinning was even more spectacular than the commencement. We found many hidden springs and a fairly broad river running into Knightsbridge. When we came to a nappe [pool of water] the bobbin would make quite a different movement. The Abbé said that he could tell the depth of the hidden supplies, their approximate volume, and directional characteristics. He could also tell whether the current was rapid or sluggish.

The descriptions given by the Abbé were confirmed by a park official.

It appears that dowsing is a way of using faculties of the mind to locate water, and indeed other minerals or objects. If, as we propose in this book, these faculties of the mind develop for survivalist purposes, then clearly dowsing serves human survival. Water is the basis of survival, and a much needed commodity in certain conditions such as when moving through new territories. Nomadic groups and the natives of non-technological cultures have long used dowsing to locate sources of water during long treks and expeditions. Both the ancient Egyptians and the ancient Chinese used dowsing. Dowsing is probably a natural ability that we all have. However, as with any other attribute, physical or mental, it becomes dormant when not used. But with even moderate training most people can be taught to dowse with varying degrees of success. It is highly likely that modern dependence on technology has allowed dowsing abilities to "get rusty" in all but a few interested individuals. We use drilling machinery to find water—and other minerals—underground, and perhaps because we invest our belief in the machinery rather than our own abilities, we cease to believe in dowsing as a reality. As we shall shortly see, perhaps this actually "turns off" the ability. Attitude of mind may well be one of the essential mechanisms of dowsing.

Apart from its uses in finding water, oil and other minerals, dowsing has been used successfully to find metal objects, even people lost on mountains. It is also a technique used during "spiritual" or "psychic" healing; the healer dowses to find the areas of the body that need attention, and the areas of the body through which to channel healing energy.

Although there can be little doubt about the effectiveness of dowsing, given its widespread success around the world for thousands of years, we still do not understand the mechanisms involved. When the West started to take an interest in dowsing— probably around the 1930s—it was known as "radiesthesia" from the Latin and Greek roots for "radiation" and "perception." At that time, it was thought that the dowser may be picking up some kind of radiation emanating from the substance being sought.

T. C. Lethbridge, the Cambridge paranormal researcher, recorded the results of a great deal of experimenting with dowsing. He believed he could identify which pendulum lengths related to certain substances and objects. In other words, a certain length of pendulum would find a certain substance. Later dowsers following up on Lethbridge's research also felt that the pendulum spin rate related to certain substances and objects.

Although there are standard dowsing tools there seem to be no limits to the devices that can be used. The most famous dowsing tools are the forked wooden stick and the swinging pendulum. But dowsing can be done with rods of plastic, metal, old coat-hangers and so on. Some dowsers just extend their hands forward and use them as the dowsing instrument. As we shall discuss later, the tool probably does not matter as long as the dowser believes that it will work and is in the right frame of mind.

So what is the dowser actually doing? Can we get closer to understanding how this ability works?

If the ability is inherent and is a survivalist instinct that served our hunter-killer, nomadic ancestors, then presumably there is a sensitivity in the human body, brain or mind that can react to the presence of certain materials. In "new age" speak we might talk of "tuning into the right vibrations" (which may turn out to be a very accurate or inaccurate description of the detected "signal"). We might speculate that, as with so many achievements, there are at least two main requirements:

- a belief that it can be achieved, perhaps based on the knowledge that it has already been achieved either by ourselves or by others
- the correct state of mind towards the operation

In considering the first of these requirements, it seems clear that those who believe they can dowse do so more effectively than those who do not. This is not uncommon in the human experience; "success breeds success" is the old adage. Another common expression from the world of personal development, "Whether you think you can, or whether you think you can't, you're probably right," also applies to dowsing. Before Everest was first conquered there were those who believed the peak could not be reached; but when one team proved it possible many others followed. Colonel Harry Gratton, whose field dowsing is described earlier, already knew that the type of water supply he was searching for existed because a family living in the area was drawing soft water from a private well; knowing that what he was searching for was really there no doubt boosted his confidence. Dowsing is no different to any other human activity; the more you do it the better you get. Paul Brown who made a living dowsing for oil for over thirty years commented: "You can develop it like learning to walk, a slow, difficult process. It takes time and practice."

The second requirement may relate to the question of which part of the brain holds the facilities that govern dowsing, and possibly most paranormal perceptions and talents. We believe that this facility is held in what is popularly known as the right brain—the creative, artistic side of the brain, which does not rely on calculation and logic but uses what we think of as the intuitive, instinctive responses.

The problem of living in a world dependent on logic, rationalism, and technology such as computers and machinery is that we have ceased to trust our instincts. Yet often when we follow our instincts against all the odds we find that we can succeed or that we are right. We suggest that perhaps the animal instincts that serve the animal kingdom so well are being suppressed in humans—to our detriment.

In this question of successful dowsing we accept the claims of dowsers—many of whom have performed very well under empathetic test conditions—that they must follow their instincts and intuition in interpreting what they perceive. Ironically, perhaps further confirmation of this claim comes from a test set up by arch-sceptic James Randi. In 1980, in Australia, he tested eleven people who claimed to be able to dowse, in this case for water. Ten pipes were laid underground through which water would or would not be channelled during the test. As part of the test the dowsers were asked to predict their own success rates; generally their expectations of their own abilities were high. In fact, the results were low—barely more than would have been expected by chance alone. Randi concluded, on the face of it not unfairly, that this "proved" that dowsing was not a "genuine" ability. He had applied the strict scientific criteria and under those circumstances the dowsers failed to demonstrate their abilities. Either he proved his point, or something was wrong with the test conditions. Our own view veers towards the latter explanation. Instinct and intuition are not perhaps at their best during nonempathetic testing. Randi is known to be aggressively sceptical and challenging to claimants. Perhaps that creates the wrong frame of mind. The dowsers almost certainly were more concerned to prove their abilities than to use their abilities; and perhaps that is why they failed. But such a suggestion is also a wonderful recipe for a scientific cop-out; in the end, some combination of testing that allows for scientific control without intimidating scientific paraphernalia must be found.

To go back to the question of "attitude of mind," perhaps each dowser uses his or her dowsing rod, pendulum or whatever not to locate substances but to act as a focus for the mind. Lethbridge was concerned with the scientific principle and believed that he could "prove" dowsing scientifically. Therefore, he needed a "scientific" way of discriminating between one substance and another; he used pendulum lengths and it seems to work for him. Other dowsers have not found that criterion important but still they are able to discriminate. Perhaps the lengths of pendulum served Lethbridge as a way of allowing his mind to believe "scientifically" in what it was instinctively doing correctly. With the obstacle of doubt removed, and his mind relaxed, he could then be successful.

If dowsing contains perceptions that we call paranormal, does it necessarily follow that all aspects of dowsing are paranormal? Probably not. Most aspects of perception are multiple; we augment hearing by lip-reading (sight) because of either impairment or high levels of background noise; we measure the danger of, say, a car closing up on us by both stereoscopic vision and listening to the increase in sounds; and so on. Dowsing is likely to involve a general use of the "normal" five senses. When a dowser finds him- or herself at a given location it is likely that the eyes scan the topography and detect more than is registered by the conscious mind, thereby subconsciously picking up clues about water courses. Perhaps it was registering subconsciously the alignments of churches, ancient burial sites and other features that gave Alfred Watkins his clues to the existence of ley lines. The other senses—hearing, smell, taste, touch—may also be capable of detecting more than is normally acknowledged. Thus the mind may be filing away data on flora and fauna that is not consciously registered. So the mind may already have at its disposal a bank of data that the mind's "owner" is not consciously aware of. Then add to that the information provided by the so-called sixth sense, or senses, whatever faculty that might be. Perhaps the whole "package" is then processed in the mind's "computer" and a result brought to the fore that seems to be the product of guesswork or intuition, simply because the individual cannot identify his or her own logical reasons for arriving at the "guess." Those who analyse their intuition may feel distrust; but those who have learned to trust their instincts might "guess" the right answers.

But what of the dowsing rod or pendulum? Why does it dip or twitch or in some other way move to "tell" the dowser that what is being sought for has been found? Does it detect some sort of radiation? Does it react to magnetism? Or barometric pressure? Or whatever? We think probably not. In fact—and this is perhaps the strangest thing about dowsing—we suggest that the dowser subconsciously makes the rod move. But how? And why?

The "how" is easy. The brain, having processed the information and come to its conclusions that, say, there is water underfoot, sends signals to the hands to make the movement. Because the processing of data has been subconscious, the signals from brain to hand are subconscious as well and feel to the dowser as if they come from "without" rather than from "within." While working with a dowser in Sweden, John Spencer was "taught" to dowse. Not that he was certain of what he was detecting, and certainly not that he was aware of how he was doing it. But one aspect was almost shocking; the power with which the dowsing rod dipped when it "found" something. It felt almost as if the rod was being physically pulled by a strong person out of the hands, ripped downwards as if by a huge magnet. It was so surprising that it left the impression that it could not have been generated from within the mind—until perhaps one considers what a powerful tool the mind is. (John was being filmed at the time and his look of surprise was clear—as was the humour of the film crew.)

But what about the "why"? We believe that the dowser makes the rod move in order to reconcile instinct and rationalism. The dowsing rod becomes the means by which we can fool ourselves into believing that dowsing is a scientific process—that something is registering on an inanimate object, thereby "proving" that it is real. In other words, the right brain dowses but the left brain won't believe it, so the right brain creates a movement in the stick that is acceptable to the left brain. Experienced dowsers—and particularly those with no interest in proving their abilities but just using them—tend eventually to leave the implements behind. Their own bodies become the dowsing rods. And that is probably closer to the real truth.

In learning to dowse it is likely that this process creates its own feedback loop. Dowsers see the results of their work, see the successes, believe in themselves more, and get better at the technique. The movements in the pendulum or rod become a reward, and a confidence builder.

Because dowsing produces such visual responses, often quite

quickly, it is a good way of developing psychic faculties and getting in touch with those aspects of the mind that are being swamped by what we call "modern civilisation."

Map Dowsing

In the section above we have largely considered "field dowsing," i.e. dowsing in a specific location, often literally in a field. But that is only one aspect of dowsing; the other aspect—map dowsing—is similar in result but may be so different in its process that it could well be regarded as a quite different ability.

The map dowser uses an implement, usually a small pendulum and not uncommonly one of crystal, and holds it over a map to locate minerals, objects, even people.

Different dowsers have their own individual ways of "reading" the pendulum. Some interpret a sideways swing of the bob as a "no" and a circular movement as a "yes," the "no" and "yes" being answers to questions they are holding in their minds. Others use left and right swings or circular swings, clockwise and anti-clockwise, to indicate "yes" or "no" answers.

For the dowser to get a correct answer, he or she must be clear about the question being asked. If searching for water, the dowser must hold a question in the mind—in word or picture form—of water. An unclear or unfocused question will produce an unclear or ambiguous response. (Abbé Lambert, whose activities finding water in Kensington and Hyde Park are described on page 97, seems to have increased his concentration by holding a small sample of what he was dowsing for: a bottle of water when searching for water; a mineral sample when searching for that mineral; and so on.)

The mind should be clear of predispositions and preconceived ideas or the pendulum will respond to the desires of the dowser rather than the actual question being asked. For example, if water is being sought, the pendulum might well indicate it is present when it is not if the dowser wishes it to be so. Under conditions of stress, or a challenging test, a lack of clarity of mind might well produce the wrong answers.

The mind must also be working in the artistic, intuitive "mode" rather than the rational, logical one. It is the "animal" senses that are used for psychic detection, not the reasoning functions.

Map dowser Georg Horak, in February 1994, located two British skiers who were lost, trapped on a mountain above Oberammergau in Germany. He was able to locate them to within 1,000 feet of the position where they were eventually recovered by a rescue team. The chief of the team, Alwin Delago, commented: "We wouldn't have found them so quickly without the diviner's help."

The Reverend H.W. Lea Wilson used map dowsing to locate water for his brother in Uganda. The Reverend was at the time 5,000 miles away at his home in England. He similarly assisted villages in India and Sri Lanka.

We have recorded in our *Encyclopedia of the World"s Greatest Unsolved Mysteries* the fascinating results of experiments we conducted into map dowsing; a summary of these results is merited here as there was a strong indication that telepathy played a part in the conclusions.

John Spencer used his diary to establish the dates when he had been present in certain locations in southern England. A map dowser with whom we were working was given the dates, but no other information. He did not see the diary nor did he have access to it. John did not look at the map, or come close to it, while taking part in the experiment so that he would not give away the locations by eye movement.

The first date was a direct hit; the dowser immediately identified the small Surrey town John had been in on the date given.

The second date was one when John had flown to Sweden in the morning. John visualised Heathrow Airport and held the images in his mind. The dowser identified Heathrow Airport quite quickly. However, we later discovered that the flight had been

from Gatwick as identified in the diary. But the dowser had identified the map site John had been thinking about.

In another part of the experiment the dowser identified the location Tunbridge Wells, but we had been in Greenwich at the
time visiting our colleague Tony Wells. The diary entry had said:
"to T. Wells." From the nature of these errors we concluded that
telepathy could have played some part in the process. But not
perhaps in the following story of the lost emerald.

The Isabella Emerald, 1,000 carats and dating from the six-
teenth century, was lost 250 years ago, somewhere off the
Florida coast while it was being transported to Spain. It was to be
a gift for Queen Isabella from the explorer Hernando Cortés.
Two untitled maps were given to two psychics, one situated on
the west coast of the USA, the other on the east coast in New
York; both maps showed the area where the ship carrying the
emerald had sunk. Both psychics, independently, agreed on the
emerald's location, and the stone was indeed found.

This takes us back to the earlier section on psychometry (see
pages 85–96); the processes, while different in appearance, are
probably closely related.

So far we have examined the mind as receiver of information
about various aspects of the world around us, or even about the
past. But can the mind reach also into the future? The next section examines the claims that it can.

Premonitions and Precognition

Both premonitions and precognitions are acquisition of knowledge before an event. A premonition is usually associated with a
"sense of doom," whereas the term "precognition" is usually applied to more "general" knowledge. In this section, we use the
term "premonition" to embrace all incidences of acquisition of
knowledge before an event. There have been hundreds, probably thousands, of reported claims of premonitions even in recent
years. Statistical studies have proven very little. However, it

should be remembered that for the most part people who experience premonitions are not taking part in experiments; premonitions often come "out of the blue" and their significance is not recognised until the actual event has happened. That said, there are cases where the level of detail and precision is high and the foreknowledge seems genuine.

One who believed that her premonitions were "instincts" was the late Diana, Princess of Wales. All she could say about them was "I have feelings about things." She had a premonition of her father's illness the day before it happened, which she confided to her friends. When the telephone call came the following day to tell her that he had had a stroke she knew without answering what the nature of the call was going to be. When Prince Charles proposed marriage to her she heard a voice in her head tell her, "You won't be queen but you'll have a tough role." In 1981, watching her husband-to-be, Charles, riding a horse she suddenly said that she thought the horse was going to die. Seconds later the horse suffered a coronary and died instantly.

Many premonitions are not reported until after the event; a plane crashes and someone then announces that they had previously had a vision of the event. Such "premonitions" are valueless for study since they offer no proof of foreknowledge and could represent wishful thinking, self-delusion, or outright hoax or attention-grabbing. But of course some after-the-fact claims may be genuine yet cannot be regarded as useful for analysis.

Many premonitions are too vague to be worthy of scientific study. If a person has a premonition of a car crash it is probably not very useful since cars crash relatively frequently. Prior to any major disaster such as an earthquake or a plane crash there are bound to be people dreaming about these events; these dreams naturally seem more significant after the event.

Studies have suggested that planes that crash have statistically fewer people on them than those that do not crash; these are thought-provoking findings and suggestive of premonition. Such premonitions may be so vague that recipients do not "understand" them but perhaps become queasy and simply decide not to take the flight. On the other hand, many planes crash because of bad weather, and the weather may be the reason why some people missed their flights, or decided not to fly. More detailed research is needed in this area before any conclusions can be drawn about the role of premonitions. For premonitions contribute to the study of the paranormal only when they are, firstly, specific enough to identify a particular incident rather than a generic type of incident and, secondly, authoritatively communicated before the event happens. A premonition is particularly impressive when, in addition, the person having the premonition acts upon it, by making an unplanned move or changing a course of action.

In the section on dreaming (see pages 38–53) we related a few of the many premonitions that were associated with the *Titanic*; some people changed their bookings and gave up what must have seemed to be the voyage of a lifetime because they felt so strongly about their premonitions. Equally impressive, in a curious way, would seem to be the handful of cases of people who had premonitions about sea disasters and, as a result, switched to the *Titanic* for safety.

Premonitions are not the domain of mediums and psychics only, nor are they a fairground attraction, though the media would often have them portrayed in that way. Most premonitions come to ordinary people in a "blast" of thought, the origin of which is usually as much a mystery to them as to anyone else. There have been some impressive cases of this type of premonition. In Plymouth, on 20 October 1966, a woman told six of her church's congregation that while in a trance she had seen a vision of an avalanche of coal sliding down a Welsh hill towards a very scared child. This was the day before the Aberfan disaster that shocked a nation, when a coal avalanche from a tip overlooking the Welsh village engulfed a school and resulted in the death of over 100 children, and several adults. It was a specific premonition: coal avalanches are hardly common and this was the day before the event. We might also consider that the woman was so impressed by her own vision that she immediately sought out people to tell it to. But, interestingly, this was not the only premonition of the disaster. Tragically, on the same day, a nine-year-old child in Aberfan, Eryl Mai Jones, told her mother: "I dreamed I went to school and there was no school there. Something black had come down all over it." But no avoiding action was taken; when the avalanche destroyed the Pantglas Junior School, Eryl Mai Jones died in the disaster.

A premonition of a different kind—a strange vision of a person present in the room—arose during the Second World War. Commander George Potter and Flying Officer Reg Lamb were used to spending time together in the officers' mess, sharing a drink in each other's company. They were stationed at an RAF bomber base in Egypt. One evening the two were in the mess, as was a third person, a wing commander known as "Roy." Potter looked towards Roy and was shocked to see something unusual: "I turned and saw the head and shoulders of the wing commander moving ever so slowly in a bottomless depth of blue blackness. His lips were drawn back from his teeth in a dreadful grin; he had eye sockets but no eyes; the remaining flesh of his face was dully blotched in greenish purplish shadows, with shreds peeling off near his left ear." Potter was brought out of his reverie by Lamb pulling on his arm. Potter described what he could see but Lamb saw only the "normal" Roy. Both knew that Roy was due to fly a mission the following night. Potter presumably feared the vision was a premonition of Roy's death but did not know how to convey his feelings in a credible way that would prevent Roy from flying. During that flight Roy's plane was shot down and he ditched in the Mediterranean, dying in the sea. Potter said: "Then I knew what I had seen. The blue-black nothingness was the Mediterranean at night and he was floating somewhere in it dead, with just his head and shoulders held up by the Mae West [life jacket]."

Returning to premonitions about the *Titanic*—for which there seems to be an extraordinary amount of psychic involvement, a point we must examine shortly—there seems to have been a very specific vision about its fate. Blanche Marshall was watching the ship sail past the Isle of Wight having left Southampton when she cried out to her husband: "That ship is going to sink before it reaches America!" Such a claim would itself be too vague, but to her husband's annoyance she started to shout to the crowd of sightseers: "Do something! You fools, I can see hundreds of people struggling in the icy water. Are you all so blind that you are going to let them drown?" The majority of the *Titanic* passengers froze to death "struggling in the icy water." This looks like a fairly specific premonition, and it is made all the more impressive by another of Blanche Marshall's astonishingly specific premonitions. This time her husband had learned to listen to her.

Mrs. Marshall and her husband were due to sail on the *Lusitania* in 1915 when she insisted that she would not sail because the ship was going to be torpedoed by the Germans and would sink. Since this happened during the First World War when there were obvious dangers, this might be thought of as more a fear than a premonition. But Mrs. Marshall's reactions prove that it was not a general fear but a very specific premonition. She was quite happy to sail on the *Lusitania* on its voyage prior to the one they had originally planned—still during the First World War and still presumably in danger of the Germans' torpedoes. The couple changed reservations and sailed safely. On the following voyage—the one they had originally booked—the ship was torpedoed by a German U-boat and sank with the loss of almost 1,200 lives.

One other case that relates to the *Titanic* is extraordinary in that it involves not only premonition but also other paranormal phenomena: ghost or spirit involvement, and physical manifestation and perhaps telepathy. It also shows how these mind powers overlap and are almost impossible to separate. On the evening of 14 April 1912, a young girl called Jessie lay dying. She called Captain W. Sowden of the Salvation Army to her room to tell him of a dream, or vision, she had had. "Hold my hand, Captain. I am so afraid. Can't you see that big ship sinking in the water?" Sowden was concerned that she was delirious and comforted her by telling her it was just a bad dream. But she insisted: "No, the ship is sinking. Look at all those people who are drowning. Someone called Wally is playing a fiddle and coming to you." Then she died. As she died she said that she could see her deceased mother coming to take her into heaven, and Sowden reported that the latch on the bedroom door operated with no one touching it. He believed that the mother had indeed come to take the child with her. But who was Wally? Almost certainly the girl was referring to Wally Hartley, the bandmaster on the *Titanic* who died after famously "playing on" with the band during the sinking. The girl had not known Wally Hartley, but Sowden had, years before. He had no idea at that time that Hartley was on the *Titanic* or indeed any ship at all—they had not kept in close touch. Even more interestingly it appears that the girl's dream and her conversation with Sowden took place approximately three and a half hours before the *Titanic* struck the iceberg.

The event made a deep impression on Sowden. He said afterwards: "What I thought was hallucination was a vision that stamped itself indelibly in my brain and changed my whole spiritual outlook."

To further research into premonitions—or, less grandly put, to try to prove there is something other than chance at work—the authors of this book, on behalf of the Association for the Scientific Study of Anomalous Phenomena (ASSAP), have started a "premonitions bureau." Anyone wishing to lodge a premonition should send two copies of their statement, one to us and one to ASSAP (addresses at the back of the book) ahead of the anticipated event. Our copy will not be opened, but ASSAP's copy will. The copy to us should therefore be marked: "DO NOT OPEN." If the event comes to pass, then the person reporting the premonition should contact ASSAP who will check the details with their copy. The unopened copy retained by ourselves will serve as evidence that the information was imparted before the event.

A similar bureau was set up years ago, though it is now defunct, by television personality Peter Fairley, Robert Nelson and Stanley Kripper as a result of the premonitions associated with the Aberfan incident. Fairley's analysis of the reports to the bureau may well offer insight into the workings of the mind. He said: "With every single person that looked interesting, the same thing happened—they lost it when they started to think they were good at it. Now there's a parallel to this in the alpha rhythms of the brain. Basically an alpha rhythm only comes through when the person being investigated is doing and thinking practically nothing. It disappears the moment they try to do something or to make some mental effort. If there is such a thing as premonition I reckon it's in some way connected with the alpha rhythm part of the brain." These observations are in line with the brainwave studies reported elsewhere in this book (see pages 39–40).

So how did Jessie—or anyone reporting premonitions—see into the future? What exactly are such people picking up? We can only speculate given our present state of knowledge, but two explanations are probably worthy of consideration.

The first explanation relates to the phenomenon of "reading" events of another time. Psychometry amounts to "reading" the past by picking up some information from an object or a location that reveals something of its history. Remote viewers often accidentally picked up events relating to a location but to a different time, sometimes into the future. It seems reasonable that we might be able to "pick up" the impressions of something that happened in the past because it has left effects and changes that can perhaps be "felt." But at the same time it seems outrageous to suggest that we might pick up impressions of something that has not happened yet.

But our outrage is based on our concept of linear time, that time is a one-way street into the future. What if it is not? What if impressions laid down in the future can be "read" from the present?

Tangential to the question of premonitions are "timeslip"

cases, which usually involve images from the past. But there are a few cases that suggest timeslips of the future. For example, while driving on a German autobahn a British family saw, travelling in the opposite direction, a long silver cylindrical "vehicle" with round portholes in the side out of which they believed that they saw startled faces peering. It seems the vehicle had no wheels and they heard engine sounds. A car of the future perhaps? If so, it seems that the British family were seeing into the future. If timeslips allow for access to future knowledge, could premonitions be a version of the same?

The second explanation rests on the assumption that emotion can create psychic impressions. If so, are these impressions also able to "travel" from the future to the present? The *Titanic* was associated with a large number of premonitions, many of them very specific, causing people to change their plans. But on the face of it there is no reason why that should have been so; special as the *Titanic* was, she was just the largest ship in the world at that time. The sinking, rather than the ship herself, is unquestionably what created her lasting fame, represented by countless books and films, including recently the most successful film ever made. And the sinking was an incredibly significant moment in history; it represented a shock to a world that had become complacent with technology and science. It presented a challenge to the existing class structure in Britain, the first hammer blow, soon followed by the First World War, after which the class structure would never be quite so divided again. Why then was there such a strong psychic impression *before* the sinking? Did the sinking, the damage to social structures, and even the suffering of 2,000 souls send a "blast" of emotion that left an impression through time, which could be read by those sensitive enough to do so?

We must look at alternative explanations. Let us take the example, again, of the *Titanic*. Possibly the emotional response to the sinking simply created a fascination for the ship, which in turn has caused interested parties to seek out premonitions.

Perhaps there have been premonitions about other ships, but because they have not been so famous no one has bothered to seek out the reports.

Added to that is the point—applicable to all premonitions, not just those relating to the *Titanic*—that the premonitions are self-selected for their success. Were there a host of "premonitions"—nothing more than fantasies, shall we say—of the *Titanic* successfully reaching New York? Of sinking after colliding with another ship? Of rolling over and floating hull-upwards? And so on? Do we only hear of the ones that match the later events? All the images that do not come to pass are then dismissed as "just imaginary fears," etc.

There is another intriguing possibility that would still be paranormal—and relates to telepathy. Is it possible that person A imagines an event, say, the sinking of the *Titanic*, and person B picks up that thought and believes it to be a premonition, which is reinforced after the event comes to pass? There is therefore no image from the future, but there is a telepathic transfer of imagery. If we take again the stories relating to the *Titanic*, there would certainly have been many individual emotions and thoughts as she was preparing to set sail.

We once received what seemed to be a premonition that "failed." A woman contacted us to tell us that she had had a premonition of a bomb planted in part of the London Underground network. We contacted officials of London Underground and they identified the areas she had described. There was no bomb, and to date one has not turned up there, but there was an intriguing detail. At the time of the premonition a team of builders was at work strengthening the area, which was considered a potential weak spot; a bomb planted there could bring disaster to the Underground. Had the woman picked up these considerations, which were obviously being thought through by the Underground authorities, and translated them into a "premonition"?

This leads us to an intriguing argument about the definition of premonition. Can there be such a thing as a "wrong premonition"? Is a premonition, by definition, something foretold that actually comes to pass? Supposing a person once had a premonition of, say, the liner *Canberra* sinking at sea with huge loss of life. It never did and since it is now being broken up for scrap it never can happen. Does this mean that it was not a premonition? Or that the premonition was wrong? Until we understand the mechanisms involved we cannot be sure.

5

Mind out of Body

People die. We can hardly argue against that; the evidence is for all to see in graveyards and funeral ceremonies the world over. But one of the most fundamental debates of the modern world relates to what follows after death. This debate has been underway since the dawn of time. In every culture there is some belief in a "life after death," that something of the deceased goes on to another existence.

A belief in an after-life implies a belief in the separation of the physical body and the mind, or whatever name is given to the non-corporeal part of the person. The physical body certainly dies, it is buried, it decays, it eventually is destroyed. But if there is a life after death, then it is some other component that "goes on." This chapter examines the claims that suggest there is indeed a "detachable" component that lives after the death of the body.

There are two experiences that may or may not be connected but which, superficially at least, seem to be. These are the near-death experience (NDE) and the out-of-body experience (OOBE).

The NDE appears to offer a glimpse of the world beyond death, though there are alternative possibilities that we shall also consider. However, if it does provide such a glimpse, it is clear that the NDE is experienced by a non-corporeal part of the person. And if that is the case, then possibly the OOBE is an earlier "stage" of that experience. The NDE also offers insight into the basis of religion and the concepts of heaven and hell. It may be a window into those realms, or at the very least the experience—whatever it is—may be the basis of the myths of heaven and hell.

Near-Death Experiences (NDEs)

We must remember that the NDE does not happen to people who die. By its very nature it happens to people who do not die—who "come back" to tell us what they experienced. Nevertheless, in many cases there is sufficient knowledge of the person's medical state to consider using the term "near death" literally, at least as we start our inquiry.

One experiencer we interviewed described his own NDE as: "Just travelling down a tunnel with a light at the end. A gorgeous light at the end like I have never seen in my life."

But there is more to the NDE than just a tunnel and light. There are several motifs that are regularly described by various witnesses. Indeed, NDEs seem to have a sequence to them. NDEs often start with a feeling of peace and tranquillity; then there is the separation of the spirit, or consciousness, from the physical body; then the awareness of a tunnel, usually dark but occasionally of light; then seeing light at the end of the tunnel; then seeing and even communicating with a being; then the person experiences a review of their life; then they have a sense of a choice: of going on (presumably to death) or coming back.

Every element of the sequence is not experienced by all witnesses, nor is it always in the same sequence, though logically some stages have to follow one on the other. Death is often defined as "entering the light," though there are claimants who say they did enter the light, even entered into the world with describable geography, and yet still returned. In some of these cases the "border" to death is represented by a bridge, fence, hedge, river or road to be crossed, or even an ocean to be negotiated.

We might look at this question of "returning" as it is an interesting part of the experience, not least because it seems to suggest that there is an element of control and choice over this part of the experience. In the following example, from *The Omega Project* by Kenneth Ring, the experiencer felt the sense of a mission to complete, seemingly a "high" motive for returning.

> Suddenly [I was] engulfed in overwhelming peace and aware of spiralling upward through a dark comforting tunnel.... [The] upward end of the tunnel had [a] luminescent glow of light and as I stepped into it, there was soft music. I found myself separated from vague forms on the opposite side of a stream of water and the Light emanating through this scene shimmered in iridescent pastels. Then came Voices telling me to return to complete my mission.

Some people have more personal reasons for "returning":

> I could see my life, from when I was born, I could see it in vivid Technicolor, the purest colours that you could ever possibly imagine. It just went right in front of my eyes, until the present day. After I went through my life, there was a long black tunnel, which I presumed was a square or a rectangle because the light at the end was in a square. The light was way down at the other end and it was pure white. As I proceeded down this tunnel the rays at the end started projecting out, beautiful rays and everything was peaceful and quiet... And there were no spoken words or anything at this point in time, but my answer to what I perceived was a question to me—did I want to stay there?—was that I screamed, "No, I want to see my son." And that's when I was back.

Although often choosing to come back against their personal desires, some do so for motives that seem almost trivial. One woman faced with a choice of a beautiful world and an encounter with God eventually decided to go back because she had a pile of ironing to do. However, we might reason that the ironing was more of a symbol for duties she personally found important—her role as wife and mother, presumably.

Sometimes the experiencer gets no further than a tunnel of light before returning, but many have reported a geography. The following description was reported to us:

> When I was around ten or eleven I had to have something done to my teeth. My parents went to the dentist and were told that I would have to have anaesthetic. The dentist wanted me to be put right out and they said, "No, she mustn't because she has a heart murmur." But anyway, the dentist went ahead and I was given a full anaesthetic. During this time I found that I was in the most fantastic place. The flowers were enormous and I have never seen such colours; they were wonderful. And the flowers were way above me. I seemed to be walking through these fantastic flowers. It seemed as if there was a light through every flower. Rather difficult to explain but that's the feeling I had. It was so wonderful. And then the dentist tried to wake me, the nurse was shaking me and I didn't want to come back. This place was so wonderful. Eventually, of course, I came back.

The being of light seen in the tunnel seems to be interpreted according to personal belief and culture. Some people have "met" their deceased loved ones and relatives who have advised them. Others have met religious figures, as described in this extract from *Life After Death* by Raymond Moody:

> I heard the doctors say that I was dead, and that's when I began to feel as though I were tumbling, actually kind of floating, through this blackness, there are not really words to describe this. Everything was very black, except that way off from me, I could see this light. It was a very, very brilliant light. It grew larger as I came nearer and nearer to it. I was trying to get to that light at the end because I felt that it was Christ, and I was trying to reach that

point. It was not a frightening experience, it was more or less a pleasant thing. For immediately, being a Christian, I had connected the light with Christ who said, "I am the light of the world." I said to myself, "If this is it, if I am to die, then I know who waits for me at the end there in that light."

Although a connection between NDEs and OOBEs is not certain, there are grounds for regarding the two phenomena as related. It may be that the same "mechanism" that brings about the NDE can also bring about the OOBE.

Joyce Hunt told us the story of her late husband's NDE while undergoing heart surgery. He "left his body" and found himself floating in the operating room. Then he went down a long tunnel towards a white light at the end. But he could still see his body on the operating table. Although reluctant to return, he did so when he saw the frantic operating team trying desperately to revive him, and heard one nurse pleading with him not to die.

We spoke to Graham James and his sister about an experience their now-deceased mother had related to them years ago. Graham began the recollection:

At the end of 1981 Chris, my partner, and I were paramedics at Heathrow ambulance station. I got a phone call from my father saying my mother had collapsed. "She's very pale, she's in bed and keeps fainting. Would you come and have a look at her?" We rushed to her; our diagnosis was a cardiac condition. We phoned an ambulance and she was taken to Hillingdon hospital. As she arrived at casualty she had a cardiac arrest: she stopped breathing, her heart had actually stopped. They took her into the resuscitation room. I followed her in there as I have done with others in the past, as it's part of my job. I had been there quite a few minutes before the Sister, who was a friend of mine, suddenly realised who I was in relation to my mother. She said: "You'd better get out of here." We stood in the doorway having an argument while the team were trying to restart her heart.

Anyway, she kicked me out of the resuscitation room. I walked down the corridor into the waiting area where Chris was. I kicked a chair and lit a cigarette; obviously I was pretty worried. After some time they got my mother round again. She was moved to the cardiac care unit, was later transferred to Harefield, and had a by-pass operation.

It wasn't until about eighteen months later that she told me about her experience. My mother told me that she wasn't afraid of dying. I said, "That's interesting. I don't think there's any need to be afraid of that." She said that when she was in hospital at that time she had thought: "I wish they would let me go" because she felt very peaceful, very calm. The word she used was serene. She remembers a very, very, bright light, a very, very sweet smell and she remembers my grandmother at the end of this "tunnel of light" as she put it.

Graham's sister added: "Her feeling was of a golden light, a golden tunnel. She found it hard to describe, but a feeling of warmth and gold. She said it was like a tunnel and she felt very warmed and loved. She said it was just such a wonderful experience." Graham continued:

But what made me prick my ears up was her description of being up near the ceiling of the room. She said to me, "One thing I noticed was your bald spot was getting bigger. And you had quite a big row with that Sister." She described looking down watching the staff ripping her clothes off—and they were literally ripping her clothes off. She remembered me standing at the doorway arguing with the Sister and she recalled me walking down the corridor—which was probably about fifty or sixty feet from the resuscitation unit—turning right into the waiting area, kicking a chair, Chris asking me if I was OK, and me lighting a cigarette. There was no way she could have possibly known all these things that were so far from the room she was in.

She said that after that she went on to this tunnel of light, and the sweet smell. She said that she remembers my grandmother, her mother, being at the end of this tunnel. Then—all of a sudden—she had a jolt back to her body. I found it very convincing from the point of view, not of the "textbook" stuff, but her knowledge of the actual things that I physically did at that time, like kicking the chair.

Graham's sister confirmed to us that this had been a life-changing experience for their mother: "She always said afterwards that she felt she had lost her fear of death; if that was what death was like then it was really quite wonderful."

Like Graham's mother, another experiencer, Philip Prewett, reported meeting his deceased grandmother in the tunnel. She ordered him to go back and he felt compelled to obey instantly. Philip has reported that his life changed for the better after the experience: he became less aggressive and has become convinced of a life after death.

But even those who encounter "beings" do not always report a "form." Avon Pailthorpe was involved in a serious car crash in 1986 and found herself transported to a "soft tunnel." There was a crowd in the tunnel, but not a crowd of people, just minds. The "minds" were debating whether or not Avon should return. The next thing she knew she opened her eyes in the wreck of her car. She admitted that she was immediately disappointed on finding she had returned, as so many other people report.

Susan Blackmore explains, in her book *Dying to Live*, her belief that the imagery of NDEs is the product of a dying brain collapsing, suffering from oxygen deprivation. We asked her why, if the NDE was just a product of a dying brain collapsing, there should be such consistency in NDEs. Why not more personal imagery? She replied:

I think the answer is that they all collapse in similar ways to some extent and also there are differences to another extent. The tunnel is an example where they collapse in the same way.

There are all sorts of things that can be happening in the brain close to death, lack of oxygen, blood pressure lowering, and so on. Several of these will have the common effect of producing disinhibition; that means the inhibitory cells will stop functioning before the excitory cells so they let off their inhibition and excitation spreads. In the visual cortex there are more cells devoted to the centre of the visual field than the outside. You will get what appears like a bright light in the middle fading off towards dark at the outside. Now this happening will be common to everybody because all brains have visual areas laid out that way, but everybody will have different visual experiences throughout their life, different favourite images of tunnels and so on, which can then be overlaid on this. Some people go down a tube train tunnel, other people go down a sewage pipe, other people seem to be inside their own arteries, those are the differences that come from the person's mind.

It would help to resolve this debate if we could find examples of people going through the experience, and the tunnel, who had no visual cortex structures; to this extent we hoped that enquiries made through the Royal National Institute for the Blind might have proved fruitful. However, the only such report we received was from someone who was partially blind and therefore had a visual cortex. The debate must continue between the anecdotal evidence and the explanation offered by present-day medical science.

One aspect of the NDE is that it may have produced the mythology of a beautiful, golden place of tranquillity, which we have come to call heaven. Or, depending on your point of view, the NDE has given some a glimpse of the true heaven. But not everyone who has had an NDE has been given such a heart-warming glimpse; some seem to have experienced the imagery that might have been the basis of, or indeed the realm of, hell.

Angie Fenimore, author of *Beyond Darkness: My Near-Death Journey to Hell and Back*, had an experience that she fully expected would mirror that of her stepmother, who had described a "pleasant feeling of floating." But Ms. Fenimore had her NDE just after she had attempted suicide, and perhaps this tainted the effects. As Ms. Fenimore reported: "Mine was initially extremely unpleasant because I had the feeling that committing suicide was the most serious action anyone could carry out." She experienced her life from birth in great detail, as is often reported. But having had a troubled life, the recall was also troubling. After going through "the tunnel" she came to a group of teenagers "entirely devoid of hope for themselves, and didn't care at all what happened to me." She met people in "dirty white robes . . . wrapped up in their own torture." But Angie was saved by meeting a being she was sure was God, who told her that life was supposed to be hard and in a scene reminiscent of the film *It's a Wonderful Life* Angie was shown what life would be like for her children if she were dead. "What was shown made me want to live," she said.

Her description, while not attributing it to hell, might well be regarded as one of the bases of the imagery of hell. A devout Christian we interviewed rejected the idea of hell as a place inhabited by demons with pitchforks and overheated by fire and suggested that it would be a place of hopelessness, where those who had rejected Christ would feel the loneliness of despair. It seems very akin to the world Angie experienced.

One woman's entry into the NDE even started with the imagery of hell. Instead of rising above her body and floating into a tunnel, she felt herself falling. Former CID officer Joyce Harvey was in hospital, sitting up next to her bed reading a book. She felt paralysed then suddenly felt a falling sensation. "I was still in a sitting position but it felt as though I was in a lift that had gone out of control." She heard the screams as though children were shrieking in a playground, and she felt heat below her "as though someone had opened an oven door." Then she felt scorching-hot hands reaching out and clawing at her feet, and a sea of faces were pulling her down a tunnel. She thought of hell and decided:

"If I'm dying, I must try to get to heaven." She was very afraid, more than ever before in her life. Then she heard a voice calling her back, felt the "lift" rise back at incredible speed, and came to in her chair with a nurse holding her. She felt that she had truly been threatened with hell, and questioned the actions she had done in her life. Indeed, she has become more overtly religious, and the experience has left her fearing death. Perhaps most persuasive of the reality of experience is the fact that her legs were bruised when she "returned." "I assume it was from the creatures in the tunnel who had grabbed and pulled at me."

Certainly it would be harder to imagine a more direct "experience" of hell, but is that the correct interpretation? We think probably not. It is more likely that experiences like Joyce's over the centuries are what have created the stories and the mythologies of hell. Perhaps having a pleasant or a fearful NDE is dictated by the state of mind at the time of the experience; her next NDE may be a very pleasant one. But the bruises are interesting. If not actually caused by "demonic figures" then either she bruised herself while struggling unconscious, or the bruises are a stigmata created by her own mind as a result of her passionate belief in attack by the entities. (Stigmata are examined in detail later in the book; see pages 228–44.)

Out-of-Body Experiences (OOBEs)

Having looked at the question of NDEs we must now turn to OOBEs. Many would argue that these are quite different and unconnected phenomena. But it appears from our study of OOBEs that some sense of consciousness moves outside of the physical body, and, if this is the case, the point of death could be a time when that happens permanently.

The classic description of the OOBE is a feeling of detachment from the physical body, during which a non-corporeal component leaves the physical body to roam freely. The following OBE account, as told to us, is fairly typical:

I was lying on the bed, above the covers. It was a warm day and I could feel a warm breeze over my body from the open bedroom window. I started to get drowsy, but I am certain I never slept or dreamt. I became aware that I was "rolling up" inside my body. I was gradually compressing into my head. Suddenly it seemed like I flew out of my head and upwards. For a while I drifted on the ceiling of the bedroom, looking down on my body laying on the bed. I could see the room with great clarity—the curtains blowing, the sunlight casting shadows across the furniture. Then suddenly I was back in my body. I can't remember how I got back there. But I was certain it was no dream, there was no dream-like quality to it. It was as real as me sitting here talking to you now.

But the OOBE is not the homogenous class of experience that it might at first seem to be. The person above described seeing his physical body, but offered no appreciation of the "body" form from which he was viewing. Other experiencers have given descriptions of the non-corporeal component that leaves the body. The late D. Scott Rogo, writing in the *Journal of the Society for Physical Research* (Vol 48, No 768, June 1976) suggested: "There seem to be three distinct forms in which the subject may perceive himself." The first of these is a human-like form that is believed to leave the physical body, as implied in this account related to us by a paramedic who had studied the subject:

One story came from a lady that I met during my time in the ambulance service who confided in me. We took her to hospital in the ambulance; she was quite ill and had to have an operation. During the operation she recalled looking down, from the theatre ceiling, to her physical body. And she recalled actually being amongst other "bodies" floating up there as well. She was under anaesthetic and she said she was floating around in the operating theatres—it was a series of operating theatres—and she said that she recalled other spirits being around. Actually she made an interesting remark: she said "It's a good job that I got the right body, I could have gone to another body in another operating room."

The second type of form is a "body" of sorts but one that is not human-like, as in the following description from Rogo's article:

I was awakened by the sun shining through the door across my face and eyes. I got up to close the door, placed one hand on the knob, the other on the door itself in order to close it quietly, then changed my mind and walked across the room to the dresser. Up to this time I didn't notice anything strange or different. I felt perfectly normal too, but when I looked in the mirror I saw the strangest thing there. It looked like me but it was just a white vapour-like image of myself. I wasn't frightened, just puzzled. I thought I must be ill and should go back to bed at once. A quick glance around the room showed both my sisters sleeping with their heads covered up. Perhaps the light was bothering them also. When I reached my bed there was I in bed and sound asleep. There were two of me.

One of Rogo's interviewes described the OOB-self as "a large, glowing ball of greenish tinted light the size of a standard beach ball."

The third type of experience Rogo describes is where there is no suggestion of any form at all embracing the "separated consciousness." Rogo offers the account of someone who tortuously avoided using the word body, clearly not believing that it was an appropriate description for the "place" from which she was viewing:

I became gradually aware that a roll of what I will call "mist" was gathering against the ceiling and wall directly above my bed. . . . I could feel its presence and its motion as though I, Helen, *was* the mist. . . .

I could see it there, though not with my bodily eyes. I was detached from it and there was no sentiment of any kind in regard to it. There was no fear, no questioning—simply a quiet acceptance of the fact that I was outside my body, hovering over it. There was a sensation of pushing against the ceiling, lightly, and of being stopped by it, as a toy balloon which has got away would be stopped. This caused a sensation of uneasiness in the centre— what I call the "thought centre"—of the mist, of light frustration but no vexation. I could see the wall, the mist spreading away from its centre, my bed, my body, other parts of the room—but none of this with my bodily eyes . . . it ended when I was aware of being back in my body.

Rogo concluded that the term we call OOBE might be a continuum of several forms, one leading to the other, or a set of quite different experiences. Our own view is that it is likely that there is only one experience but it is being viewed and interpreted differently according to personal predisposition. At its simplest, perhaps the form of the OOB-self is dictated by personal imagery rather than a set of external criteria.

There is a case that implies this (though it could imply a range of other possibilities also, we must admit). Caroline Larsen reported that in 1910 she separated from her body and discovered that she was in a beautiful, younger and more vibrant body. Her face glowed so brightly it illuminated the room. Such was the experience that she became quite depressed at having to return to her ordinary, middle-aged body.

"Repeater" cases of spontaneus OOBEs are rare, but they do arise. In July 1993 the *Daily Mail* newspaper reported the case of three-year-old Ami Greenstead whose rare heart condition caused her heart to stop periodically. Her mother stated: "She told me that she goes up to the ceiling and can see the room. Then she says she 'clicks back in.'" Within a minute or so Ami "returns to her body" and announces: "Don't cry, Mummy, I'm back now."

Perhaps what is generally not appreciated is that OOBEs are very common. Estimates vary, but one survey suggested that one in eight of the population experience them at some time in their lives. Estimates have included figures of one in three. For some the experience is so frightening that they deliberately seek to prevent it from happening again. For example, "Gillian" reported having an OOBE and floating above her body in bed, watching her husband try to "revive her," thinking that she was dying or dead. She made a conscious effort to return to her body to end his discomfort. But after that she reported: "I'm afraid of it happening again; a couple of times I've had to fight it by waking myself up. I'm afraid that I might float away forever."

Although the phenomenon of OOBEs may be fairly common, there are many variations of the experience. For instance, the state of the physical body is not always the same. In many cases it is inert (perhaps undergoing an operation or simply sleep), and the OOBE is perhaps a product of an altered state of consciousness, or the liberation of consciousness from the corporeal form. But these are notable exceptions. Lorraine Parry related to us her account of her OOBE when she was five years old:

> I was at the top of the stairs and looked down; and I wanted to fly down the stairs, I really wanted to fly. I jumped off the top of the stairs and I flew down and landed very gently just below the last stair . . . while I was flying down the stairs I was very close to the ceiling and looked down and there was me, slowly holding on to the banister and very slowly going down the stairs. And when I landed just below the bottom of the stairs I entered into my body from above going in with a kind of a slight jolt.

Lorraine felt that she had left her body while it was still "normally" active. Similarly, in 1984 Audrey Bourne was out walking when she suddenly found herself high above the street and looking down. She could see her own physical body walking along the pavement and then cross the road after carefully looking left and right. Afterwards she slipped back into her body. Whether it was significant or not she noted that she had just undergone an extremely painful hospital examination. Another similar case was reported by an experiencer, John Migliaccio, who was eighteen years old at the time. He was swimming off the New Jersey coast and got into trouble. "As I was swimming I suddenly found myself looking down on my body from a few hundred feet up. I could see myself in my wet suit, the scuba equipment on my back. The first thought was, how can this be happening? It was the strangest thing I had ever experienced, because not only did I see myself swimming but I realised in my body that I was looking down at myself. It was like being in two places at once."

The inference that can be drawn from these OOBE accounts are as follows:

- The consciousness was still housed in the physical body, perhaps "transmitting" to the disconnected "self."
- The disconnected "self" was transmitting to the physical body.
- The body was being run by "automatic" functions in the temporary absence of the "true self."
- Consciousness may have been split between the two selves.

There is, therefore, still the question of where the "higher" intelligence is seated during the experience. Ms. Violet Tweedale reported waking up and catching a glimpse of her astral body returning to her physical body at that moment. Her description suggests that she was viewing from her physical body.

Earlier in the book we looked at the phenomenon of alien abductions, a relatively modern experience. Many of these reports contain parallels to NDEs and OOBEs and some directly overlap. What this might represent is as yet unclear. Are aliens "using" the astral world? Are they the beings that inhabit it and always have done? Is this a new version of religion? Or—more probable in our view—are we looking at modern interpretation of an ancient experience, a new twist to an innate natural ability.

The UFO abduction experience is generally held to involve

extraterrestrial aliens visiting the Earth. However, there is an alternative view that the "flying saucer" and extraterrestrial qualities of the experience are an interpretation, even a symbolism created by the mind, to explain an extraordinary form of experience that the person is not familiar with in everyday life. As such, therefore, the abduction experience may be a special, or specific, form of OOBE.

The following cases show the overlap between these two types of experiences:

- In a famous abduction case in Aveley in Essex, which took place on 27 October 1974, "John and Sue Day" described themselves being "drawn out" of their car towards the UFO. They experienced a floating sensation, during which they could see themselves in their car although their "selves" were apparently located elsewhere.
- In an abduction case in October 1955, in Nebraska, "Jennie" reported being moved through the bedroom wall with such detail that she could even see dirt and cobwebs inside the wall as she passed through it.
- Rauni-Leena Luukanen-Kilde, a Finnish doctor, was for years a leading light in the medical world. She has worked as a medical adviser in Indonesia, and has been acting director at the Finnish Department of Health and Social Security and has represented the Finnish government at the World Health Organisation in tropical medicine. Clearly she has impressive credentials; and she has no doubts about the experiences she had. Like many who claim to have had an OOBE, Dr. Rauni-Leena was undergoing surgery at the time. "I saw the whole operation 'from above' and knew in advance what the surgeon was about to do. Just as he, by mistake, was about to cut an artery in the abdomen I tried in vain to warn him!" She believes she was lucky to survive. Rauni-Leena also believes that she was abducted by a "flying saucer," but that it was her astral body that boarded the spacecraft.

The bridge between the reports of OOBE and abduction seems to be that the astral body leaves the physical body. The physical scarring some abductees report is not irreconcilable to this claim. Rauni-Leena speculates that "damage" to the astral body can manifest on the physical as psychosomatic images. Take the example of American abductee Barney Hill. He reported developing a ring of warts when aliens clamped a device to his groin, which flared up years later when he re-lived the experience under hypnosis—even though the aliens and their machinery were not present (assuming they had been the first time).

Such cases beg the question of whether UFO abductions are physical or astral, or both (ignoring alternative arguments, which do not concern us here). Most abductions are reported by the person undergoing the experience, who often describes the abduction as physical; however, they may be in no position to determine what is and is not physical.

Despite all the descriptions of *what* happens, we have yet to consider the question of *why* such abilities exist.

We are arguing in this book that the so-called paranormal abilities of the mind have developed—as have most attributes, it would seem—as an aid to survival, arguably the primary function of all living creatures. We might, therefore, look at the needs that OOBE serve. Generally, the experiencer acquires information that is otherwise difficult to acquire. Audrey Bourne, for example, reported that while floating above her physical body she saw a small bald patch on her head, which she had never known existed; when she checked in the mirror when she got home she discovered it was indeed there.

The following accounts given to us in 1993 by a reporter living in Australia are also examples of using OBEs to acquire information:

> I was in bed, asleep, and I dreamt—or so I thought—of five people gunned down in somewhere like Spain. The place had the types of villas that gave that impression. They were in a room and they

were being shot by machine guns with silencers on. I woke up and thought it must be a dream but later when I was driving to work I heard on the car radio that five people had been assassinated in just that way in those kind of surroundings.

We established that she could not have heard the announcement in her sleep from a radio or television; she had just moved house and she had not bought a radio or television at that time. Here is her second account:

When I was in Perth I had a first-floor flat. There was a lovely old lady in the flat underneath me. She had a beautiful Siamese cat, and she came to me—in a dream—and said "I think I'm dying and I'm really worried because there'll be no one to look after my cat." I woke up concerned for that feeling, knocked at her door to see if she was all right and she told me she had been ill all night, had thought she was going to have a heart attack and had been really worried about her cat.

And her third account:

A friend was ill and I "went" and saw them. It put my mind at rest to know they were all right. It was a long trip—from Perth to Sydney. When I spoke to her about it I told her she was wearing her blue nightdress and she confirmed that she was.

Obviously, gaining information through OOBEs is useful for individual and tribal survival. Such information might relate to enemy action, food and water supplies, the approach of predators and so on.

Graham James, a former paramedic, has researched OOBEs among pregnant women. Such a "sample" is inevitably skewed, but his work suggests that OOBEs during pregnancy perhaps meet a need, as in this following case reported to us:

> When [Tina] was aged 25 she was pregnant with her second child. She remembers lying on the bed in the afternoon, going into a semi-sleep state and then she remembers being on the ceiling and looking down to her body, panicking and coming back to her body suddenly, and waking up. But she distinctly remembers looking down at her body, and distinctly remembers that something was on the floor that she had been unable to find from her sitting position. I thought that was also quite relevant because she remembers getting off the bed feeling slightly dazed and picking up whatever it was had fallen on the floor that she had dropped.

We would suggest that either the body during pregnancy needs extra rest, which is afforded by the absence of the non-corporeal body, or perhaps the OOBE is a defence mechanism: the consciousness watching over—literally—the physical body.

Perhaps a slightly different version of survival is implied by the account told to us by Stan Conway, who suffered from poltergeist activity as a child:

> At Newark Street [where he then lived] my greatest delight was not being in my body. I used to be out of my body looking down at everything else that was going on. I didn't want to be in the room but I was safe when I was out of my body, or so I felt. And where I was I was powerful. I was in the room, looking down, and nothing there could touch me. And at will I could get into my body any time I wanted to. I remember I used to go into bed and I used to close my eyes. And if I didn't want to be in my body I could just turn myself out through my head and I could look down on my body. And I could do it at will. This ability gradually stopped; I lost the ability as I lost the need to do it.

There have been attempts to test the claims of OOBEs, and the extent to which OOBEs can be made to happen to order. The most important aspect of such testing is that knowledge should be acquired which is not otherwise readily available. Such knowledge would rule out the main alternative explanation for the OOBE state—that it is a fantasy construction.

It is believed that when a person is dreaming the muscles are automatically "paralysed" in order to prevent self-damage. Some scientists believe that the "detached consciousness" of the OOBE is a fantasy construct designed to provide the person with the illusion of movement during these periods of paralysis, which allows for dreaming and the benefits of that state and also prevents the fear of constraint. If so, then the OOB-self should have access only to information known to the "real" person. But there are claims that information is sometimes gleaned that is not ordinarily known to the subject. Such is the case, for example, with the Australian reporter whose accounts were described earlier.

It would also appear from the following accounts that some people can consciously and deliberately make an OOBE happen. Graham James successfully trained for what he calls astral travel, one of many terms for the phenomenon of OOBE. Here's what he told us:

> When I was quite young I joined a group of elders, a coven as it was known then, and part of my training was to have more control over not just my physical body but also the psychic side, to help me to develop my psychic strengths. Part of this was learning to astrally project. I found fasting extremely important if you want to develop a higher sense within your psyche; fasting for twenty-four hours before you deal with these experiments is very, very important because then your metabolism is not concentrating on digesting food. You must every hour take liquids so you don't dehydrate, but that's all. I took a week off from my regular work, which was to be my "psychic week," part of my training if you like. I fasted for two days solid and I found that I felt almost elated, almost slightly as if I was walking on air. And then did some breathing exercises to further enhance my mind. What I would do is lie on my bed, I would breathe, I would do mantras.

I was trying to get my psychic carburettor tuned as finely as possible. And I found it was very easy to feel this experience of lifting away from the body.

I did learn to project. Actually I didn't go up to the ceiling (as is often reported); I went into the lounge, into the next room. The idea was that you would travel a little bit further each time in order to get used to it. We were told that there was a silver cord that was, if you like, your safety line; that was the popular way of describing it at that time. I have travelled away from my body probably as much as half a mile. But it did take me something like a year to achieve that, at different intervals. It wasn't something I consistently did, something I may have left alone for a month or two and then tried again and so on. When I became more relaxed about it, more in tune, I found it very easy to put myself into a state even without fasting. It was as if I had more control.

Once while travelling I saw somebody slip up in the snow outside the flat, it was the lady from across the road. Now I was actually in bed on that occasion and she was walking towards the top of the road. She slipped over some ice and somebody helped her up. I heard about that incident about three days later, "old Mrs. So-and-So has broken her ankle down the road." I know I actually saw that incident take place.

Graham's father, Frederick, also explained his own experiments with out-of-body travel.

I personally prefer to do any projection at night and usually I go to bed reasonably early when I am going to do it. I sit bolt upright at the head of the bed in the lotus position and meditate for some considerable while, starting of course with the usual breathing procedure. This will allow your pulse to drop. When you get adept at it you bring your pulse down to as low as forty or so per minute. And your breathing will slow right down, in fact the whole metabolism drops to a low level. When you reach this point you begin to get a feeling of a lightness. Not necessarily a physical feeling of lightness but a spiritual feeling of lightness. This is awfully difficult to describe and must be experienced to really be known. When this occurs, thinking of a particular person you are going to visit or wherever you wish to go or do will allow your spirit body to leave your normal body, your earth body. You will proceed on whatever it is you wish to accomplish.

Remote Viewing

If OOBEs can be controlled at will, then the implication is that the experiencer can "travel" to remote locations and obtain information that would not otherwise be available to him or her. This hypothesis has been the basis of many years' research and the reason for military interest in OOBE—where the more clinical term "remote viewing" is used.

In July 1973, at the Psychical Research Foundation, tests were conducted with Keith Harary who claimed to be able to "go out of body" at will. His target was to project himself to a specified location where he would attempt to affect the actions of a cat. The cat was seen to change its behaviour during the time when Harry was alleged to "be" there in an out-of-body state; the cat displayed a calmness that was typical when Harary was present and then reverted to "edginess" after Harary "left." One experimenter at the site also reported seeing an inexplicable "darting shadow" at the time of Harary's visit, although the witness did not know when Harary would make the attempt.

In the 1970s a rather sceptical police detective, Rodney Roncoglio, happened to be visiting the American Society for Psychical Research during an experiment into OOBE conducted by Dr. Karlis Osis. Psychic Dr. Alex Tanous was attempting to project himself from within a sealed, windowless cubicle into the laboratory where Osis and Roncoglio were. Tanous was in intercom communication with Osis. Over the intercom Roncoglio heard Tanous say, "Right, I'm leaving my body now. I'm coming along the corridor. Excuse me Rodney." Roncoglio stepped aside to admit Tanous through the door before he realised what had happened. Tanous, sealed in a room and supposedly unaware of Roncoglio's presence, had asked him to move aside, and Roncoglio had responded before he realised there was "no one there," at least in the usually accepted sense.

Even if ESP were the explanation for Tanous' knowledge of Roncoglio's presence in the building, it is still impressive that Tanous knew, correctly, that Roncoglio was blocking the doorway. The simplest explanation seems to be that Tanous had projected out of the room, had moved down the corridor, and had passed by the detective. Any other explanation involves either ludicrously complex fraud or some other equally amazing paranormal ability.

A most famous case of acquisition of unavailable knowledge arises in the case known as "the tennis shoe on the ledge." The subject—Maria—was in hospital having had a heart attack. She drifted above her body, watched staff working to save her life, and then apparently floated out of a window, drifting towards the back of the hospital. Her eyes were drawn towards a window ledge where she saw a tennis shoe. When she revived, Maria told of her experience and described the shoe's position and even its worn condition and its laces. The shoe was located where she had indicated and was exactly as she had described it.

Ian Wilson, in an article in the *Daily Mail* of 18 August 1997, reports on the case of Dr. Josef Issels of Bavaria's Ringberg Cancer Clinic. One morning he was doing his rounds when an elderly woman, near to death, told him that she could "leave her body" and offered him proof. After a moment's silence she described a woman in another room writing a letter to her husband and gave Issels a detailed description of what she had seen after leaving her body. Issels hurried through to check out the claim and found it exactly correct in all details. When he returned, however, the woman who had demonstrated her abilities had died.

Remote viewing has been tested by Princeton Engineering

Anomalies Research Project (PEAR), who have concluded: "Even casual comparison of the agent and percipient narratives produced in this body of experiments reveals striking correspondences in both their general and specific aspects, indicative of some anomalous channel of information acquisition, well beyond any chance expectation."

In recent years there has been admission from members of the American security services and military that they have used the technique for espionage. Fearing ridicule, they avoided such phrases as "telepathy," "out of body" or "clairvoyance" and coined a more scientific-sounding description: remote viewing. Jim Schnabel, in his book *Remote Viewers: The Secret History of America's Psychic Spies*, related the opinions of one of the programme managers, Dr. Harold Puthoff: "The old terms carried unwanted baggage, full of hysterical mediums, palm readers, and all those dead, dry card-guessing experiments."

Not that remote viewing for military purposes is a new idea. One early incident of what seems to be a deliberate such use of OOBE is recorded in the Old Testament of the Bible:

> Once when the King of Syria was warring against Israel, he took counsel with his servants, saying, "At such and such a place shall be my camp." But the man of God [Elisha] sent word to the King of Israel, "Beware that you do not pass this place, for the Syrians are going down there." And the King of Israel sent to the place of which the man of God told him. Thus he used to warn him, so that he saved himself there more than once or twice.

The implication seems to be that Elisha used this technique a few times, much to the consternation of the Syrian king.

> And the mind of the King of Syria was greatly troubled because of this thing; and he called his servants and said to them, "Will you not show me who of us is for the King of Israel?" And one of his

servants said, "None, my lord, O King; but Elisha, the prophet
who is in Israel, tells the King of Israel the words that you speak
in your bedchamber."

It seems therefore that it was not the servants who caused the
"information leaks" but Elisha, who is said to have remained in
Israel, while "hearing" the king in his bedchamber. The fact that
the king's servant thought it a quite plausible explanation for
military espionage to offer their master implies that such a technique was known and accepted at that time.

We could argue that actually Elisha used telepathy to "tune
in" on the Syrian king. But this might be too fine a distinction; we
do not know where the boundaries of OOBE, clairvoyance,
telepathy and the more clinical-sounding "remote viewing" overlap. Possibly they are all versions of the same attribute.

The US Pentagon, under code names such as "Gondola
Wish," "Grill Flame" "Star Gate" and others, authorised the use
of remote viewers for espionage. In one case, the USA Central
Intelligent Agency (CIA) requested that the remote viewers examine the new US embassy in Moscow, checking for electronic
monitoring devices ("bugs"). The Russians had insisted that only
Russian workers undertake the construction and would not
allow Americans to do the work. The remote-viewing unit found
masses of bugs and even described certain girderwork construction joined in such a way as to turn the building itself into a
broadcasting antenna. These findings were confirmed when the
building was "physically" checked out.

The remote-viewing unit was asked to experiment through
time as well as space, something that remote viewers believed
they sometimes could do. But this proved difficult, and the remote viewers could arrive at no clear image of the buildings future. The long-term result was that the building was torn down
because it could not be de-bugged. The remote viewers had perhaps been right: they couldn't see the building's future because
it didn't have one.

The remote-viewing unit had another clear success in September 1979. Joe McMoneagle was shown a "spy-satellite" photograph of a building and asked to view inside. He saw a huge submarine under construction. ("This sucker is big," he commented.) He described its revolutionary drive mechanism, its double hull, the specialist welding techniques used on it, and its missile payload. The unit even projected ahead in time and saw the manner and time of its launching. The data was originally rejected by the National Security Council; the submarine was so big that they did not believe it could have been developed without coming to their attention. In fact, some months later satellite photography confirmed the remote viewers' information. The "Typhoon" class submarine was all that they had "seen" it would be.

The programme had high-level support. Major General Edmund Thompson, the US Army Assistant Chief of Staff for Intelligence 1977–81 and Deputy Director for Management and Operations DIA 1982–4, said of the use of remote viewing: "I never liked to get into debates with the sceptics, because if you didn't believe that remote viewing was real, you hadn't done your homework." Harold Puthoff put it more succinctly: "There were times when they wanted to push buttons and drop bombs on the basis of our information."

But were the remote viewers travelling out of body or is this a different, if no less spectacular, technique? Individual remote viewers seem to each have their own way of getting into the right state of mind for the job, of explaining what they are doing, and of interpreting their impressions. Perhaps remote viewing is a different process to OOBE, or perhaps it is just a different way of interpreting the same technique. There is certainly one example from Schnabel's *Remote Viewers* that implies something closely akin to OOBE from the way the percipient described his own "viewing position." It is the case of Hartleigh Trent who was asked to view a building in what was then the Soviet Union. Once in the "altered state" that was his way of viewing he told his monitor who was supervising the session: "I'm here." He was asked to look to his right and he said that he could see a metal building. Asked to say what he could see to his left he described a parking lot. "And what do you see straight in front of you?" he was asked. Hartleigh replied: "A transmission. I'm lying under a truck."

The USA is not the only nation to admit to using "psychic spies." The Czech army, for example, used psychics in 1919. "It was a great advantage in battle," stated a spokesman for the army. "The clairvoyant research party safeguarded the troops in action."

Miroslav Ivanov in his book *Not Only The Black Uniforms* claims that psychic spies were used during the Second World War by the Czechs to monitor concentration camps and the German occupation. "Many facts given us by the clairvoyants were right," he states. "The abilities of telepathists were used in war with excellent results to get information about the enemy, his intentions, his bases, his aerodromes."

In our studies of various paranormal phenomena, from ESP to the perception of ghosts, poltergeists and even alien abduction reports, we have found at least some evidence that it is the intuitive, creative side of the brain that seems most alert to these experiences. The rational, scientific part of the brain does not seem to be able to grasp how these things happen. The military units discussed above that engaged remote viewers found similar results. Their research concluded: "Artistic talent, visual-spatial intelligence, and creativity all tended to be associated with high remote-viewing scores."

Here is Schnabel's description of one remote viewer: "Mel Riley was valued for his artistic skill: Atwater knew that if Riley saw something in his mind's eye, he could render it on paper in sharp detail." So Riley was artistic. But it was his intuition that had led him to discover his talents. "As an aerial observer, he seemed to have an unusually accurate intuition about where to head the plane or point the cameras. And as a photo analyst, he seemed able to see things in a reconnaissance image that no one else could see." Sometimes his intuition would lead him to make guesses about things hidden in the photos, and subsequent events would prove his guesses right.

Curiously, the attitude of the military—not usually associated with such open thinking—might have helped to make their remote viewing successful. In our experience, those attempting to prove their paranormal attributes in test situations often fail even though they are successful otherwise. We believe that the attitude of mind brought to the experiment is important; trying to prove something is not the same as just doing it, and perhaps the mind-set in challenging tests causes the failure. But creating objective test situations was not a priority for the military. They would often give a remote viewer encouraging feedback during his sessions, which seemed to promote and improve the output. This would not happen in a strictly controlled scientific test, but that was not the military aim. According to Schnabel, the military "weren't so much interested in the rigor of the process as they were in the accuracy and reliability—and above all, the usefulness—of the results."

The military found that the remote viewers had trouble seeing names and numbers: quite possibly our fixation with alphanumerics is a trait that is connected with rationalism and scientific thinking rather than with intuition. It has often been a claim of "crystal ball gazers," psychic healers and the like that they cannot use their "powers" for self-gain—and often will not take money—because if they do their abilities will be "taken away from them." The army's remote viewers felt that way. Of one remote viewer, Ken Bell, it was said: "Psi could never be used to make money; he [Bell] had read too many stories about psychics who had become failures as soon as they had tried to strike it rich. There was something about psi, he believed, that was intimately connected to human morality." We doubt that there is an entity that doles out and regulates paranormal abilities, but the underlying reasoning might be correct when we consider our theme in this book of right-brain and left-brain functioning. Seeking financial gain is very rational-brain thinking; quite probably those who try to make money from their psychic abilities are pursuing them with the wrong frame of mind and might well find that their abilities desert them.

6

Receiving from the Dead?

It is the "detachable" component of the person that seems capable of the NDEs, OOBEs and remote viewing discussed in the last chapter. This "detachable" component is also sometimes taken as evidence for life after death. However, it is not the aim of this book to enter into the debate about the existence of a reality beyond death. So when, in this chapter, we look at alleged communication with the dead, our discussion is limited to two aspects of the phenomenon: the nature of the mind that might be reaching back from the dead; and the nature of the mind of the receiver that is "picking up" something in a paranormal way, which may or may not be from the dead.

Mediumship

Mediumship is the ability, claimed by some, to contact spirits of the dead, or in ancient accounts to contact the gods, and bring from them messages to the living. The person acts as a "go-between," hence the term medium.

Like many aspects of the paranormal, evidence of the practice of mediumship stretches far back in time, certainly to the writings of early religions, and even beyond written records. The oral traditions of early religions contain accounts of channelled messages from "higher powers" or the spirit world.

In the modern Spiritualist Church there are mediums bringing messages from those who have passed over. The Spiritualist movement started, in 1848, with the Fox sisters responding to "poltergeist-like rapping noises, which they were convinced were messages from the dead. They "communicated" with the spirit of a man who claimed to have been a pedlar who was murdered by a former occupant of the house. He also claimed that his remains had been buried under the cellar floorboards. A maid who had previously lived in the house confirmed that a pedlar had spent a night there, but as no missing pedlar was known to the police, no murder enquiry was pursued. Digging in the cellar, however, uncovered some human teeth, hair and bones, and later, in 1904, a skeleton was found there, and a tin box, allegedly a pedlar's box, was found nearby.

When mediumship had its "heyday" in the parlours of Victorian houses, the fashion was for what we now refer to as physical mediums. They produced apparently physical effects: ectoplasm, spirit photographs, levitations, apports, and communication with the dead through rapping and table tilting.

The history of the paranormal has had many fads; and physical mediumship has not been fashionable for many years. It might be said that physical mediumship went out of style following the trial of Helen Duncan in 1944. Even now, over fifty years after that trial, she is the subject of much controversy. The Society for Psychical Research (SPR) more or less rejected her claims, but at least one current council member of the SPR, Manfred Cassirer, believes that some of her claims were genuine. Duncan was tried under the 1735 Witchcraft Act, which made it an offence to falsely claim paranormal abilities, though quite why a medium should be so tried is unclear: the act was usually invoked against those who were becoming a public nuisance. (Some have speculated that the real reason the authorities pursued Duncan was because she revealed the sinking of a British warship before it had been announced through proper channels.) Duncan was convicted and sentenced to nine months imprisonment. Several requests to set up a seance in the court for the benefit of judge and jury were rejected, not the first or the last time that the authorities would refuse to look at evidence. As Duncan's senior counsel, C. E. Loseby, observed: "My offer of a demonstration, which I regarded as the acid test of Mrs. Duncan's powers, was refused. This demonstration would have been short, easy, and practicable. How can this test, in justice, be refused?" Perhaps if the test had been undertaken in open court we would today have a better understanding of the mechanisms of physical mediumship. This would be very helpful because physical mediumship is becoming fashionable again, and many sitting groups around the country are claiming successes.

A second type of medium, known as a "transfiguration medium," takes on the look and mannerisms of the spirit contacted, often speaking as the spirit once spoke when alive. The characteristics exhibited are recognised by the sitter as belonging to a certain individual. Some of this is true of the Sutton case mentioned below; however, Mrs. Piper, the medium, did not take on the appearance of the child. Apparently some transfiguration mediums actually change the shape of their faces and heads and "become" the person being contacted in spirit.

And there are "mental mediums" who rely for corroboration of their abilities not on manifestations but on the gleaning of information that seems to come from sources not readily available to them.

One well-known trance medium was Mrs. Leonore Piper, whose claims were thoroughly investigated. She was twenty-five years old when she first realised her potential as a medium, and she continued up to her death at the age of ninety-three. She was studied by the sceptical researcher Richard Hodgson for eighteen years. In order to ensure that her claims were genuine, he would often organise her sittings in detail and even went to great lengths to ensure she could not obtain her "information" from conventional sources. For example, he had her followed by private detectives prior to sittings. Hodgson was forced to conclude that she had special abilities, but whether Mrs. Piper was in contact with the dead or whether she was receiving her information through telepathy was a distinction he could never make. After Hodgson died he apparently made contact with Mrs. Piper and acted as a "guide" for her, a term we shall explain shortly.

Mrs. Piper had also been examined in England by Frederick Myers and Oliver Lodge of the Society for Psychical Research. They, too, did not detect fraud on her part, and again rigorous precautions had been taken.

Mrs. Piper made contact with the spirit world by means of a spirit guide, or control, called Dr. Phinuit. Most trance mediums have a spirit guide who acts as a sort of "master of ceremonies" between the spirits and the living; the guide resides in the spirit world. (Most express no purpose other than to assist, though medium Eileen Garrett's guide, Uvani, specifically announced that he was there to try to prove the existence of a life after death.) Dr. Phinuit was never identified with a living person and many, including Hodgson, believed that he was a sub-personality of Mrs. Piper.

One example of Mrs. Piper's trance mediumship is given in the case of a sitting for The Reverend and Mrs. Sutton in 1893. They were present at the sitting, and trying to contact their deceased daughter, Katherine. When Katherine "came through," Mrs. Piper/Dr. Phinuit picked up a button from the table and began biting it. The Suttons recognised that gesture as a mannerism of their deceased daughter. Mrs. Sutton commented of "Dr. Phinuit": "He exactly imitated her arch manner." Many other characteristics of the daughter were also apparent. For example, the deceased Katherine referred to her brother George as "Dodo" as she had done in life, and she referred to herself as "Kakie," also as she had done while alive.

Whether or not the "information" was coming from the deceased or the minds of the parents present at the sitting is unprovable; but either way, some paranormal ability appears to have been in evidence.

Eileen Garrett (1893–1970) was one of the most famous modern trance mediums. As a child she appears to have made contact with her own deceased relatives; she thought little of it and assumed that everyone else could do the same. An example of her work comes from research into the case of Captain W. G. R. Hinchcliffe. In March 1928, Hinchcliffe, together with Elsie Mackay, daughter of Lord Inchcape of the P & O shipping empire, set out to fly across the Atlantic in an attempt to make the first east to west trans-atlantic aeroplane flight. They never made it; they were presumed to have crashed somewhere near the Azores. Garrett passed on many messages from Hinchcliffe to his wife that were recognis-able to Mrs. Hinchcliffe and gave her valuable information relating to lost documents. Mrs. Hinchcliffe was convinced that the mes-sages had originated from her deceased husband.

The information gleaned by mediums is not a straight deliv-ery of facts; often it is couched in symbolism or clues. An experi-enced medium therefore seeks to understand the true meaning of the clues and symbols. In our interviews with medium Bar-bara Wright, she gave us several examples of the type of oblique information that mediums receive:

> The spirits . . . give you impressions. For example, I could be here talking to you and all of a sudden I could feel as if I am growing large and I might say to you, "I know that there is a gentleman here because I get that impression . . . I feel I am so large." You might say, "Yes he was a large man." When the impressions come and we are able to say to the recipient, "I've got your mother here, or a lady, whatever," they give you the details of how they died, they describe themselves usually. They rarely give a name. You can't demand anything from a spirit. Remember we are the chan-nel, we are in the middle like a telephone. We can only receive what is coming through from those who have passed over.

Barbara Wright told us a story of a reading with an apparently mysterious clue. A couple came to her for a double reading. Everything flowed smoothly and all their loved ones came through, giving names and descriptions of what they had died of. Then she started to tell them about a young lad who was putting his arms around the woman, giving her all his love and calling her Mum. This was the couple's son. Barbara went on to describe his last hours in an intensive care unit. The couple were overwhelmed with their grief. Here was the proof they had been desperately looking for—proof that their son still existed.

Then Barbara said: "Oh, by the way, he says I am to remind you of the lovely rose bush." But the couple did not understand the message; they had no recollection of a rose bush in connection with their son. But Barbara insisted that the spirit was showing her a beautiful pink rose bush. She could see him hanging on to one of the roses with a beautiful smile on his face. Again, the couple insisted that there must be a mistake in the information because they had never had a garden and could not remember any incident with a pink rose bush. Barbara again asked the spirit about the rose bush. He said his parents would remember it.

Naturally Barbara felt quite disheartened about this, because everything else had gone so well in the reading. But she told the couple to keep it in memory because their son had told her he would help them remember. After the reading, as the couple were about to leave, the woman showed Barbara a picture of her son. It was the last one taken of him, while they were on a family holiday. Barbara said: "When I looked at the photograph I didn't see the boy. The first thing my eyes saw was the beautiful pink rose bush. And his hands were hanging on to the rose." When she pointed the bush out to the couple, they were amazed. Neither of them had remembered the rose bush, yet this was the picture they always carried with them and looked at almost daily. They saw only their adored son, not the background. The mother told how when she had taken his photo, her son had said: "Wait, Mum. Let me hold one of these flowers."

Barbara Wright had another reading in which she was able to interpret the images and relate some good news. The client was a woman whose son had emigrated to Australia but she had lost contact with him. She started going to mediums to see if they could tell her where he was. Some of the mediums had told her that her son was in spirit. But Barbara disagreed with this because she was in tune with his sister, who was in spirit. Barbara told the woman that her son was in the United States, that he had married but it was disastrous and he hadn't wanted to worry his mother about it. She also said that the son would make contact with his mother at Christmas time. She knew it would be during the Christmas season because she could hear carols being sung. The following Christmas Eve, the woman phoned Barbara to share her joy. She had received a card from her son, saying he was alive and well, but that much had happened in his life and he hadn't wanted to disturb her with his problems. But now he was planning to come to see her.

As to why the spirits offer clues rather than clear messages, Barbara suggested: "They want us to work on this level to prove survival." A more challenging interpretation of mediumship could be that the medium is in touch with faculties in his or her own mind. If this is true, then being forced to interpret "clues" could represent the left brain trying to rationalise the intuition of the right brain.

Most messages received through mediums, while often crucially important to the recipient, are mundane, and there is rarely any information imparted that is not already known to the recipient. The lady whose son was alive, described above, might well have "felt" his presence herself telepathically or intuitively. The boy in front of the rose bush might have seemed surprising to the mother, but she had the photograph with her—even subconsciously she had seen it. But occasionally the recipient receives a message that it seems unlikely they would have knowledge of. "Carol" related to us just such an account. She had been through an impressive reading with a medium, who had offered many items of information that related closely to her family, when suddenly one item seemed quite out of place. The medium was in contact with Carol's deceased brother. Then he referred to Carol's sister. "I don't have a sister," Carol stated. The medium sought confirmation; but the spirit brother insisted that this was correct. To Carol this was so disappointing; such a wrong item of information perhaps meant that the rest of the seemingly good reading was valueless. Later she discussed the sitting with her parents. She told us:

> There was a stunned silence. And they were obviously very uncomfortable. I started to wonder if there had been some stillborn child in the family, or an early death I had never been told about. I had no idea what was to come. When I think back now I can hardly believe they did what they did. Eventually Mum said: "I think we had better tell you something. Laura is your sister. We had to give her away at birth." Laura was a friend I had gone to school with, everyone used to say how alike we were. We were told we were distantly related, cousins or something. Apparently something had happened in the family and Laura had been adopted by friends. I never found out quite what the family circumstances that caused it were.

But it would be possible to argue that even in this extraordinary case there were of course people alive who knew of the events: Carol's parents. Could the information have come to the medium "via" them? Or could it have come from Carol's subconscious, her own "knowledge" having been acquired telepathically from her parents? If telepathy exists, perhaps such information-transfer through the living rather than from the dead is possible.

But are mediums actually in contact with a person now dead but with the ability to think as he or she did when alive? There have certainly been some impressive cases; Leonore Piper and Eileen Garrett—tested by the Society for Psychical Research and the American Society for Psychical Research—were not found to be cheating. Cases in our own files have also proven difficult to discount. But there is no conclusive proof that the information comes from a person now dead. In Barbara Wright's case of the boy and the rose bush, the living members of his family had seen the picture many times, even if they had not "acknowledged" it in their own minds. Barbara Wright might have been gleaning the image in a paranormal way but it is hard to understand why a dead person would offer it as proof of his existence; there must have been more impressive moments in his life shared with his parents.

The mediums, though, are receiving information that has not been passed to them in any "normal" fashion. They may be picking up, telepathically, thoughts and knowledge of the dead from the living. There can be no doubt that the medium has mind power. But it does not follow that they are in contact with the dead.

To quote Eileen Garrett, whose work impressed so many: "In all my years of professional mediumship I have had no 'sign,' 'test' or slightest evidence to make me believe I have contacted another world. . . . I do not believe in individual survival after death."

Channelling

The medium acts as a "channel" between the spirits and the living; and the receipt of the messages is sometimes known as "channelling." We continue this examination of this mind power by looking at this phenomenon.

In 1907 the ruins of Glastonbury Abbey were acquired for the nation, and architect Frederick Bligh Bond was given the job of supervising excavations. Bond contacted John Barnett who, through automatic writing, received instructions for the excavation of the abbey from long-dead monks, and in particular one called William. The writing was highly accurate and the information of great use to those who had commissioned Bond—the Church of England. Unfortunately Bond felt justified in publishing his story of how he had provided the Church of England with their information, and they were—to put it mildly—not best pleased. They dismissed him immediately.

The medium Rosemary Brown claims to channel compositions from dead composers, including the former Beatle John Lennon. A UFO contactee and a musician acting in "partnership" claim to channel the compositions and the voice of the late "King" of rock and roll Elvis Presley. Interestingly, some of the composers that modern mediums act as "channels" for may themselves have alluded to the same claim; Mozart said that his music would often walk into his head unannounced, and Saint-Saëns said that in order to compose he only had to listen.

The following account of channelled "guidance" from the spirits is a curious one indeed, not least because, if true, it accurately predicted future events. And if that is so then there is presumably no one from whom the information could have come telepathically (unless we speculate information across a time barrier). It is the case of Morgan Robertson and the *Titanic*. The story is more usually treated as a prediction, and indeed perhaps that is where it belongs, except for Robertson's own assertion that he channelled it from "spirits."

Morgan Robertson was born in 1861 in New York. His father was a shipmaster on the Great Lakes. His early years are reported to have been brutal and full of deprivation. At the age of sixteen he first went to sea, perhaps to put distance between himself and the then-recent deaths of both his sister and his mother. At twenty-five years old he was back on land, working in a shop. Ten years later he began a writing career that was extraordinary to say the least. He admitted from the start that he wrote as an easy way to make money. At the age of thirty-six he apparently became convinced that he was not actually doing the writing at all, but that he was channelling his writings from spirit guides. His relationship with his guides seems to have been unusual: chastising them for not giving him inspiration; swearing at them; and pacing up and down in his apartment pleading with them. Many thought him crazy, and apparently he considered that possibility himself because he had himself admitted to the New York Bellevue Psychiatric Hospital where he stayed for two months.

In 1898 he wrote his first short novel called *The Wreck of the Titan, or Futility*. It was to turn out to be an astonishing piece of prediction. The comparisons below between the fictional ship, which he called the *Titan*, and the real *Titanic*, whose fate is probably the best known of all maritime disasters, is compelling:

Titan	*Titanic*
British	British
Owned by an company whose main shareholder was a wealthy American	Owned by White Star Line, whose main shareholder was J. P. Morgan, a wealthy American
Was the most luxurious ship in existence	Was the most luxurious ship in existence
Regarded as "unsinkable"	Claimed by "The Shipbuilder" to be "practically unsinkable"
Huge loss of life	An estimated 1,522 died
Nineteen watertight compartments	Fifteen watertight compartments
Watertight bulkhead doors operated automatically with flooding	Watertight bulkhead doors could operate automatically with flooding
Three propellers	Three propellers
Displacement 70,000 tons	Displacement 60,000 tons
40,000 horsepower	Approx 50,000 horsepower
Three triple expansion engines	Two triple expansion engines and one steam turbine
Top speed twenty-five knots	Top speed twenty-three to twenty-five knots
Capacity 3,000	Capacity 3,547
2,000 aboard	2,227 aboard (sources vary slightly)
800 feet long	882 feet long
Twenty-four lifeboats (could only hold 500 people)	Twenty lifeboats (could only hold 1,178 people)
Struck iceberg, leading to sinking	Struck iceberg, leading to sinking
Location of incident: North Atlantic off Newfoundland Banks	Location of incident: North Atlantic off Newfoundland Banks
Happened on April night	Happened on April night
Sea was calm	Sea was calm
Travelling at high speed (trying for a record)	Travelling at high speed (not trying for a record but trying to better the time of her sister ship)

But there were also differences: *Titan* struck in thick fog; *Titanic* had a clear night. Titan had left New York; *Titanic* was heading for New York. *Titan* grounded on the iceberg; *Titanic* sailed on. And the list goes on.

The reason Robertson added "Futility" to the title was, he declared, as a comment on shipping lines that cared more for profit than people and did not put safety first. But even given that many of the book's assumptions were a logical extension of actual or speculated shipping development, the comparison between the fictional and real-life events is impressive and deserves consideration.

The size and general capacity of the ship was a natural extension of the developments of the time: Cunard Line and the large German steamships were creating a climate where speed and size were the "space race" of the day. Even the insufficient number of lifeboats was a known factor for those who did a little research. What is often not realised is that the *Titanic* in fact exceeded lifeboat requirements of the time—ships of over 10,000 tons were required to have sixteen lifeboats or more—but the regulations had not been updated as the ships had grown in size.

And even the circumstances might have been predictable: April is the most dangerous month for icebergs because the warming spring months cause them to cleave off the glaciers. And a calm sea might well be a dangerous time: the crew of the *Titanic* made it clear at the two subsequent inquiries that the dead-calm, millpond-like sea meant that with no breaker waves crashing against the icebergs they were that much less easy to spot.

But certain factors are less obvious: the fact that the ship was on its maiden voyage, for example, was an unlikely piece of fiction as it was an astonishing and poignant fact. We might also consider just how unlikely the sinking was, given what we now know of the *Titanic*'s fate, making the fictional precursor all the more strange. Many small factors combined to create the disaster, and changing any one of them would have produced a quite different outcome. For example, had the iceberg been seen only moments earlier it would probably have been missed. In fact, had the iceberg not been seen at all *Titanic* might have avoided sinking—had the ship struck the berg head-on it would have been severely damaged but would probably not have sunk because of its watertight compartments. Had the lookouts been provided with binoculars ... had the arrangement of propellers and rudder been slightly different ... had the water been less calm ... and so it goes on. The more it is studied the more it is realised that the sinking of the *Titanic* was an incredible piece of bad luck and a bizarre combination of factors. To have predicted such an event so closely fourteen years earlier is undoubtedly food for thought.

And we have Robertson's own insistence that he was channelling from the spirit world.

Nor was Robertson's "success" with this prediction an isolated occurence. In 1909 he wrote about a war between Japan and the USA that commenced with a surprise attack on the American fleet—as happened at Pearl Harbor in 1941. He also seems to have "predicted" airships, rocketry used in warfare and submarines.

The irony might well be that if these messages did come from the spirit world, the spirits must have been very frustrated at how futile their efforts were; there is no indication that Robertson's work influenced the course of actions at all. Even *Futility* was little read before the *Titanic* disaster. And that is one aspect of channelling that we have to consider. Wherever the knowledge comes from, however it is obtained, we do not yet know how to deal with it usefully.

However, one useful application of channelling is demonstrated in the next account. (It is also another example of "paranormal overlap"; it could just as easily appear in Chapter 8 in the section on "guardian angels.")

Patient X received coverage in the *British Medical Journal* in 1997 because of the unusual circumstances that led to her operation to remove a brain tumour. It seems she channelled information about effective action that needed to be taken. The story began when she contacted Dr. Ikechukwu Azuonye at Lambeth Healthcare NHS Trust after hearing a voice that told her it was a friend and that it wanted to help. She was counselled, given some medication and, having no history of psychiatric disorder, was discharged. Then, while on holiday abroad, she heard two voices telling her to go back to England because she was ill. The voices gave her an address to go to, which she did. It turned out to be the brain scan department of a London hospital. The voices told her, when she got there, to ask for a brain scan and to cite two reasons: that she had a tumour, and that the brainstem was inflamed. She was examined, the two diagnoses were found to be correct, and she was immediately operated on to remove the growth. When she recovered from the operation the voices said to her: "We are pleased to have helped you. Goodbye." Dr. Azuonye was impressed enough to write up the story. "This is the first and only instance I have ever come across in which hallucinatory voices sought to reassure the patient of their genuine interest in her welfare." He points out that in this case the voices "offered her a specific diagnosis [and] directed her to the type of hospital best equipped to deal with her problem."

Sceptics of channelling point out that many channelled messages are vague; but the case of Patient X is clearly difficult to dismiss. Psychiatrist Dr. Susan Blackmore stated: "Having a brain tumour will make you feel odd in various ways." Perhaps so, but that does not explain where this level of specific information came from. In fact, Dr. Blackmore's other comments are more in line with our own thinking. She suggests that given a vague feeling that something is wrong, a voice "pops up" to tell you intuitively what is wrong. If channelling is accessing a huge store of memories, consciously forgotten but capable of recall when needed, then perhaps even the address of the hospital and a guess at the diagnosis is possible. The attitude of sceptics is generally that "paranormal" means something that cannot be explained; we disagree. Everything paranormal will be understood by a science one day—perhaps in a thousand years' time—and channelling may well be understood as a memory-access device. But it remains outside of today's accepted "normal" science and is, therefore, paranormal by definition. The case of Patient X is a clear indication of the reality of channelling. But of spirits? That is a conclusion not to be jumped at, but given the level of detail in this case, not one to be summarily dismissed either.

A stroke can also cause astonishing repercussions, some of which may explain perceived channelling effects, or may be a part of the process. In particular there are several cases on record of "foreign accent syndrome." One such case is that of Anne Bristow-Kitney of the BBC World Service. Her clear English accent was a defining feature. One morning she awoke with a severe headache and a stiff neck. By the time she was taken to hospital by ambulance she was losing consciousness. At the hospital it was discovered that Anne had suffered a cerebral haemorrhage and an operation was necessary. When she awoke from the operation she spoke French, not just fluently but with such a perfect accent that some of the hospital staff thought Anne was French. She had spoken French earlier in her life, but not so fluently. Anne had also suffered an aneurysm—a swelling in the brain's main artery. Just after the operation to remove it she suffered a stroke that created hallucinations—she believed she was in India, for example—and she also started speaking with a Scottish accent. She is not Scottish, nor are her friends and close relatives, and she has never lived there. Her great-grandfather was a Scot, though she had never met him.

Ian Pople, consultant neurosurgeon at the Frenchay Hospital in Bristol, commented that there have been other such cases of people with head injuries speaking in other accents, such as American and German. Pople believes that Anne possibly picked up the Scottish accent from meeting someone earlier in her life, perhaps only once. "It's to do with the left side of the brain that controls our ability to talk. The speech control centre is left intact, but the part which links up to it is damaged, so you get a re-emergence of a first language or maybe simply a memory, as in Anne's case. It could have been someone she met only once."

Such conditions generally cure themselves over time and the person's "normal" speech re-emerges.

We must remind the reader that Anne is not channelling, but what happened to her might offer an explanation for those instances in channelling and mediumship when a person starts "speaking" (or channelling) in a foreign accent. It might explain some cases, but oddly enough it might also strengthen the case for channelling. Let us take the claims of mediumship at face value for the moment. The medium channels via a "master of ceremonies"—the spirit guide—who in effect connects the medium to the spirit wishing to communicate. Is the spirit guide able to select a medium with some background in a particular language and "use" the pathways in the brain to effect communication?

Or perhaps we must acknowledge that probably throughout our lives we all hear a huge variety of accents and languages, often subconsciously. If so, then perhaps we can all access those memories when called upon to channel.

But if channelling is from within the person's own mind—and we believe there is a strong case for this viewpoint—then why does the mind choose to use foreign languages and accents? We have a tentative suggestion to offer. We suggest that the process of channelling allows for more efficient accessing of the mind's information store, developed originally for survival. Is the mind automatically creating a way for the conscious mind to "trust" and rely on the information by making it appear to come from an external source? When the person is in danger or difficulty and the mind is drawing from a pool of information for help, how much more reliable that information might seem if it purports to come from the deceased (who are usually attributed with far more knowledge and wisdom in death than they had in life), from aliens, guardian angels or whatever. So perhaps the mind builds on a variety of memories to create a mask to hide the information behind.

Victoria Holt, a successful advertising executive, responded to the *Daily Mail* survey of the paranormal in 1998, indicating that she had built her life and career on the advice of psychics. "I can honestly say I owe my success to psychics," she comments. She is far from alone; we have spoken to many people who have taken direction, or given direction, on the basis of psychic information, with great success. Perhaps Victoria is brave to have admitted the "source" of her success; employers might think someone who listens to mediums "a bit strange." But such employers would be well advised to think twice; whether Victoria and those like her are actually receiving guidance from "elsewhere," or from their own heads or the intuition of psychics, it is highly likely that they are using the best part of their brains in the most efficient way, and success is likely to follow.

Channelling takes many forms and it is easy to understand how a message "heard" in the head might be the brain accessing different areas of itself and transmitting the result to another section. But what of messages that seem to come through from "elsewhere"—spirits, aliens, God—in the form of writing? And not just messages but art forms such as music, writing, painting and so on. Are these part of the same process? We can start our consideration of these questions by looking at the phenomenon of "automatic writing."

The recipient of automatic writing—the writer—is often in an altered state akin to a trance when receiving the writings. Often writers do not remember writing. They may "come to," for example, on a sofa surrounded by sheets of paper covered in writing that they presume they have written but which they believe has been channelled from, say, spirits. They have no memory of doing the writing, and often find it represents a subject or even a depth of knowledge that they do not believe they possess.

We have interviewed several such automatic writers and have found their accounts of their experiences very similar. Because of the report of a third-party witness we have been particularly drawn to the writings of Heather Woods. Heather, who died in

1993, was a stigmatic and her writings were of a religious nature. Her main focus was her stigmata, which she took to be a sign that Christ was drawing the world's attention to her healing work (she was also a spiritual healer), which she believed was the continuation of Christ's ministry. Over time she received more than 60,000 words of channelled writings.

The first channelling was coincident with the arrival of the stigmata. In May 1992 she noticed blistering on her hand, which eventually formed the first stigmata marking. Two days later she had a vision of the Lord being baptised. She saw it as if she were present, a part of the experience. That night she dreamt the same vision and in the morning she found she had drawn it. The same evening she had a feeling of being on the cross with Christ, effectively inside his body during the suffering, all of which she felt. Again, she found she had channelled a drawing of the scene. She described the feelings she could remember about the channelling:

> It was just an urge to draw. I could only remember reaching over for the pencil. . . . I wasn't even aware I was drawing. But it got to where the urge to draw and write was so strong that it was distracting me. I would be coming downstairs and I would miss some of the steps in my urgency to reach pencil and paper, to get it down in black and white. It wasn't as though there was an urgency or that I was going to run out of time; it wasn't that if I didn't get it down I wouldn't get it at all. It was just that these feelings were so compelling. So I started to keep paper and pen upstairs, or anywhere I might be. . . . During the time the writing or the drawing comes through I am oblivious. Those who have seen me writing, or drawing, say that I do it with my left hand. I don't know, I'm not aware; but normally I'm right-handed. And when I have to write it's like a need. I've grabbed anything that comes to hand; I've written on a Christian Aid poster, on a piece of cardboard box, on old envelopes and cards and all sorts of papers that were lying around.

One witness, the wife of Heather's priest Father Eric Eades, commented: "From what I've seen I've no doubt whatsoever. She didn't do those [consciously]; she could do little faces and so on, but what she did with her left hand was amazing." Father Eric had asked Heather to record the times when she received these messages and how long it took to draw or write them. She was never very successful in that, but the effort of trying to note the time as she went in or out of trances seems to have had the effect of giving her slightly more awareness of the process. She commented:

> [One] night I had gone to bed, but I was awakened. I found myself coming down the stairs again and just sitting down. The urge to write was strong. I knew I was going to write and I reached for the pen. I was trying to remember to look at the clock to note the time, remembering that Father Eric had told me to try to note times down in case it was important. But I couldn't. I was fighting inside myself, trying to look at the clock and yet I knew then that it wasn't me any more. I wasn't taken over but I had lost my own will. I was under another will. So although I was aware of picking up a pencil or pen and finding some paper, and I was aware I was writing, I couldn't move. I was aware I was writing but not what I was writing. And I wasn't able to look at the clock. And then it just seemed as though I picked up the paper, as if there was no break. But there was writing on both sides of the foolscap paper. The pen was still in my hand.

The speed of Heather's writing was first implied by an incident that happened over the Christmas holidays. She was with members of her family, watching television:

> On Boxing Day I was watching *Orphan Annie*, about ten minutes before the end I got this really strong urge to write. It was strange because I got a bit angry that I was going to miss the end of the film. As I left the room I asked them to video the end for me so

that I could watch it later. I went upstairs. Hazel [her sister] gave me some paper and I went in my bedroom and just let the writing come. Then I went through to Lucy [Hazel's mother-in-law] and asked her to witness that I had just done the writing. And I came downstairs and Hazel said, "You weren't very long. Weren't you given anything?" [I replied] "What do you mean, I wasn't very long?" I felt as though I had been up there about half an hour. She told me that I had only been up there for a few minutes. I showed them the writings. I think there were three sheets covered on both sides and another sheet that looked as if it was just plain. I told them that I mustn't have used that page. But then we saw faint marks on the paper; there was a faint pencil drawing on the paper. You could only see it when you held it up to the light, or caught it at the right angle.

Hazel remembers being astonished at the short time that Heather had been gone given the prolific output she created. Lucy was similarly astonished; it is burned in her memory because of the strangeness. As she put it: "I wasn't very well on Boxing Day, I was in bed, and Heather came upstairs. In a matter of ten minutes she came into the bedroom and said she had just had this . . . prophecy, or whatever. I was absolutely staggered by the short time it had taken and how beautiful the writing was. It really was remarkable."

The speed of writing was not at that time actually witnessed, though there seems little reason to doubt the claims. Nonetheless, shortly after this incident, two people were present in the room when Heather went into a trance and watched the writing as it happened. Witnesses to automatic writing are quite rare, and what these two people saw was astonishing. One of the witnesses was a close friend called Helen. As Helen described it: "I gave her a large piece of white cardboard. She wrote with her left hand, and using a red pen, which she'd never used before. . . . She was writing quite furiously on this piece of white card—at an abnormal speed, I can definitely confirm that. [Father] Eric and I sat with her in the lounge, ate sandwiches and drank tea, and watched her doing this writing. Then all of sudden she dropped the pen, looked up and said, 'Oh tea.'" Helen said it was like watching the "Superman" movies when he moves at "super-speed" and she demonstrated what she meant by moving her own hands in a furious, seemingly uncontrolled manner. But with these movements Heather had produced elegant, clear writing.

There seems to be no reason to think that the process of automatic writing is any different from channelling through speech. The channeller is in an altered state, and we believe that possibly the unconscious mind is accessing its own data bank and feeding it to the conscious mind at high speed, or as in this case bypassing the conscious mind altogether. Heather had possibly read the scriptures and poetry that she later "channelled." Perhaps the by-passing of the conscious allows for the speeding up of muscle reflexes and therefore the fast writing.

The messages that are received also fit the usual pattern of channelling. Although the channellers may not think they have the knowledge to produce the messages themselves and, therefore, feel an outside entity is at work, the fact is that most messages are supportive of the beliefs of the recipient. Aliens warn ecologically concerned people to take care of the Earth; the deceased bring much needed comfort to the living; and in Heather's case all of her writings and drawings were supportive of what she saw as an all-consuming mission in life. Again, there is no reason to believe that the source of Heather's material is from other than Heather herself, albeit from a subconscious store of information that even she could not believe in. However, to be dismissive of "external" input might be too impulsive given our present state of knowledge. There are cases of channelling that are thought-provoking, and at least suggest an outside influence:

· When Father Eric, Heather's priest, died she channelled a message from him to his wife Betty. Heather questioned "his" use of the word "Bet" to describe his wife, which she was sure was inaccurate. But Betty told us: "In fact he always called me Bet when we were alone together." The message contained references and items that Betty thinks Heather would have been unlikely to know. She believed the message truly came from her late husband. Betty also told us: "it was in his writing. . . . I have no doubts whatsoever about that message. Eric didn't very often write his sermons but when he did, the faster he wrote the bigger his writing; and this is exactly the same. The 'y's are the same . . . it is all just the same."

- Luiz Antonio Gasparetto is a Brazilian who channels, and paints, pictures in the style of several famous painters. Like Heather, there are descriptions of him working at "breathtaking speed."

- Another Brazilian, Francisco Candido Xavier, has channelled books for over fifty years, never taking payment for the works. The earnings are donated to the country's poor. The language style is more complex than might be expected of him, and he does not even understand some of what he writes. Again, witnesses say he writes as if his hands were "driven by a battery."

- Channelling music has become the "trademark" of the medium Rosemary Brown, despite the fact that she has no formal training in the subject. She has received compositions from many deceased composers, including Beethoven, Liszt, Chopin and, more recently, John Lennon.

- Matthew Manning, a well-known psychic, had a history of automatic writing, which then "switched" to automatic painting. He produced drawings in the style of deceased artists such as Albrecht Dürer; some of the drawings were of existing paintings that Manning claimed never to have seen before.

An interesting example of "self-healing" through automatic writing is the case of Sarah Cartwright, written up in the book *Shamans, Healers and Medicine Men* by Holger Kalweit. At the age of twenty-three, Sarah Cartwright had become a virtual invalid. For five years she had been unable even to raise her feet over a small step. She was also emotionally on edge, prone to fits of hysteria. Conventional approaches by her doctor had not eased the problem. Then she claimed that "a new and strange element suddenly invaded my life." Automatic writing started first when one evening her right hand became numb and she saw her hand—as if independent from her will—take a pencil and start writing.

Often automatic writing takes on quite different characteristics but in this case Sarah described the writing as looking like her own. The words however were meaningless to her. In fact, what she had written out was a medical prescription that listed plants and their applications. The descriptions were even accompanied by a few drawings of the plants. Later she commented: "I know now that the prescription was the antidote calomel and a remedy for nervous debility." Other automatic writing informed her that she should go into a dark, quiet room; after following that advice she found that she was able to walk in a way that she had not been able to do for many years. This case has many parallels to the "voices" heard by Patient X mentioned earlier (see pages 157–58). Perhaps, as we speculated in the account of Patient X, Sarah Cartwright found the details of the cure within herself and in her case used automatic writing to channel the messages to herself.

Ouija

Perhaps the most common form of channelling is to receive messages through a Ouija board. Although its use is not recommended, many people admit to having "played" on one while at school or in their teenage years—sometimes with frightening results. The famous case of the possession of Robert Mannheim began with the use of a Ouija board (see pages 192–94).

There is a report of one researcher, Alan Vaughan, who used a Ouija board for entertainment with a friend and ended up believing himself possessed for a time by a number of entities. One was allegedly the wife of a Nantucket sea captain who resented being dead.

Indeed, experienced researchers can fall foul of the technique. On 9 November 1948, the third of a series of seances was held in Barnwell Castle in Northamptonshire. Spirits came through dramatically; there was a crack like a whip and the vision of the upper torso of a monk. The researchers left at a pace, to put it mildly, and one later commented that he wished he'd not undertaken that investigation.

We know of sittings, and have undertaken Ouija experiments ourselves, that have suggested that the minds of the sitters might play a part. On one occasion we were part of a group that received a coherent communication, but which one of the group admitted was from a fictional character he had invented for a film script he was developing. This seemed to suggest strongly that what we had contacted was an aspect of his mind. When a famous personality comes through it is tempting to consider that it is a member of the group's image of that person that is being received, rather than the actual spirit of that person. Certainly if every teenage group in a dark basement that has successfully conjured up the spirit of Adolf Hitler is correct then he has been busier since his death than he ever was in life!

That said, there are, as always, cases where information passed over is of a calibre that forces us to consider the possibility that a "real" spirit has been contacted. At the seances of mediums Madame B. Bricout and Jacques Brossy in the early 1930s, a French soldier killed in the First World War communicated a spirit contact—perhaps a control—called Juliette, when the couple were using the Ouija board. The soldier was introduced by Juliette to prove her abilities; she hoped that since the mediums using the Ouija board could have no knowledge of the soldier it would rule out telepathy from their own minds. Juliette told Brossy and Bricout that the soldier, Robert Marie, had died in 1914; prior to that he had lived in Villers-sur-Mer, that his father had been the caretaker of a villa. Robert's own son, also named Robert, had suffered meningitis that had left him deaf and mute. The dead soldier was apparently a bit annoyed about his former wife's remarriage. Brossy wrote to the authorities at Villers-sur-Mer who confirmed many of the points raised.

Electronic Voice Phenomenon (EVP)

One form of channelling which also offers the suggestion of an external source is known as Electronic Voice Phenomenon (EVP). Channelled messages, generally from the deceased, are heard on radios and even recorded on audio, and recently video, tape recorders.

Thomas Edison tried to record the voices of the dead, believing that if there was survival of spirit there should be a scientific way of communicating with them. In his view: "If our personality survives, then it is strictly logical and scientific to assume that it retains memory, intellect and other faculties and knowledge that we acquire on this earth. Therefore if personality exists after what we call death, it is reasonable to conclude that those who leave this earth would like to communicate with those they have left here. I am inclined to believe that our personality hereafter will be able to affect matter. If this reasoning be correct then if we can evolve an instrument so delicate as to be affected or moved or manipulated by our personality as it survives to the next life, such an instrument when made available ought to record something." Edison was never successful, nor has there been any reasonably supportable claim that he ever communicated through EVP after his own death, which would have been a logical progression of his thinking.

There have been many proponents of EVP and many experiments with it, some of which have produced thought-provoking success. None, however, has produced results that were irrefutably the product of the deceased. Nevertheless, for devotees of EVP the deceased remains the true source of the signals.

The first EVP recordings are attributed to Friedrich Jorgenson, a Russian-born painter, film producer and musician. When living in Sweden in 1959, and out in the country recording birdsong, he recorded a voice speaking Norwegian discussing lifestyles of birds. Later he conducted experiments to see if the recordings were an accidental receipt of some radio transmission or if they were paranormal in origin. He succeeded in recording a voice he recognised as that of his dead mother. It is notable that the first recorded communications were about birds while Jorgenson was recording birdsong and presumably thinking about birds. Also, something about the moment suggested to Jorgenson that it might be paranormal, but at face value it is hard to see why. Electronic equipment often picks up spurious signals; we have heard police radios from cars passing outside our house "coming through" our hi-fi, the computer and even kitchen equipment. But because Jorgenson thought the voice was paranormal he sought other evidence to prove it and found it. Either a coincidence is at work here or Jorgenson's role in the incident is more central than it first appears. Jorgenson later recorded the sounds of his own mother, so there is no doubt that he became central to the experiment in some way. That he recognised his own mother's voice means, *ipso facto*, that he had a memory of it and, therefore, it was present somewhere in his own head.

But that leaves us with the problem of how they got onto magnetic tape. Voices in the head are heard by the person: automatic writing—wherever it comes from—is done by the recipient of the message; but magnetic tape is a third party and a nonintelligent mechanical one at that. Can a thought be impressed on magnetic tape? The glib, but unsatisfactory, answer to that question is: why not? If telepathy is a reality, then some transfer takes place into the electrochemical processes of someone else's mind. It has to make an impression there, to become a "recorded memory" of sorts. So why could it not be recorded on other materials? The claim of thoughtography is that mental impressions can be recorded on photography film. Ghosts are allegedly recorded on both photographic film and magnetic video tape and their source is uncertain. So while we would have to accept that the mechanism might not be discovered for some time, EVP remains a possibility as long as there is unexplained evidence. We might also consider that Jorgenson spoke in trance, even taking on the voice of his mother; if so he might not have remembered it, just as automatic writers do not remember writing. And Jorgenson's experience offers the suggestion that it was Jorgenson's mind that produced the recording.

Reincarnation

Another phenomenon relating to the survival of mind after death is reincarnation, the belief that the soul—or whatever term is regarded as acceptable—is born again into this world to live other lifetimes. In the East, the belief in reincarnation is part of the major religions: in the West, it is viewed as possibly "real" but not part of the major religions. The German philosopher Arthur Schopenhauer said: "Were an Asiatic to ask me for a definition of Europe, I should be forced to answer him: 'It is that part of the world which is haunted by the incredible delusion that man was created out of nothing. And that his present birth is his first entrance into life.'"

Nonetheless, as a belief rather than specifically as a part of religion, reincarnation has gained a wide following. In the 1998 *Daily Mail* survey of belief in the paranormal, one-quarter of the people surveyed believed in reincarnation, slightly more women than men. In the West the re-emergence of reincarnation as a belief was less dependent on religion and more on "paranormal research." Arguably the starting point for a reappraisal of reincarnation were the claims of the "sleeping prophet," Edgar Cayce. Between 1923 and 1945 Cayce gave something like 2,500 life "readings" to people, many of which involved past-life recall. Cayce suggested that many current-life problems arose from past-life experiences. Psychologist Morey Bernstein set out to prove Cayce a fraud; he ended up being the man who "brought" reincarnation to the West in the way only the West knows how—through the media.

Most events in science, entertainment and, in this case, the paranormal have a "start" point that is not the first of its kind but is the event that suddenly promotes the topic because it is exposed to the public at just the right time.

In 1956 Bernstein published *The Search for Bridey Murphy* describing his work with a Colorado housewife Virginia Burns Tighe—pseudonym Ruth Simmons in the book (see also page 63). Bernstein used hypnotic regression techniques to take Mrs. Tighe back to an earlier life when she was Bridey Murphy, a peasant woman living in nineteenth-century Ireland. The book was a bestseller and brought the subject of reincarnation, and the technique of hypnotic regression, to public attention.

During the sessions Mrs. Tighe spoke in a thick Irish broque, and when describing the end of Bridey's life her voice becomes very flat and "old." She described several relatives and historical sites. Research indicated that while some of the details may have related to nineteenth-century Ireland, others seem to have been drawn from Mrs. Tighe's own childhood. There was some suggestion that even the name was taken from a neighbour, a Mrs. Bridie Murphy Corkell, though it is unclear what knowledge, if any, Mrs. Tighe would have had of that person.

Despite the fact that some of her recollections may have been overlaid by her current life-style, there were some seriously thought-provoking features: she recalled the names of shops she, as Bridey, had frequented and which later turned out to have been in existence at the time. There was nothing in the recall that could not have been discovered, nor could cryptomnesia (forgotten memories) be ruled out, but the detail was such that it was an impressive case. But it was the use of regression hypnosis in retrieving the memories that was to be the cause of much debate.

It is important to explain a few caveats about the use of hypnotic regression, and to remove a few misconceptions. General concerns are covered in a separate section of this book (see pages 53–59). Specific to this case, it is sometimes held that under hypnotic regression the subject is taken back to a specific time and relives it as if the subject were there at that time, with all subsequent memories removed. That is not so; even in *The Search for Bridey Murphy* Mrs. Tighe—as Bridey Murphy and speaking in her strong Irish accent—refers to sweets as "candy." This would clearly seem to be an overlay from her life as a 1950s' American.

A boy who had spoken only German until the age of six, when he learned English, was regressed to an age of six or earlier when he would only respond in German claiming that he could not understand English. Nevertheless, he was responding to questions from the hypnotist given in English!

Despite these doubts there are many cases, particularly in the East, that do not involve hypnotic regression but seem to suggest that reincarnation is true. Therefore, if people do have past lives, it must be possible that regression can reach back to those lives; but the degree of accuracy of retrieved memories is doubtful. The problem is that the hypnosis might not be reaching just past lives, it may also be enhancing other psychic areas of the mind such as telepathy, clairvoyance and so on. If so, the information that comes out under hypnosis may be from an extremely complex source—even unremembered memories in the hypnotist's mind.

One fascinating case was researched by Arnold Bloxham, who started investigating reincarnation in 1940. His subject's name was Jane Evans; she was regressed to seven past lifetimes. In one, she lived in York in the twelfth century as a Jewish woman, Rebecca, during the persecution of the Jews. She was able to describe a great deal about the attitude and oppression of the Jewish communities of the time: some details took a great deal of verifying through archive records. Furthermore, her recall apparently had a "true ring" to it because it was highly personal and missed out on well-known topical aspects of the massacre. For example, she recalled being forced to wear a yellow badge used to identify Jews. In the finale of her story she was caught up in the Jewish massacre of 1190, when anti-Semitism was pervasive and violent. Gangs of York residents rampaged through the streets and into the homes of Jews, killing and destroying. Jane's former self and her children sought refuge in the crypt of a local church but they were discovered and murdered. Subsequent research discovered the church where Jane's former self had died—St. Mary's Church in Castlegate. Her recall seemed to be seriously flawed, however, by the fact that this church had no crypt; indeed most churches of the time would not have had. However, workmen renovating the church, long after Jane's recall was taped, discovered a previously unknown crypt.

But what looked like good evidence turned out not to be; the "crypt" was in fact a charnel vault used to lay out bodies of the dead, and it almost certainly dated from a time long after that of Jane's recollections. The detail of the badge was also challenged by historians who do not believe that at that time Jews were forced to wear identifying badges.

Several researchers have argued that the recall could have been from "hidden memory" (cryptomnesia)—a recall of past reading and other learning, which are consciously forgotten. Jane might have, they thought, read a novel set in the time of the Jewish massacre. Certainly the detail of one of Jane's regressions—in the Roman era—was traced to a novel she had read.

Beliefs about past lives can be triggered by a wide variety of stimuli. A story told to us by "Fleur" seems supportive of reincarnation. It was triggered by a painting:

> When we moved to Ilford about twenty years ago I was shopping, and I went past Harrison and Gibson and there in the window was a copy of a painting by the artist Holbein, a portrait of his

daughter. I stopped in my tracks, I thought: "That's me." I can remember sitting there in those clothes, and being painted. When
we went to Paris, the original was hanging in a gallery there. I
have now got a copy of that painting in my lounge and every time
I look at it I remember sitting down and being painted. And fun-
nily enough I've got a photograph of me when I was sixteen—
taken long before I saw the picture—a side profile with my hair up
in a "beehive" style. And my eyes are exactly the same at that
same angle. I know that is me in the picture, and therefore Hol-
bein must have been my father.

We spoke to Frederick James, now in his eighties, who throughout his life has had specific recurring dreams that he believes
show himself in past lives. Frederick identified a different quality
to these dreams compared to "normal" dreams; they had exceptional clarity and never changed in detail, as he believed "normal" dreams would do. He believes they represent memories.

Frederick first described the geography of the surroundings
he sees in these dreams:

> There is a large white temple, and two large front doors which look
> as though they are bronze from where I am. On one side there is a
> white pillar on the doorway, on the other side there is a large black
> pillar. The temple is approached by a large "driveway," I suppose
> you'd call it, which I am walking down. On each side there are
> sphinxes which also look as if they are in bronze, and statues of
> various Egyptian gods; making it a very impressive avenue.
>
> It is obvious to me that I am a lower member of the priesthood
> because I am wearing their pleated skirt with the blue motif at the
> bottom. I have a man on each side holding my arms. Looking up to
> them I realise that they are both rather large men. They are wear-
> ing full regalia normal to priests; the white pleated skirt, and so on.
>
> They march me down this long aisle and almost at the door of
> the temple we take a left turn down into an alleyway to a side en-
> trance. Down there is a big doorway and we go through that into

a room of, I suppose, around twenty-four feet square. In the middle of this room is a statue of Isis, a gold statue strangely enough, which is unusual for Egyptian statues. Usually of course they are painted in blue and other basic colours. I am roughly thrust down on my face, down on my knees, in front of the statue by the guards, or priests. And the statue speaks. I cannot understand what the statue says because it's in the ancient intonation of the Egyptians and of course these days we have no knowledge of exactly how they spoke. We have plenty of things we can read but we have no knowledge of the spoken tongue. Therefore I do not know what the statue says to me but obviously it's not a very good thing because the priests at the finish suddenly pull me up off my face and take me to the side door which we exit through. What I have done, what my sin was, I don't know. The dream ends right outside that doorway. We go through the doorway and . . . blank.

I have visited that scene so many times endeavouring to extend beyond it, without any success whatsoever, though I am quite sure that the final chapter is outside that door.

Frederick said that he has always been very strongly drawn to the Egyptian period; he has studied it throughout his life, read innumerable books, studied the various writings, and so on.

Frederick told us of another dream of similar quality that he thinks originates from a somewhat earlier time:

This dream I have had time and time again. It starts in exactly the same way every time and again it stops short of the end. The details are just as clear. There is the sea on the left-hand side, or in front of me. Behind me is desert. There is, on the edge of the sea, a stone-built quay or unloading bay. About a hundred yards from where I am standing there is a deck-loaded ship. I have a feeling that it was probably a Phoenician ship. When I say ship, of course, it was an open-deck ship of the time and it was loaded with all sorts of things in wood; long planks, small planks. There are stevedores, obviously slaves by their dress, unloading it.

Standing over them and occasionally using a heavy whip he holds is a large man wearing a rough, leather-like skirt or kilt. Over one shoulder he has a sort of shirt top; it looks also like soft leather. His hair is black. His face is a typical face of the time. He is flourishing the whip and occasionally using it on anyone he sees lagging a little in the unloading.

I am about a hundred yards away from this on the other side of this stone quay which is about, I suppose, fifteen to twenty feet wide. It has rather a worn condition by the way, as though it has been there many, many years. It was obviously an outlying port which was not used a great deal. There was no other shipping to be seen.

I am on the other side of the quay to the sea side, on the sand side, and peering just over the top of the top stones. It looks as though, by my dress, I am one of the gang who are unloading this ship and I have got away from it. Obviously the foreman, or overseer, has missed my presence—presumably by counting the number of people there now and again—and he comes walking down towards me flourishing his whip and shouting.

Where I am standing, just in on my side of the stone wall, there is a worn indentation where stones have fallen away just enough to allow me to press my body into it and therefore not be seen from the top unless somebody deliberately leaned over and looked straight in. He passes by where I am, walks back again, still shouting and obviously not seeing me, towards the ship. That is the moment when I finish; I have never managed to get past that point in the dream. I wish I could but I have tried many times without any success.

Probably the most important work undertaken in the field of reincarnation study is by Dr. Ian Stevenson, a psychiatrist and parapsychologist working at the University of Virginia. He does not believe that the use of hypnosis in this field is very useful, and his work is not dependent on this technique. He has been analysing cases that suggest reincarnation since the 1960s and has examined over 2,500 cases. Despite the fact that he is responsible for an important body of evidence relating to reincarnation, he views only a small percentage of his cases as valuable and even then leaves the door open for alternative explanations.

Dr. Stevenson has examined children who have reported an earlier untimely death, and they seem to have reincarnated very quickly. The possible implication of this is that an untimely death provokes a speedy return. Often the subjects exhibit physical features that are suggestive of their previous existences and their previous deaths. Many of these children—brought up in an environment where belief in reincarnation is not challenged—have detailed recall; adults seem to lose this recall. In the West, recall seems to be lost at an early age, perhaps because of resistance to the belief by parents, peers and so on.

The following are some of the cases investigated by Dr. Stevenson.

- Gopal Gupta was born in Delhi in August 1956. At a very young age he began acting in a way not consistent with his social class. It should be pointed out that the caste system is extremely embedded into Indian culture. When asked to pick up a used glass of water he refused to do so claiming to be a sharma. A sharma is a member of India's highest caste, the Brahmins. The boy went on to explain that he had once owned a company called Sukh Shancharak, that he had lived in the city of Mathura and that he had been shot and killed by one of his brothers in his former life. It was not until Gopal was nine that his father investigated the claims when he was on a trip to Mathura. He discovered that there was a company called Sukh Shancharak and that one of the owners had been shot and killed by his brother in May 1948. Gopal's former family were impressed by Gopal's recall of incidents, many of which had never been widely reported. It should be pointed out that the killing itself was widely reported as the company owner concerned was of some standing. As Gopal grew up he seemed to lose his involvement with his former family and acted more within his own caste than the Brahmin caste.

- Indika Guneratne was born in Sri Lanka in 1962 and at around two years old described his past life as a wealthy citizen of Matara. He described his beautiful home and a Mercedes-Benz car together with memories of pet elephants. Many of the facts turned out to fit the description of a man who had lived in Matara, K. G. J. Weera Singhe, who had died in 1960. Indika's memories were highly accurate when applied to Weera Singhe's life and death. But there were also inaccuracies: he had only owned one elephant, not a great many, and he had never owned a Mercedes. However, Indika was able to recall the car's registration number and a Mercedes bearing that registration number had been owned by someone living in a nearby town to Matara.

- Winnie Eastland was killed in a car crash in 1961 at the age of six. Her mother, Charlotte, had another child in 1964 and during the pregnancy dreamt that Winnie was back in the family. In the delivery room her husband thought he heard Winnie's voice saying, "Daddy, I am coming home." During her life Susan appears to have exhibited several memories of Winnie's life, such as school events, family outings and so on. At one time she also said of a photograph of Winnie, "That was me." Quite how much influence the family might have had in creating some of Susan's images is probably impossible to tell; certainly the father's experience in the delivery room might have been significant in his attitude towards his daughter in later years.

In recent years, in Britain, there has been a claim that has promising characteristics. Jenny Cockell, born in 1954, believes that she is the reincarnation of Mary Sutton who died in 1935. She was able to track down "her" previous children, some of whom are still alive and in their sixties and seventies. Jenny lives in Towcester, in England, and remembers her life—and death—

near Dublin. She was able to identify the town of Mallahide from her memories and when visiting it recognised her former home. From there she tracked down her former children. One of them, Sonny, apparently produced nine pages of memories that matched her own exactly. How her own researches will continue only time will tell.

"Linda" told us of her own memories of a past life, which included details less commonly reported:

> After a death as a fighter pilot [a former existence] I spent a period of about three years between that lifetime and this one. I was with a friend, neither of us having a body, but we were actually looking for a body each. There was a frantic feeling of being desperate to find one because there were then so many "people" looking for bodies to be born into. I picked the body that I've got now and there was another one that was due to be born about the same time in the same house. We decided we wanted to be together so these were the ones we'd go for. I remember fighting for mine. And when the person, who is now my cousin, was born about five weeks later my auntie brought the baby in to me where I was in my cot. And I remember being absolutely horrified that this was not my friend. Obviously he had lost the fight to get that particular body. My friend and I have never been able to reunite since. The feeling of loss was tremendous—I remember it now. This cousin and I were brought up closely together for many years but I never did forgive him. I didn't know this person who had become my cousin—I was really quite put out having him there.

The implication of this is to suggest that people who are "close"—whether friends or relatives—may have selected their relationship prior to birth. An interesting twist to the saying that "you pick your friends but not your relatives"!

There is a case from Hexham in the north of England that also suggests choice. A Mr. and Mrs. Pollock had two daughters, Joanna and Jacqueline, who were killed in a car accident, on 5

May 1957, at the ages of eleven and six. Mrs. Pollock had been told by her doctor that she could not have any other children. However, her husband dreamt that they would have twins and that these twins would be the reincarnations of their lost daughters.

Twins were indeed born, named Jennifer and Gillian. Jennifer had two birthmarks that matched marks Jacqueline had had. She had a white line across her forehead that matched the shape of a scar Jacqueline had received in an accident, and she had a birthmark on her hip similar to a birthmark Jacqueline had had in the same place.

When the twins were around three years old the family visited Hexham—from which the family had moved just after their births. The girls knew shops in the town and described a white-haired lady in the park who was known to the parents from their former time there. They also knew of the park's existence before they saw it and said it had swings, which it did. The twins were able to describe their old home, and they showed fear at the spot where the former daughters had been killed. Indeed, the parents heard the twins talking about their former deaths, describing blood oozing from the body and commenting "that's where the car hit you." They could also recognise toys from their "former" lives. For example, they were given two dolls that had been packed in the loft, and immediately one of the twins, Jennifer, identified them as "Mary" and "Suzanne"—the names the dolls had previously been given.

If these two people together chose their new bodies to be born into, did the husband's dreams also amount to their giving an "advance notice" of their impending rebirth?

It must be said that the husband had strong beliefs about reincarnation but like his wife he was a Catholic; he thought that the earlier girls' deaths were a punishment on him for holding these unorthodox beliefs. How strong a belief system this may have set up is uncertain, but it must be considered.

When the twins were about five years old they began to lose memories of their former lives.

Nor is this an isolated case. In 1910, Alexandrina Samoa of Palermo, Sicily, died at the age of five. One month later her mother, Adela, had a dream in which she saw Alexandrina holding a baby and saying that she was "coming back." Adela had previously accepted that she was unlikely to have any other children, but after the dream she knew intuitively that she was pregnant. And so she was; in fact she gave birth to twins. The elder twin had identical birthmarks to Alexandrina, and indeed her mother named her after her deceased elder sister. As she developed it became apparent that she was left-handed, as her elder sister had been, and she seemd to have similar likes and dislikes and enjoyed the same games as the deceased girl.

When the twins reached the age of ten, Adela told them they would be visiting Monreale. They had never visited that town before. But immediately Alexandrina told her mother that she had been there before, and described the town accurately. She told her mother that in Monreale they would find the "red priests." Her mother asked her how she knew these things; Alexandrina told her mother that she had taken her there when Alexandrina was young, and they had been accompanied by a woman described as "the neighbour with scars on her forehead." In fact the only time Adela had ever visited Monreale was with the original Alexandrina; and at the time they had gone with a neighbour who had been suffering quite bad cysts on her forehead. Adela then remembered that there was one thing in which her original daughter had been interested when they had visited the town: Greek priests wearing unusual red clothes rarely seen in Italy.

These cases seem to present very strong evidence in favour of reincarnation, and if so, there is a valuable question here—one of choice. It seems that once a person goes "into death" they have a wide variety of choices at their disposal: to stay there or move forwards, or to be reborn, and according to these cases into the bodies and the families of their choice.

But there is of course a strong argument against reincarnation as an explanation in these cases when one considers the very strong emotions that might follow the death of a child. The grief must be intense, and the desire to seek the rebirth of the original child or children would be normal. Perhaps for some parents it becomes so strong that they imagine every nuance of the new child's actions against their memories of the former child. Perhaps they even steer the new child into certain games or preferences, or lead the child in fantasy to seemingly recall events that belonged to the former child.

But there are cases that match the Pollock and Samoa case with one vital difference. The identification of the "former" child was not by the grieving parents but by a new family taken wholly unaware by the recollections. We mentioned earlier the case of Gopal Gupta, for example. The following case of Jasbir Lal Jat is similar. In India in 1954, Jasbir Lal Jat, then three years old, apparently died of smallpox. The following day his body seemed to come to life. But the child, revived, spoke with a quite different accent and used different language styles. He claimed he was in fact Sobha Tyagi, the child of a nearby family. Indeed he called out to one of Sobha's relatives, calling her his aunt. Over time the child proved that he knew all of Sobha's relatives even though Jasbir had never met them. Investigation showed that Sobha had died from a head wound at exactly the same time as Jasbir has died.

A similar case arose with a girl named Sumitra and her rebirth as Shiva. But in this case we shall see an overlap between reincarnation and possession, which leads us to speculate that perhaps these claims might relate to powers of the mind rather than a "natural" inevitable process. This case relates to the "rebirth" of a twenty-two-year-old into the body of a deceased seventeen-year-old. It cannot be a clear-cut case of reincarnation because there was a long period when the two girls were both alive at the same time.

Sumitra, an illiterate seventeen-year-old, apparently died on 19 July 1985. While arrangements for her funeral were being made she re-awoke, but demanded to be called Shiva. Shiva had been a twenty-two-year-old woman who had died two months earlier, on 17 May. When Sumitra—now Shiva—met with Shiva's father she recognised him immediately; she identified Shiva's mother despite a "control" attempt to trick her. She also recognised many relatives and neighbours. She was able to identify clothes and belongings of Shiva, wrote letters in the manner of Shiva and convinced the family that she was, in fact, Shiva. "We never had any doubts that our Shiva had come back to us," her father said.

She was also quite clear about the manner of her former death. Shiva had been found dead on railway lines with severe head injuries. There had been suspicions about the manner of her death; her in-laws claimed she had committed suicide but her own family pressed for an enquiry. Her body was cremated before it could be examined. Sumitra—now Shiva—insisted that she had been murdered, hit across the head with a brick during a family quarrel. The next thing she remembered was waking up in the body of Sumitra.

The evidence for the case is seemingly strong: Sumitra—as Shiva—recognised over twenty people Shiva had known; she was no longer illiterate as Sumitra had been; she knew of details that had not been published in the press reports of Shiva's death.

But what of Sumitra? If her body was capable of sustaining a spirit, why did she leave it and allow Shiva to take it over? How, in fact, do we define death in this instance?

And perhaps more importantly, will Sumitra return one day? Did she make a pact in the world of spirits with Shiva to allow her to use her body for a time, complete a mission such as telling of her murder? Is it the intention of Sumitra and Shiva that Sumitra might one day return to her former body? If that sounds far-fetched then the Lurancy Vennum case amounted to exactly that.

The case arose in the USA in 1878. It is highly complex and seems to include an extraordinary "relationship" between the subject—Lurancy Vennum—and one particular spirit—Mary Roff.

In 1878, in Watseka, Lurancy Vennum, who had had several months of fits and trances, claimed, while in a trance, to have made contact with the spirit of a dead child, Mary Roff, who had died in 1865. Mary Roff's father was in the room at the time, apparently invited to be there simply because he was a respected member of the community. What his being there on that occasion might indicate about "manipulation" from the world of spirits is interesting given what was to follow.

During the session Lurancy became possessed by several spirits and eventually Lurancy became host to Mary Roff's spirit. The morning following this event Lurancy's father, Asa, told Mary's father that Lurancy was still claiming to be Mary Roff, and that "Mary" was asking to go home—to the Roff home. As in the case of Sumitra/Shiva, Lurancy—now Mary—recognised her former home, family and friends. She was able to tell Mary's family about many incidents in their lives, in some cases in incredible detail; for example, she was able to tell Frank, Mary's younger brother, about an accident where a stove had burnt his arm; she was even able to point out the exact spot on Frank's arm that had been injured. Interestingly, "Mary" was not eating and told the cook that she didn't need to as her health would be taken care of "on the other side." A doctor indicated that Lurancy's body seemed to be well taken care of by Mary and presumed that, if nourishment was needed, Mary would take it for the body's sake.

Sometime earlier Mary Roff's parents had visited a medium to contact the spirit of their dead child. They were successful and "Mary" gave them some information through the medium. When Lurancy Vennum was claiming to be Mary, she was able to recall and recount the details of that seance.

"Mary" announced that she would be able to stay just twenty-one days; when the time came to leave she went around saying goodbye to her friends and family. She started walking to Lurancy's home, and by the time she got there she was Lurancy again. Mary Roff had left her body.

In recent times there has been a trend towards the search for past lives, as a form of new-age therapy.

We know of a case where a man felt dislike for his brother but could never logically reason out why. He sought therapy and was recommended to past-life regression. In a past life it was "discovered" that the brothers had been antagonists, and the elder brother had been openly hostile. This "explained" the problem to the patient's satisfaction, who passed this information on to his brother who agreed with it. They were able to "understand" their difficulty in this life and indeed resolve a conflict of personality. But does this represent proof of a past life? This past-life situation might happen to be true, but this account is not sufficient as evidence. Clearly there is a possibility that the "story" could have been a convenient device for the two to "agree" on a way forward, which perhaps both wanted. This would make acceptance easy and would prove very little.

There are similar cases of a more physical nature, such as curing muscle pains by treating the "previous" personality under hypnosis and curing the "previous" ailment by allowing the cure to "come through" to the present life. Again, the reservations must be similar; people are quite able to react to what they believe rather than what is.

Sometimes medical work itself triggers a past-life memory. Take for example the following case that was related to us: "I injured my back and went to a chiropractor. She put a heat-lamp on the spot on my back and went out of the room and left me. The pain became even more intense, and I felt fear. I turned round and there was a Norman knight behind me, holding a big broadsword, about to plunge it into my back. I think that was a memory of a former death, particularly given the size of the sword and the area he was going to plunge it into!" Did the attention to the back trigger a genuine memory or did it begin the construction of a fantasy? There is research to be done in this area but at the present time there is no objective evidence. These accounts indicate that reincarnation is perhaps more complex than first thought; in Sumitra's case there seems to be a permanent take-over of a dead body by a spirit searching for a way back, perhaps needing a mature form in order to complete a mission. In the Vennum/Roff case a deal seems to have been struck to "lend" a body for a time. There seems to be a link, therefore, between reincarnation and possession.

There may be other "overlaps" to consider. Plato suggests in his writings that the body is the prison of the soul and that death is the release of that imprisoned soul. He recounts a legend, in the *Republic*, which shows a similar link between the near-death experience and reincarnation. It is the story of Er, a soldier. He was a Greek soldier who, believed dead, was placed on a funeral pyre. He awoke before being cremated—back in his own body— and told of a time spent in the after-life. He had been with other spirits; they had gone on to their future lives but he had been sent back to tell people about the world after death. While on the other side Er found people who were waiting to choose their own new bodies and found that the wisdom of their decision depended on the wisdom they had accumulated in their lives.

Before rebirth the souls drank from the river of forgetfulness, the River Lethe, to erase their former memories. We might consider the logic of such an action; psychologists make the point that suppressed memory can be a form of protection. As with most aspects of the paranormal, the best evidence is the knowledge acquired by a person who could not have obtained that information by "normal" means. In reincarnation cases this is extremely difficult to verify; the information is often available in books or histories if the subject wants to seek it out; indeed, the fact that it is available is how the researchers verify the statements in the first place. The cases discussed above are thought-provoking, but while they might constitute evidence for "something paranormal" they do not offer proof of reincarnation.

Rarely is a person or family given information of a highly personal nature from the supposedly reincarnated person that satisfies the recipient, such as the case of Shiva. These rare cases are nonetheless very important.

Less valid, we think, are cases where people—usually parents—are impressed that a person is the reincarnation of their dead child. These may well be true, but must be considered in the light of wishful thinking and the desire not to lose their dead child.

In the West, since the work of Morey Bernstein on "Bridey Murphy," there has been an increasing use of regression hypnosis. This is a flawed technique of research as we have already discussed (see pages 57–59). Where past-life research is concerned, information obtained through regression is no more reliable than that obtained through dream-memory, visualisations, and so on. It is the quality of the recall that may have significance, i.e. is the revealed information something that would not otherwise be known to the subject?

We end this section by considering possibilities other than simple re-birth to explain the reincarnation phenomenon. If we assume for the sake of argument that reincarnation is not a reality, then we must ask: how does a person acquire such indepth knowledge about a former life, to the extent of being able to "fool" previous friends and relatives? The alternative explanations listed below all relate to the mysterious powers of the mind and cannot be ignored in seeking to understand reincarnation:

· ESP by the family looking for that loved one. Perhaps those who have lost loved ones are psychically calling out so strongly that a recipient of the message, telepathically received, thinks the images and impressions he or she receives are pre-natal memory.
· Trace memories. If apparitions are, as some people speculate, the visual "recording" of a person who once stood where a ghost is now perceived and if sounds can be similarly "recorded"—hence the term "recordings ghosts"—can memories, emotions and impressions also be similarly recorded?

The feelings and even memories that used to belong to the dead person might "linger" and be picked up by others. This is what happens in psychometry, and it is possible that people who believe they are the reincarnation of another are, without realising it or being familiar with the paranormal process they are experiencing, actually just receiving the lingering impressions of the former person.

· The Akashic records. Do aspects of a person's personality at death get transferred to some sort of collective data bank (known as, for example, the Akashic records or perhaps it is Jung's collective unconscious) that can be accessed by individuals?

· Possession. Mediums are sometimes taken over, temporarily and by invitation, by spirits. Could reincarnation be the possession of a living person by the spirit of a deceased one? The person would then experience and relate the spirit's memories as if they were his or her own. The subject might not even be able to tell if they were genuine pre-natal memories or the memories of an "intruding" spirit. The phenomenon of possession is discussed in further detail in the next section of this chapter.

One way to test reincarnation would be to set up a very long-term study. Perhaps we have to give special information to a subject in a "double-blind" way and then wait for them to die, track down their next incarnation, and then hope they have remembered it!

This may sound bizarre; however, one religion has made just this the cornerstone of its leadership. In Tibetan Buddhism it is accepted that the two most prominent Lamas—the Dalai Lama and the Panchen Lama—must be located in their new incarnations whenever one of them dies. A search is immediately undertaken to find the successor. The "new" Lama identifies himself in a number of ways but one area of proof is the new child's acceptance of the "old" Lama's belongings.

Possession

Possession is a word that conjures up images of demons and people under the control of evil. It is not a state that is generally regarded as desirable. However, some types of possession are regarded by their proponents as welcome because they form part of their religion. Voodoo worshippers invite gods into their bodies in order to perform their rituals; mediums invite spirits to speak through, and even temporarily take control of, their bodies as a form of communication; shamans invite spirits as a way of gaining knowledge. There is also the class of possession, as we have suggested calling it, which involves the specific "invasion" of a living person by a recognised individual now deceased, as in the cases of Sumitra/Shiva and Lurancy Vennum/Mary Roff discussed in the previous section on reincarnation.

We shall first examine the classic images of possession.

Early literature deals with many accounts of possession, often the possession of a human by a demon or god. In the *Bacchae* by the ancient Greek dramatist Euripides, the god Dionysos possesses the bodies of his female devotees—the bacchantes—and his detractors who resist the cult building up around him. His devotees sing and dance in an ecstatic religious experience; those who still resist are deemed "mad" and sent raving to the mountains. Plato attributed this type of madness or frenzy to poets inspired or possessed by the Muses, and to the priestess possessed by Apollo when she prophesied in trance.

In the Bible demonic possession and exorcism by Jesus—followed by a rather bad decision on the part of the demon!—is recalled by the apostles. Here is a passage from Luke 8:26:

> Then they arrived at the country of the Gerasenes, which is opposite Galilee. And as he stepped out on land, there met him a man from the city who had demons; for a long time he had worn no clothes, and he lived not in a house but among the tombs. When he saw Jesus, he cried out and fell down before him, and

said with a loud voice, "What have you to do with me, Jesus, Son of the Most High God? I beseech you, do not torment me." For he had commanded the unclean spirit to come out of the man. (For many a time it had seized him; he was kept under guard, and bound with chains and fetters, but he broke the bonds and was driven by the demon into the desert.) Jesus then asked him, "What is your name?" And he said, "Legion" for many demons had entered him. And they begged him not to command them to depart into the abyss. Now a large herd of swine was feeding there on the hillside; and they begged him to let them enter these. So he gave them leave. Then the demons came out of the man and entered the swine, and the herd rushed down the steep bank into the lake and were drowned.

The Catholic Church identified the states of possession as follows:

- infestation: demonstrated by the poltergeist-like scratching and rapping noises, followed by
- obsession: tormenting the subject, and finally,
- possession: the demon using the body for himself. (The demon sees through the subject's eyes and speaks using the subject's vocal chords, and so on.)

The Catholic Church considers certain signs to be proof of demonic possession. These include the following:

- speaking in tongues
- some comprehension of a foreign language (particularly Latin) unknown to the subject
- clairvoyance, the knowing of secret matters
- excessive physical strength
- blasphemy
- aversion to holy objects
- levitations

Perhaps the most famous relatively contemporary case is that of Robert Mannheim, which occurred in 1949 in the USA. The story provided the basis of one of the most graphic, and exaggerated, fictional images of possession: in 1971 the story was fictionalised by William Peter Blatty and made into the film *The Exorcist*.

At the age of thirteen Mannheim was encouraged to use a Ouija board by his Aunt Harriet, who was a member of the Spiritualist movement, which was then enjoying its centenary. Shortly afterwards poltergeist-like rapping noises were heard around the house, precisely the same phenomenon as the sounds that had started the Spiritualist movement in the homes of the Fox sisters 100 years earlier (see page 146). There were other sounds like dripping water, for instance. One night Robert and his grandmother, who lived in the house, watched a painting of Christ being "bumped" as if from behind. Robert's parents had been out that evening and on returning they could hear sounds like scratching and clawing. This continued for several nights.

When Mannheim's aunt died eleven days later the rapping seemed to develop into a communication with her. Further classic poltergeist activity then started: spontaneous movement of items in particular. The movements were not just limited to Mannheim's house; even his school desk would spontaneously move.

A Lutheran minister, The Reverend Luther Miles Schulze, was called in to help and took Mannheim to his home where he could study the phenomenon at close range; he watched the boy's bed and other furniture spontaneously moving. The minister returned Mannheim to his home because the force seemed too powerful to handle.

The activity moved on to the spontaneous appearance of scratches on his skin, which looked as if they had been scratched from the inside. Eventually the scratches formed words as if from under the skin. A Catholic priest was called in to help.

As the possession evolved, many classic signs manifested: Mannheim spoke in Latin to a degree far more complex than he should have been exposed to up to that time. He spoke in "a deep gravelly voice" that claimed to be the devil. When an attempt was made to sprinkle holy water around Robert's bedroom, the bottle was somehow flung and smashed, a common response in these cases.

The Catholic Church identified the case as one of demonic possession and the rite of exorcism was eventually approved. It was conducted by Father E. Albert Hughes. During the exorcism Mannheim severely slashed Hughes' arm. The exorcism was not successful.

The activity stopped when the family moved home, and when it re-started they decided to try a different tack, calling in a Jesuit minister. Eventually Father William Bowdern was appointed as the exorcist to rid Robert of his demons, which he did.

So what started with poltergeist activity eventually became possession. We must consider why this should be. Presumably there was a link between the two phenomena—for Mannheim to have been the victim of two types of unrelated but similar manifestations seems improbable. The Church believes that possession develops over time, and it seems clear that poltergeistery could fulfil their definitions of the earlier stages of infestation and obsessions. But not all cases of poltergeists end in possession, so what made this one do so? It could well be the intervention of the Church itself. If possession is not the action of demons or the devil, it seems likely it is unconsciously generated from within. The attentions of the Church might, if they were not handled delicately, have encouraged Mannheim to promote his manifestations.

The book *Deliverance*, edited by Michael Perry, presents the Church of England's experience with these phenomena. It has this to say: "Possession...cannot just 'happen' unwittingly. Man cannot catch demons as he catches the common cold. He has to put himself at risk and in a vulnerable position. The greatest risk is that of straightforward invitation." Mannheim was already well on that road by using the Ouija board.

We believe that both poltergeists and possession are manifested from within. But what will manifest will depend on belief systems. Mannheim's Aunt Harriet may well have encouraged the boy towards Spiritualism and the possibility of communicating with the dead, hence the use of the Ouija board. When the Catholic Church entered the scene they brought their teachings to Mannheim. By instructing him in the Catholic faith, they of course trained him to believe in the power of evil and the existence of demons. This encouraged him also to believe in the power of exorcism. Mannheim eventually became a devout Catholic.

Such demonic possession is not always restricted to individuals. There have been several instances of multiple possessions, most of them involving nuns. In 1554, nuns of the Nazareth convent near Cologne, France, were afflicted with convulsions. They saw apparitions and were believed to be possessed by devils. Four years earlier in a monastery at Uvertet, Belgium, nuns had been allegedly possessed by devils. Their condition was attributed to food deprivation which caused hallucinations. But an alternative explanation, for those who took this as a case of possession, was that the lack of food may have created an altered state that allowed contact with demons.

Probably the best-known case took place in the seventeenth century at Loudun in France. Seventeen nuns, including the prioress Sister Jeanne des Anges, together with their students, were allegedly possessed by demons. They exhibited many symptoms of possession: their bodies writhing out of control, they blasphemed, and so on. However priests who examined the convent were unsure if possession was the answer because "classic" symptoms they expected were not apparent: extraordinary strength, levitation and speaking in tongues.

But one Jesuit priest, Father Jean-Joseph Surin, believed the women were possessed and exorcised the demons by inviting them into his own body. As a result, Surin found himself possessed and was driven almost out of his mind for the next twenty-five years. There were times when he would be attacked by his own body; he would find himself biting his own hand, apparently unable to stop. Many thought he had been driven mad; and he attempted to take his own life at least once. The manner of the attempted suicide was of interest; he seems to have tried to throw himself out of a window while under the control of "something else."

But Surin was in control enough to record his emotions and describe his possession. "I find it almost impossible to explain what happens to me during this time, how this alien spirit is united to mine, without depriving me of consciousness or of inner freedom, and yet constituting a second 'me' as though I had two souls. . . . I feel as if I had been pierced by the pricks of despair in that alien soul which seems to be mine. . . . I even feel that the cries uttered by my mouth come from both souls at once; and I found it hard to determine whether they are the product of joy or frenzy."

If possession reflects a form of Multiple Personality Syndrome—different aspects of one's own mind not "in touch" with each other—then Surin might well have suffered from this. Whether these sub-personalities developed as a result of his experiences at Loudun or whether it was his personality disorders that gave him the desire to be the exorcist is unclear.

The cases discussed so far have depicted "classical" possession—unwanted invasion. However, cases of invited possession are more common. The first of these relates to religious rituals.

Voodoo is the religion of the vast majority of people of the island of Haiti. It is a hybrid of African and Christian religious influences. The main characteristic of Voodoo worship is the possession of worshippers by their gods during ceremony. At the climax of the ceremonies one or sometimes several worshippers attain an altered state of consciousness engineered by rhythmic drumming and frenzied dance. They then enter a trance-like state and are possessed by a god. The Voodoo gods include the Guede—the gods of death, such as Nibo, Baron

Samedi, Baron Cemetery, Baron Cross and others. They are also the gods of obscenity and licentiousness. Those possessed by them dress as corpses for the ritual dances, strap imitation penises to their loins, tell bawdy stories, sing bawdy songs and enact rape scenes with female worshippers, or dance the banda—the most sexually explicit of ritual dances. Other Voodoo gods include an Earth-force depicted as a snake-god, Damballah. Worshippers possessed by Damballah never speak but only hiss, and they wriggle along the ground or climb trees.

But not all possession is religious. There is an interesting case of a specific deceased spirit apparently possessing a living person for a time.

In 1905 Frederic Thompson suffered what he first believed were hallucinations. He felt compelled to sketch and paint, though he had never previously been interested in art. It was his own view that this activity, including his choice of subjects, was being forced on him from outside. For eighteen months this continued, and Thompson came to believe he was under the influence of the deceased artist Robert Swain Gifford, who had died at more or less the same time Thompson started having the compulsions. It was while looking at paintings of Gifford's in a gallery that Thompson heard a disembodied voice say, "You see what I have done. Can you not take up and finish my work?" Gifford and Thompson had in fact previously met, but Thompson knew very little of the artist's work.

Thompson confessed that during this period of compulsion he was beginning to lose touch with reality. He sketched and painted, his skills ever increasing. He sold several of his works, and many people commented on the similarity between his work and that of Gifford. A medium that Thompson visited claimed he could see a figure—a man who loved painting—standing behind him. And through a trance medium it appears that Gifford told Thompson: "I will help you, because I want someone who can catch the inspiration of these things as I did, to carry on my work." He began to follow in the artist's footsteps. On one occasion while in a park he felt drawn to a tree and discovered that it had Gifford's initials carved into it. Gifford's influence eventually faded but the artistic talent that it had "created" in Thompson stayed. Thompson remained an accomplished artist thereafter.

One curious case is not possession in the "Catholic" sense but nevertheless has elements that make it worthy of inclusion here. A woman called Claire Sylvia had a combined heart and lungs transplant. Over a short period after the operation she developed a craving for cold beer and fried chicken. She found that her favourite colour was now green. And she dreamt of a man with the initials TL who "visited" her in a dream and kissed her. "As our lips met, I sucked his entire body, Ghost-like, into my own."

The changes in her diet and other habits made Claire want to know who the donor was. She started her quest after recovering from the operation. Although the hospital refused to tell her, she found the answer and the hospital confirmed she was right. She then discovered that the donor's favourite meal had been cold beer and fried chicken, and that his favourite colour was green.

The donor whose organs she received was Tim Lamirande who had died in a road accident. Claire impressed his family with what she knew about him. Tim's sister said: "Claire never met Timmy. She didn't even know our family, so how could she know all these things?"

Claire's association with Tim strengthened. She yearned to visit France, which she had not previously considered, and then found out that Tim was born in France. She became interested in Russia, where, it turns out, Tim's grandparents were from.

Claire became so moved by her experiences that she decided to set up a programme to bring together people who have been similarly influenced. Dr. Robert Bosnack of the Carl Jung Institute in Boston is assisting her. He commented: "Tissue carries a certain kind of memory. Hearts and lungs in particular have strong psychological imprints." There was more scepticism at

Britain's primary transplant facility: Harefield Hospital. They point out that people often ask if they will take on the characteristics of the donor, so it is clearly on the minds of patients for whom the operation is a huge emotional undertaking as well as a physical one. They had not received any reports of this type of "possession" or "memory imprinting."

No commentary on possession can fail to consider alternative explanations. Earlier in the book we described the complexity of Multiple Personality Syndrome (see pages 35–37). It is possible that such a condition could explain the apparent possession of an individual by another entity. However, psychotherapist and author Adam Crabtree, who encountered "possession type" cases in his practice, decided that if the patients thought they were possessed then treating them as such was, whatever the underlying mechanism, the simplest and quickest way to effect a cure.

Dominic Walker, the Anglican Church's leading Deliverance Minister—they do not use the term exorcists—believes that possession cases need pastoral care that treats the whole family. He takes the view that exorcism is not driving out entities but rather it is exorcising "unhealed parts of the unconscious which manifest in unusual ways." He uses counselling techniques rather than religious symbols such as holy water. "An exorcism is not a form of Christian magic," he told us.

This second section of the book has looked at the mind as a super-receiver, picking up information from the world—and perhaps the world beyond—so that the mind's "owner" has the best possible data bank of information from which to make decisions. We have examined the information, the methods of reception, and the interpretations of where that information came from. While the quality of the received information is impressive, the latter two points—how it is received and where it comes from—are still the subject of study. We know what the mind can do, but we are not quite sure how it does it.

The next section has similar unresolved considerations. We shall see what the mind can do, but we shall not always be sure how it does it. But this time we look at the mind not as receiver, but as transmitter, to see what the human mind can do when it seeks to influence the world.

III
Mind as Transmitter

7

Transmitter of Energy for Change

If the mind is a transmitter of its energy, then it is logical that its first "reach" is to the human body that houses it. In this chapter we examine how the mind seems to have developed astonishing abilities to mould and manipulate the body it is "married to," for better and for worse.

Holistic Healing

One of the main criticisms of science and medicine in the modern day is that it has become mechanistic, that doctors deal with the body as a physical object more akin to, say, an automobile than a living organism. Medicine and treatment amount to service and repair rather than care.

But some doctors are more open to alternative ideas than others. One medical doctor, Kit Pedler, commented: "I am bound to confess here that of all the aspects of the paranormal I have written about, healing is the one I had most personal trouble with. This is entirely due to the irrational prejudices and biases implanted in my mind during my training as a doctor. There is still a part of my head that is trying to dismiss the whole thing as a human indulgence. Another part of my head is convinced by a considerable volume of well designed and conducted experimentation."

Later we shall discuss the claims of psychic and spiritual healing, but in this section we shall look at evidence: the mind's ability to heal the body.

The person is not a mechanism, like a motor car, but rather is a complex combination of mind, body and spirit. There seems to be little doubt that positive and negative influences emanating from any of these three components affect the well-being of the whole. In the West we have adopted the name "holistic" healing to reflect this, holistic simply referring to "the whole." In the ancient language of Sanskrit, this concept is known as "ayurveda" which refers to the "science of life." The name, and the concept, originated over 4,000 years ago. Embracing ayurveda in the West has created both alternative and complementary approaches to healing. Alternative healing includes, for examples, homeopathic medicines as opposed to "conventional" drugs. Complementary healing might include, say, reflexology, acupuncture and psychic healing, all of which can be undertaken while still following a course of "conventional" treatments. Some of these practices have been accepted by some "conventional" doctors in the West.

The principal objection to the claim that the mind can heal the body is that it seems to work for only a small section of the community. So-called spontaneous remissions arise in a tiny fraction of cases; most cases are cured not by inner feeling but by drugs and surgery. These statistics cannot be disputed; therefore, the claims of most doctors that they must administer conventional treatments must be accepted. Perhaps their rejection of alternative healings is valid because they cannot maintain a system of medicine that does not work for the vast majority of their patients. But homeopathic practitioners, for example, would also argue that their methods work for everyone.

This debate is taking place against the background of 150 years of mechanistic thinking. The problem for modern, Western people is that they have come to believe in the mechanistic approach, that drugs and intrusive operations are the best cure. Psychic healing, for example, is regarded by the main-stream as music-hall entertainment, alongside mind-reading acts and stage hypnotism. It is true that of all "paranormal" subjects psychic healing is gaining increasing acceptance, and so it should, but it seems that the main reason that it still only works for a small number of people is because most people do not expect it to work and therefore do not try it, or go into it half-heartedly. To say that holistic healing depends on belief is putting it too blandly, but it is also a truth that belief is the start-ing point for the inner strength that the mind/body/spirit com-bination needs for self-healing.

Doctors are right to warn people that faith will not cure them because those same doctors and their predecessors have spent too long deconstructing faith and replacing it with science. But should we be blaming the doctors? Probably not. Western soci-ety is also a "sound bite" society and the world of the "quick fix." People demand drugs and immediate solutions rather than spend time healing themselves.

One study showed that psychiatric patients improved in their condition more when on a waiting list to see a psychiatrist than when they actually underwent treatment. The implication is that it is the patient that does the healing, not the doctor. Studies un-dertaken at the end of the Second World War showed that many patients left Yale Medical School hospital more ill than when they were admitted; something in the mechanistic hospital process had not worked for those patients.

It would seem that the belief system of the patient is a factor in true, inner healing. Religion itself seems to play a part, but not always with the result that might be expected. Studies on people who were seriously ill, taking into account the strength of their religious beliefs, showed that those with strong religious beliefs did less well in recovery than those without such beliefs. The im-plication might be that those who have a firm belief in survival of spirit are more "content" to die than those for whom death is a final end. An alternative might be that those with strong religious faith might leave their cures in God's hands, whereas those with no one else to turn to fight hardest for themselves. We cannot be sure of the cause and effect here, but the fact that non-medical criteria can affect the statistics suggests that something other than hospitalisation and drugs is playing its part in the healing process; and that something is an attitude of mind. But at the individual level there are also spontaneous remissions that may be linked with religious belief, at least in the minds of the patients. Take the following case, for example.

After a routine breast screening in January 1997, Pat English was told that she had a malignant tumour; the following month it was removed. That could have been the end of her story, but in April she received the awful news that cancer had spread into the lymph nodes in her arm. The lymphatic system can carry cancers around the body and such cancers are hard to target and eradicate. She was given chemotherapy treatment but by June the cancer was attacking her liver. The doctors broke the news to her that it was inoperable and that she had only months to live. Most people receiving that news would be hard pressed to think of anything worse to worry about, but Pat did. Only days earlier she had been overjoyed to learn that her own daughter was expecting a child; she now feared she would never see the grandchild but prayed that she would. Pat was a devout Roman Catholic. Her friends at work collected £1,000 to send Pat to Lourdes, where she bathed in the holy water at the world-famous shrine. When she returned she began making her own funeral arrangements. She also re-visited Lourdes in the September. A month later she had a scan to check on the progress of the cancer; the doctors could find no sign of it. Indeed, they checked their equipment to ensure that it was not faulty. The absence of the cancer was shortly afterwards confirmed. Pat commented: "If I was to die next year, at least I have had the joy of holding Rebecca [her granddaughter], which is what I prayed for." She also made this observation: "I have no doubt that faith has played an enormous part in what has happened to me."

Perhaps it did, and perhaps it did not. There are cases of spontaneous remission without religious overtones, so perhaps religious people who "happen" to have lucky remission attribute it to God. But perhaps every remission reflects an attitude of mind and religion is just an easy one to label.

Let us step away from belief for a moment and consider technique. Can thoughts alone cure physical illness; that, after all, is at the heart of the debate. And the answer would seem to be yes.

In 1971, a radiologist at the University of Texas, Dr. O. Carl Simonton, encountered an elderly man with seriously advanced throat cancer. The man could hardly swallow. He was given only a slight chance of surviving for more than five years. He was already so weakened by his condition and presumably lack of nourishment that the doctor thought radiation treatment, which is usually recommended for such cancers, to be dangerous. Anything that could cut down on the dependency on radiation over the long term would be beneficial. Somewhat backed against the wall and interested to see what alternatives there were, Simonton suggested visualisation therapy—attacking the cancer by imagination. This would operate alongside the radiation treatment. The man was taught to visualise his cancer; he chose to imagine it as a large black rock. He was taught to imagine his immune system as a blizzard of snow that could cover the rock, gradually diminishing it. Sure enough, over a period the tumour began to diminish in size. Also, he suffered fewer side-effects from the radiation treatment than the doctor expected. Within two months the tumour was gone. Impressed with visualisation, the patient took Simonton's advice to try it against his arthritis; the condition was relieved within weeks. For six years after that date there was no return of either condition.

In another, unrelated case a patient with blocked arteries was taught to imagine himself in a canoe "white-water riding" through his own arteries and using the oars to knock the deposits from the arterial walls. In a short period there was a measurable improvement in his blood flow; the arteries were clearing

without the need for intrusive operations. In recent years, visualisation techniques have become more commonly recommended by conventional medical practitioners.

There is of course the well-known "placebo effect" that might
be relevant here. In experiments, groups of people suffering
identical illnesses were given the standard prescribed medical
drugs or a placebo of bicarbonate of soda or sugar pills. In the
tests neither the doctor nor the patient knew who was getting
which treatment until the experiment concluded. The groups
were found to respond equally well to treatment whichever they
received. This suggests that the drug is not necessarily doing the
job; rather, the mind is using the drug as a prop with which to
heal itself. Nor is such experimentation confined to drugs alone.
Placebo surgery has produced interesting results. Angina patients have been taken into the operating theatre, opened up and
then stitched closed again, no actual surgery on the angina having been performed. A good percentage of such patients reported relief from their condition. There is also the concept of
the "nocebo," a negative placebo. In this situation valid and appropriate drugs are administered to a patient but he or she does
not improve because either the patient has no trust in the doctor
or the doctor has transmitted a negative message that is in effect
saying "this treatment will fail to cure you." Even if doctors
choose to lie positively to their patients about their "chances" it
is likely that the patient will pick up the true message; eighty per
cent of communication is in the eye contact and body language.
The message of both the placebo and the nocebo is clear: belief
and attitude are playing some part.

Deepak Chopra, a pioneering and open-minded doctor, admitted to a situation that suggested attitude of mind was important.
In his book *Quantum Healing* he tells the story of a man in his sixties who had had a small lesion on his lung for five years. He was
unaware of the cancer, and it was growing quite slowly. Dr.
Chopra told him of the cancer, and he "became agitated." Just a
month later he was coughing up blood, and within three months

he was dead. Dr. Chopra commented: "This patient could live with his tumour, but he couldn't live with the diagnosis." A totally negative attitude seems to have accelerated the damage.

Our earlier comment that statistically conventional medicine is the safer bet for a cure is also borne out. One statistic indicates a ninety per cent cure rate for breast cancer detected while still in the early stages using conventional treatment. Spontaneous remission arises in probably 0.1 per cent of cases. But we contend that these statistics reflect our mechanistic thinking rather than anything inherent in the techniques. The doctor/patient relationship is still probably the most important single factor in recovery; those who believe their doctor can cure them and have a strong "will to live" fare better than those who distrust their doctors and have a pessimistic outlook.

Dr. Deepak Chopra tells of an almost accidentally double blind experiment conducted at Ohio University in the 1970s. Healing was not the subject of the experiment; it was merely a test to measure the effect of cholesterol on the arteries of rabbits. The results were consistent in all rabbit groups except one; in that group the rabbits had sixty per cent less arterial blocking than in the other groups. The experimenters could not find anything different about those rabbits to account for their cholesterol resistance. Then they discovered that the student that fed those rabbits liked to cuddle and stroke them for a while each day; it was the only difference they could come up with. They tested to see if this was the cause of the difference by separating two groups of rabbits and dealing "neutrally" with one group and giving the other group loving attention; the same difference was noted. It seems that something in the "gentling" procedures activated the rabbits' immune system. Either the student was transmitting something to the rabbits or, what seems more likely, the rabbits' positive emotional response to the caring treatment had triggered their own best healthcare.

Not that caring for patients is ignored by the Western health services; that is one of the roles of the nurse after all. Unfortunately, certainly in the UK, an over-stretched National Health Service has left nurses with little time and energy to exercise their "caring" role as effectively as possible. If modern hospitals cannot create an environment that is conducive to self-healing, people will need to depend more on their own immediate environment of families and friends. This could be a positive trend were it not for the prevailing mind set that at present sees the hospital as the primary place for healing.

To summarise at this point, a positive attitude to health aids recovery and the mind plays a part in healing the body. We now move on to show that the attitude and role of the healer may also be important and that perhaps something "real"—more than just an attitude of mind—is involved in certain areas: as demonstrated by experiments at McGill University in Canada, to be described later. We shall also look at an extreme situation where it seems the mind, with sufficient conviction, can physically alter the body. We will begin this exploration by looking at the field of psychic, or spiritual, healing.

Psychic and Spiritual Healing

Psychic healing is a form of alternative or complementary treatment. The process has several names—spiritual healing, psychic healing, faith healing and so on—depending on the beliefs and interpretations of the practitioners. But psychic healers are all agreed on one aspect of the process: the ability comes *through* them rather than *from* them. The source for this healing is the natural world around us, "cosmic consciousness," God, etc.

One such healer, Graham James, explained to us in interview, and while we sat in on several healing sessions with him, how he believed the process worked:

> We open a channel in order to receive power from the cosmic consciousness, and we channel energy into a patient. I teach healing and I teach my students we all have an energy force field

around us. We have to learn how to control it, how to direct it, how to channel into it. You have a patient who is hopefully receptive but it's not important that the person believes or has faith in what you are doing.

I remove my watch, my ring and jewellery, clear my mind, and work up a force field of energy between my hands for about four or five minutes. When I have done that I ask the patient to put their hand out and I hold one hand below and one hand above. Then I ask that patient: "What do you feel?" And I wait to hear three responses from that patient. The first being an electrical, tingling feeling. The second thing is weight, the feeling as if I am taking over their hand, and the third thing is heat. So we have electricity, heat and weight. Not weight in the traditional sense but weight as in energy. In other words I have a control over their hands. What I am doing is I'm working not just on the aura but, if you like, a little like psychic surgery. In other words I'm getting into the spot that's got a problem.

Graham described his healing technique as being to "open the aura." He said people are bathed or surrounded in an aura. Before beginning a treatment, he opens a flap in his aura above the crown of his head and allows the energy to come down into his body. He makes sure after each healing session to close that aura again, like hanging up a telephone and closing off the line when the conversation is finished.

I open my mind, I pull down energy from the cosmic consciousness. I don't know if I get in touch with some sort of guide or spirit, I don't honestly know. What I do know is I have this ability to open up to receive an energy, to enhance the energies in me and to project that energy into the patient. I can run my hand an inch away from the patient's body all over the body and they can tell me exactly where I am and yet there will be no physical contact at all, and they cannot see what I am doing. So they are feeling something. After identifying an area or I am told what the clinical diagnosis is—somebody has cancer of the stomach for instance—I usually place one hand physically on the body, on the stomach, and I will draw through behind and I work up a very, very heavy force field around the body. Then I put my other hand on the body and the patients feel something almost like an electric charge going from one hand to the other. They sometimes experience quite intense pain in that area.

Graham has successfully treated several cancer patients. In some instances the cancer growth has either been reduced or disappeared; of these patients, some were undergoing conventional therapy such as chemotherapy but others were not.

He spoke of a forty-seven-year-old woman, known as Jessica, who had come to him with several cancer growths. At that time, she had been told she had three months to live. Graham, as well as his group, worked with Jessica. Jessica seemed to prefer the passive energy channelled to her from the group members. She felt Graham's energy was a bit too powerful, and it left her with severe pain for days afterwards. However, in Graham's opinion, "a little zap" of energy gives the best results. The group spent an evening and the whole of the next day treating Jessica's stomach cancer. Two weeks later she was tested at the hospital and the cancer cells had disappeared. After three to six treatments, Jessica went back to hospital and was tested again; there was no evidence of the secondary cancer that had previously shown up in biopsies. Today, Jessica is alive and fit.

Graham always encourages his patients to continue their conventional treatment and to inform their doctors that they are working with a healer. Graham works with the doctors, not against them. He sees himself as the patients' back-up treatment. However, Jessica refused all conventional treatment for about three months while she was having healing sessions with Graham and his group. And it was during this period that most of her growths had disappeared. Her consultant at the hospital at first claimed the improvements were the delayed response of her conventional treatments and not the result of the healing sessions. But the consultant was intrigued to find that she continued to improve during her three-month break from hospital treatment.

Graham has also worked with muscular dystrophy patients. One of his patients was so stiff she could hardly walk. After about thirty sessions with Graham, her muscles were far more supple and she could walk almost normally.

Not everyone feels pain during a healing session with Graham, although many people do. Graham talked about one painless session with Jessica. He was working on her neck, where a growth, about the size of a conker, had appeared during the secondary stage of cancer. He put his hand and a magnetic lodestone on the left-hand side of her neck. On her right-hand side he used only his hand and channelled the energy through two of his fingers straight through to the core of the lump. He worked this way for about forty-five minutes. Jessica did not feel any pain, but the next day the growth had shrunk to the size of a pea; the following day it had disappeared, never to return.

Graham has also used a pendulum over a patient's body to pinpoint areas that cancer hospitals have missed. One woman reported Graham's diagnosis to her doctors. They dismissed the information from a spiritual healer until they investigated and found that she did indeed have a growth where Graham had indicated.

Graham does not believe that his healing is simply a matter of faith healing—of the patient's faith in the power of the healer. The basis for this assertion rests mainly on his success in curing sick animals. He cured his sister's cat of yellow jaundice. The cat was left with him for one week and he practised psychic healing on it. The jaundice completely disappeared, to the amazement of the vet. He also cured an old English sheepdog called Bumble, who was brought to Graham by a very sceptical owner. Bumble had a growth on the side of his groin about the size of a golfball. His tummy area, which is normally pink, was black. The dog had to be carried up the stairs to the healing room. After four sessions, the dog could slowly walk up the stairs. After nine sessions he could walk fairly normally, but with a limp. On the twelfth session, Graham felt a build-up of energy, and when he put his hand over the dog's growth there was a strange sensation in his hand. He said it felt as if an elastic band were being snapped into the palm of his hand. The following day, Bumble's owner phoned to say that the dog's growth had completely disappeared. When he brought Bumble back a few days later, the dog's tummy had returned to its normal colour of pink and the growth had vanished.

Graham never charges for his healing session. "It's something that's been given to me to use, not to profit from."

Perhaps the most impressive psychic healing experiments are the ones that remove the human patient from the tests altogether. Such work was undertaken with Dr. Bernard Grad of McGill University, Montreal, Canada. Mice were the subject of the first tests. Small pieces of skin were taken from forty-eight mice. The mice, having been weighed and measured, were separated into three groups. The groups stayed apart from each other in their cages. The healer, Oskar Estebany, never made physical contact with the animals throughout the experiment. The technique of psychic healing—placing the hands in close to the patient to "channel" healing energy—was to be used. Estebany would "heal" one group of mice; as a control, the second group would be treated in exactly the same way by a "non-healer"; and the third group of mice would be ignored for healing purposes. The control of a non-healer would ensure that if the healing were merely a product of care and attention or of temperature of the hands in proximity to the mice, then they should exhibit the same results as the ones Estebany healed. In all other respects the mice were identically treated. After twenty days the groups were checked and the healing of the wounds measured.

Estebany's group showed a considerable increase in tissue healing over and above the results of the other two groups, which did not vary greatly from each other. A second version of the experiment was repeated, with the control group being treated by those from the medical profession who were sceptical of Estebany's claims; this experiment produced the same results, with Estebany's group still showing increased healing.

In order to eliminate even the animal-to-animal responses, an experiment was devised using barley seeds. Estebany had even more astonishing results. Two groups of barley seeds were separated and dealt with identically. The only difference was in the water given to the two groups. One group was watered with "ordinary" water; the other with water that Estebany had "healed," i.e. had gone through a healing process with. Estebany did not do the watering, nor did he contact any of the plants. Those watered by the solution he had "handled" grew significantly faster.

As Dr. Grad indicated: "Something must have passed from [Estebany's] hand to the solution which was then delivered to the seeds. And since the treatment in most of the experiments was through the barrier of a sealed glass container, it cannot be a material substance in the sense that it is a chemical of any kind. I know of no other way to explain these experiments, and so I am inclined to feel that there was something from the hand that was being radiated and this penetrated the glass bottle and went in and altered the water. There is some evidence now that properties of water themselves are changed by this process." So regardless of whether the "something" came *from* Estebany or *through* him, there is evidence that the healing power was related in some way to the individual healer.

Sorting out the causes and effects in these situations is difficult precisely because there are so many unknown factors, but it seems clear from the evidence that state of mind can affect the body's health. It is tempting for some to stop there and adopt an almost mystical interpretation, or even an overtly religious interpretation. But that does not have to be the case. There is nothing about this theory that runs counter to our current knowledge of the human animal, and we contend that one day we will understand the exact causes and effects of this, and all other, branches of the paranormal.

Consider the disorder known as SAD—Seasonally Affective Disorder. In simple terms, a person suffering from SAD feels depressed during the winter months. When the condition was first speculated on as a recognisable disorder, there were critics who disagreed. They argued that it was easy to feel more depressed in winter than summer and left it at that. Their recommendation for a treatment would presumably have amounted to telling patients to "snap out of it!" But further analysis showed that SAD is a "real" disorder where cause and effect can be examined. The presence or absence of sunlight affects the output of the very important pineal gland, and for a small group of people the winter absence of sunlight causes the gland to give off too much melatonin, creating a state of depression. So chemicals cause changes in the body, a strikingly obvious statement of course.

It is not unreasonable, therefore, to assume that other changes in the physical body are caused by chemicals. Indeed, chemicals act as the body's messengers within and beyond the brain, so it is clear that chemicals must carry the commands that heal or damage the body, or do a host of other things. It is only one stage further to assume that one specific attitude of mind, perhaps even a response to the attitude of others, can cause different chemicals to flow and do different work to another attitude. And we know that "mere thinking" can produce many such effects. For example, if a person sees another person naked, by accident, he or she may blush. No assault or contact has been made, the cause is entirely in the imagination; yet the effect is that the physical blood flow is changed and a host of hot, flushes, or other "feelings" arise. A second common example is being shocked by, say, a sudden sight or sound. It "makes us jump." The physical response in this case is based on a purely imaginary set of possible scenarios constructed by the mind. Responding to fear and, in some cases, memories, the brain quickly activates adrenaline ("the drug of fright, fight and flight") to enable us to be ready to deal with possible threat. It is a survivalist response, to give us the edge in case the shock proves to be a genuine threat. But there has been no actual attack; the chemical changes and the body's physical changes have all been caused by chemicals activated by the imagination.

In the case of psychic healing, the process is intangible and the effect uncertain despite the interpretations of the healers. Whether or not something real "passes" into the patient in psychic healing, whether faith is involved, and whether it is the patient or the healer that does the healing is debatable. Nonetheless, people are cured by these processes, which is evidence of a mind power that deserves further analysis. But now we must look at a type of healing that is allegedly more direct—and more controversial.

Psychic Surgery

Psychic surgery is the name given to the performance of paranormal surgery using only bare hands or simple instruments. The psychic surgeon's hands are allegedly plunged into the patient's body, seemingly without leaving a scar or even a mark, and substances removed, resulting in cure. The surgeon often claims to be controlled by spirits. In the West psychic surgery has been challenged as fraudulent and a sleight of hand trick, but there are many claims of success and patient cures.

There are unquestioningly improvements in many conditions after psychic surgery, but whether or not the patient becomes well as a result of the actual surgery or whether it is an example of the placebo effect is unclear. If the latter, then the skill of the surgeon lies in convincing the patient that he or she has been cured in order that the person's own mind takes over the healing process.

Psychic surgeons can be divided into two types: those who actually perform operations, and those who appear to do so but in fact seem to be using sleight of hand and illusionist tricks. Some psychic surgeons do both at different times, presumably depending on the patient. Both techniques are relevant for this study; indeed, arguably both appear to heal.

One of the best-known claimants to psychic surgery was the Brazilian Jose Pedro De Freitas, who was known as Arigo. He performed his surgery in trance—many psychic surgeons do—allegedly under the guidance and "control" of a deceased German doctor who had died in 1918—Dr. Adolphus Fritz. In trance Arigo would write out prescriptions for medicines; these were found to be for old-fashioned drugs. Arigo used no surgical instruments; he would often use an unsterile penknife or rusty implements such as scissors. He used ordinary cloth to wipe wounds. Yet patients healed quickly and never suffered infection. Although prosecuted and jailed twice, in 1958 and 1964, for "practicisng medicine illegally" it was never claimed that in twenty years of work he ever caused harm to a patient. He was treating up to 200 patients a day at the peak of his activities.

Judge Filippe Immesi undertook to study Arigo and stated, of an operation he watched to treat a woman almost blind with cataracts: "I saw him pick up what looked like a pair of nail scissors. He wiped them on his sport shirt, and used no disinfectant of any kind. Then I saw him cut straight into the cornea of the patient's eye. She did not blench, although she was fully conscious. The cataract was out in a matter of seconds. The district attorney and I were speechless, amazed. Then Arigo said some kind of prayer as he held a piece of cotton in his hand. A few drops of liquid suddenly appeared on the cotton and he wiped the woman's eye with it. We saw this at close range. She was cured."

A modern, and well-known, psychic surgeon is Stephen Turoff who channels the spirit of "Dr. Khan." He works at a centre in Essex, England. We have interviewed both patients and witnesses to his surgery; they were impressed by their experiences and convinced that conditions had been cured by him.

In the 1990s Turoff was featured on the Spanish television programme *Otra Dimension*. In front of an audience of several million people Turoff operated on a patient, Isabel, who was blind in one eye. He cured her. The fact that she could read after the operation was demonstrated on the programme. But Turoff was challenged by sceptics; some claimed that he had even bribed the woman to pretend blindness. But the woman was able to produce her medical records on a subsequent edition of the programme showing that her blindness had been medically recognised.

But the sort of work Arigo did, and Turoff still does, is only part of the story of psychic surgery. The mind power involved is at least partly the surgeon's in channelling the technique, or knowledge, from somewhere. However, the patient's own mind power is also at work.

Other surgeons have been seen to operate using sleight of hand, not actually piercing the skin but showing blood clots as if from wounds. When tested this blood and tissue have been found to be of non-human origin. But the healing capabilities should not be dismissed simply because it is a trick. The fact is that many people are cured or feel better after visits to psychic surgeons using these techniques. The practice has a long history in the Philippines and South America.

Shamans and healers of tribal societies cause cures often by sucking from the patient's body an item—say, a stone—that, according to the healer, had been causing the problem. It seems unlikely that the patient had a stone within the body and far more likely that the stone was a prop concealed in the shaman's mouth. But the fact is that the patient has been given a reason for the pain, and has seen it removed, and believes that he or she is cured. Then the patient becomes well. The shaman, or psychic surgeon, creates the healing circumstances and the patient does the work.

The fact that it is an illusion may look like fraud to Western eyes and has been dismissed as such by stage illusionists and scientists who, in doing so, demonstrate that they have missed the point completely. The question is not the validity of the surgery; the question is the validity of the healing. The suggestion is that people have within themselves a mind power strong enough to change their bodies, to break up and remove tissue damage and growths if they have strong enough belief. If this can replace the need to open up the body and remove or destroy malignancies, then it is a far gentler and less harmful form of cure. Destroying kidney stones by mind power is obviously preferable to even modern surgical techniques.

But the remaining question is an obvious one. Can a person, by power of the mind alone, physically change the body? And the clue to the answer might lie in other forms of paranormal phenomena that demonstrate extraordinary mind power: firewalking, the abilities of fakirs and stigmata.

Firewalking

Firewalking is simple to describe. Beds of hot coals are heated to high temperatures and people walk across them without suffering injury or pain. Indeed, they seem to be using mind power to override the pain and warning sensors. And there is some evidence that they actually prevent damage to the body by force of will.

The use of firewalking in the modern day is probably divided equally among three different groups: certain religious or spiritual practitioners; business management trainers, as a modern version of "outward bound" self-development courses; and stage magicians, more often than not as a way of trying to "disprove" its paranormality.

Its religious associations are long standing and widespread. It formed a part of the religious ceremonies associated with the god Apollo in ancient Rome. In Hawaii it represents a way of ensuring that the individual is protected by—and therefore in the favour of—the god Pele.

In the Bible there is a description of fire resistance that also seems to represent protection by God. Nebuchadnez'zar threw three people he regarded as disrespectful—Shadrach, Meshach and Abed'nego—into a flaming furnace. But the outcome was far from that which Nebuchadnez'zar had hoped for. Those who took the three men to their punishment died from the heat of the furnace, but Shadrach, Meshach and Abed'nego were unharmed. Nebuchadnez'zar watched them walk safely through the furnace and observed: "The fire had not had any power over the bodies of those men; the hair of their heads was not singed, their mantles were not harmed, and no smell of fire had come upon them."

Each May, at Langadhas in northern Greece, there is a religious-based firewalk that has become something of a tourist attraction. The selected participants fast for days prior to the firewalk and appear to enter into some kind of altered state for the time of the firewalk. The altered state is enhanced by a long sequence of ceremonial dancing and animal sacrifice; no doubt this also serves to get the watching crowd in "the right mood" also. Each firewalker tends to spend around twenty minutes walking on and off the coals over the period of the "walk," and emerges unharmed.

In Father Herbert Thurston's 1952 work *Physical Phenomena of Mysticism* he describes a firewalk that took place in Mysore, southern India, in 1921 or 1922. This was originally recorded by the Catholic bishop Monsignor Despatures who watched the event. Monsignor Despatures was careful to check for signs of trickery, and was satisfied there was none. When the event started the Mohammedan who was in charge of the proceedings pushed an obviously reluctant servant into the "pit." The servant tried, panicking, to get out of the pit when "suddenly the look of terror on his face gave place to an astonished smile, and he proceeded to cross the trench lengthways, without haste and as if he were taking a constitutional, beaming contentedly upon those who were standing round on either side of him. His feet and legs were perfectly bare." Having watched this astonishing feat, 200 people then walked over the embers. One "walker" was the head of the Maharaja's police force and another a civil engineer; they commented: "We felt we were in a furnace, but the fire did not burn us." Monsignor Despatures concluded: "I am forced to believe in the influence of some spiritual agency which is not God." Interestingly when the walkers did not have the blessing of the Mohammedan they did come to grief. At a later firewalk he warned people not to enter the coal pit but three ignored him; they were all badly burned.

Harry Price, perhaps more famous for his research into ghosts and poltergeists, arranged two firewalks to enable the phenomenon to be studied. The first "walk" was observed by a physicist from the University of London. The coal pit was twenty-four feet in length, and heated to a temperature of around 800 degrees Fahrenheit. The firewalker, Kuda Bux, walked through the pit four times. He apparently took no precautions that anyone could see and cleaned the ash off his feet at the end of each "walk" to avoid any suggestion that he was using a build up of cold ash as an insulator. Bux showed no sign of injury, nor did his feet show a rise in temperature. Two of the observers, Digby Moynagh and Maurice Cheepen, attempted the walk for themselves, copying Bux; both were badly blistered. During the second "walk," another firewalker, Ahmed Hussain, duplicated the feat. According to Price: "Any person with the requisite determination, confidence, and steadiness can walk unharmed over a fire as hot as 800 degrees F. The experiments proved once and for all that no occult or psychic power, or a specially-induced mental state, is necessary in a firewalker. "But, as we shall see, there are those who are harmed by firewalking and those who are not, and the key seems to be a mind power—a belief in the safety of the process that translates into reality."

Firewalking has more recently become a positive technique for self-development and consciousness-raising, used even in training for businesspeople. It increases their self-esteem and their ability to concentrate their minds. Further still, it provides a sense of accomplishment, which can then be channelled into other areas of development. Clearly there is no religious connotation here; but perhaps there is a spiritual one.

Firewalking in this context was popularised first in the USA in the late 1970s and early 1980s, as part of training and development workshops. It is believed that there are anything from thirty-five to one hundred training instructors practising this technique as part of their development programmes at the present time. One estimate suggests that over a quarter of a million people have firewalked as part of such training. Each workshop, depending on the leader, could have around twenty "walkers"; some have reported up to a hundred. One practitioner, Tony Robbins, author of *Unlimited Power*, reports as many as 1,200 participants at one firewalk.

Generally, before the actual walk there is a period of team-building and individual confidence boosting. Techniques to get people to face their fears are employed, and there are smaller workshops designed to show that people can often achieve beyond their expectations. Not least, there is a description of what to expect, and what attitude of mind to bring to the experience.

First to walk through the glowing coals is the leader/trainer. If nothing else this reinforces their leadership, which itself generates trust in the leader. Furthermore, there is no better way to instil a feeling of possible achievement than to see a thing being done. History is replete with examples of how a commonly held belief that a thing "couldn't be done" is shattered once one person breaks the barrier—the four-minute mile is one such example.

So is the firewalk a piece of stage magic? Or is there more to it than that? Two propositions suggest the former.

The first is the "Leidenfrost effect." Johan Leidenfrost observed that water on a very hot surface evaporated more slowly than water on a cooler surface. This suggested that sweat that might form on the soles of those doing the firewalk, or water picked up from wet grass before commencing the "walk," might not quickly evaporate but form a water barrier of cool insulation that would protect the firewalker. Dr. Jearl Walker, professor of physics at Cleveland State University, put this theory to the test and did a firewalk while carrying a copy of the book *Physics*. He had some successes. Walker wrote up his theories in "The Amateur Scientist" column in the August 1977 issue of *Scientific American*.

The second proposition is that stage magicians have found a way to do a firewalk without coming to harm, and they believe that this "trick" allows others to do the same. Several stage magicians have gained a great deal of publicity during recent years, when "the paranormal" has been a popular topic on television, by doing "firewalks" openly stated as being "tricks" performed in just that way. A witness to Kuda Bux's walk, Charles Darling, commented: "Firewalking is really a gymnastic feat." He believed that Bux went through the fire in such a way, and manoeuvring his feet in just such a way, as to minimise contact with the coals and therefore also risk of injury.

If this were true then the speed of firwalking would be an essential factor; the walker must go through the coals so fast that the heat does not have time to transmit through the skin or damage the skin in any way.

Some stage magicians also claim that the nature of coal—chunks of rounded lumpy material—makes the feat all the easier. They believe that only small pressure points of the feet are in contact with the uppermost surfaces of the coal and that there is the double advantage of air pockets of lower temperature and the fact that only the coolest sections of the coal touch the skin surface. Others have suggested that the dry wood coals used in some firewalks conduct heat poorly. Although these coals themselves are very hot they do not transfer heat well to something touching it. Furthermore, they argue, blood is a good conductor of heat and will quickly transfer heat away from the soles of the feet.

Perhaps so, but these explanations would not seem to explain other types of firewalkers, those not set up by these illusionists. For example, Hawaiian kahunas who walk across hot smooth lava rock; Fijian shamans who walk across glowing river rock; several well-authenticated cases of firewalkers who walk very slowly, and even stop for periods, in the firepit, sit and lie down, and even allow their hair to touch the coals, all without harm. Some walks are for very long distances also, some of over 100 feet. Some people pick up and hold coals for over half a minute. The well-known, nineteenth-century medium Daniel Dunglas Home was able, on occasions, to handle burning coals and to pass these round his group of sitters and no one would be burned.

But there are some possible explanations for these phenomena, which we examine below.

We have a colleague, Philip Walton, whose experiences helped us to understand part of the complexity of firewalking. Having damaged his hands in an accident many years previously, Walton could not feel pain in them and could, consequently, hold coals or put his hand into a flame for some period. But such people are rare. We learned from him that the ability to limit damage from fire can be developed and it seems to be under some kind of mental control. Walton was frequently burned in his work, a natural hazard of his job and not usually serious. He had found that when he saw himself getting burned he would blister, but when he did not know it had happened he would not blister but only find a red mark representing the "damage area." Possibly, then, blistering is to some degree a self-generated response to burning, at least at the first "level" of damage.

What this suggests is that providing you can "block" the pain you probably can last in the firewalk for some time before damage sets in. But can you block the pain?

Perception of pain varies from person to person. There are those who seem to be able to take great levels of pain, and those who can take very little. But there is evidence that some degree of control over the perception of pain is possible, hence the use of firewalking in self-development training. Those who believe that they have a certain amount of control over the situation seem to be able to control the pain. Those who feel out of control, who are panicking or are afraid show a very low tolerance to pain. Those who "walk" as part of a religious observance presumably believe that what they are doing is for a good purpose and perhaps that the pain is even part of that process. They are

POWERS OF THE MIND

testing their faith, proving the protection of their God or purifying themselves in the fire. For those people, tolerance of pain is probably higher than for the average person.

In 1980 German scientists from Tübingen examined the famous Langadhas firewalk that takes place each May in Greece. Examination showed that the coal surface temperature was around 1,000 degrees Fahrenheit. However, measuring equipment on the soles of the firewalkers' feet showed only around 350 degrees Fahrenheit. Interestingly when the firewalkers' brainwave activity was monitored, it was discovered that there was an increase in theta activity in the brain. It is possible that this represented a mental "pain blocking" process; similar results have been found when examining the abilities of fakirs who pierce their bodies with metal spikes, as we shall examine in the next section. Two scientists decided that they would try the most obvious control test; they walked onto the coals and immediately suffered third-degree burns.

Those scientists did not believe in what they were doing. But the common denominator among those people who were successful is their belief in the forces that would allow them to walk through fire without coming to harm. Religious firewalkers see it as part of their religion, perhaps some believe they are divinely protected; a physicist carried his physics book knowing that he has the "Leidenfrost effect" on his side; stage magicians "know" they are doing a trick. Is the ability to firewalk simply a matter of belief? If so, that belief takes many forms depending on the firewalker.

The Abilities of Fakirs

The fakirs of India and the zanies of Libya are only two examples of many groups of people who, with strong religious convictions, bear pain in almost unimaginable circumstances. When the Italians, in the 1930s, watched the zanies they were repelled by what they saw. They reported: "The perforation and burning of the flesh, walking on fire, the swallowing of poisonous animals, broken glass, nails and prickly pear leaves, and the placing of rings through the noses of children, must be considered repugnant to the principles of morality and modern civilisation."

Fakirs have had themselves crucified for hours at a time, been buried alive, and undergone the most excruciating body piercing. One fakir was tested by Dr. Wolfgang Larbig at the University of Tübingen in the 1960s. The fakir thrust four metal spikes into his stomach, chest and neck without any sign of bleeding. Based on observations of his behaviour, the testors concluded: "There was no evidence that he experienced any pain whatsoever." When the spikes were removed there was still no bleeding, and very little damage to the body.

Somehow the fakir had controlled physical characteristics of his own body. Hypnosis used as an anaesthetic in operations (described earlier in this book, see pages 56–57) also has the effect of slowing blood flow. The evidence is that a state of mind can control the body.

Tests conducted on the fakir and fourteen other subjects suggested that a pain-blocking technique was being used. All fifteen people were asked to prepare themselves for the forthcoming pain of forty electric shocks as best they knew how. They were wired up to monitor their brainwave patterns. Then they received the shocks. It was the fakir who came out far ahead of the others; and Dr. Larbig found a reason. The brainwave patterns of the fakir were quite different to those of the other subjects in the test. Every time pain was induced, the brainwave recordings of the fakir showed theta waves—the waves usually associated with sleep. It was as if during moments of pain he had put himself—or some part of himself—into sleep.

Furthermore—and this might also have relevance to the firewalking described in the previous section—the conductivity of the fakir's skin was different from that of the other subjects. By using mind powers, the fakir had changed both his perception of pain and the character of his skin.

Stigmata and Spontaneous Body-Markings

We were told the following story first-hand by "Bill." While working in the garden he pricked his arm badly on a thorn. He admitted that he immediately feared he could get "lockjaw." During that night his arm puffed up into a huge blue and black swelling. Even worse, he found that he could not move his jaw, he could not even talk; his worse fears appeared to have come true. At the first opportunity that morning he went to the doctor who checked his tetanus jab history. He was fully up to date. The doctor told him to go to the dentist, which he did. The dentist found that he had a long-term problem, a bad habit of eating to one side of his mouth, which had caused the stiff jaw. After simple treatment (the temporary removal of a small denture) the mouth and jaw were perfectly free again. But note that the problem was a long-term one; that it should have "locked" his jaw that night of all nights seems an impossible coincidence. The implication was that Bill "locked" his own jaw, his attitude of mind creating the appropriate "proof" of his fears.

We all at some time get a bit hypochondriacal, creating the symptoms of what we fear. But how much can a mind—convinced of a reality—affect the body? Stigmata might be the ultimate proof of the mind's incredible power to affect the physical body.

Over the past 770 years, between 300 and 350 people have reported an extraordinary phenomenon. They have displayed for all to see wounds on their bodies, and particularly their hands and feet, that they believe represent the crucifixion wounds of Jesus Christ. Research shows that within religious circles there may have been many more stigmatics; many believe that their suffering is a private experience not to be made public. Certainly one stigmatic, Heather Woods of Lincoln, only made her marks public when she was "told" in a message from the Lord that she should. The vast majority of the claimants have been female; one estimation indicates a figure as high as eighty-five per cent.

The first person to show stigmata was St. Francis of Assisi.

In 1224, two years before his death, he received the marks on his body. According to St. Francis' biographer, Thomas de Celano, the marks were described by witnesses as having the appearance of the nails themselves, the points and the nail heads showing through the skin on both sides of his hands. They were alleged to have existed after St. Francis' death; many pilgrims filing past his body witnessed "not the prints of the nails, but the nails themselves formed out of his flesh and retaining the blackness of iron."

Other stigmatics, such as Giovanna Bonomi in 1670 and Domenica Lazzari in 1848, have reported similar marks. However, the appearance of the marks is not consistent. Some people have exhibited red patches that do not bleed; others have claimed deep holes that, in some cases, are alleged to go right through the flesh. There have been reports of circles, ovals, oblongs, indeed many shapes. The marks may include representations of the spear mark in Christ's side and the crown of thorns on his forehead.

In addition to the "usual" marks, Georgette Faniel of Montreal recently reported a pain that she believes represents the injury caused to Christ when he carried the cross on his shoulder as he walked to his crucifixion. Other stigmatics have displayed arm elongation corresponding to the stretching of Christ's arms while on the cross. Some have displayed bruises on the knees, which allegedly originate from Christ's stumbling while carrying the cross. There are a number of stigmatics, such as St. Catherine of Siena, who have died at the age of thirty-three, the age of Christ when he died. Therese Neumann, in addition to exhibiting stigmatic marks, has also wept tears of blood. Several reports have been made of marks found on the hearts of stigmatics during post-mortem. St. Teresa of Avila's heart is preserved as a sacred relic and displays marks believed by some to represent the piercing of her heart by a spear. Charles of Sezze, in 1671, and Caterina Savelli, in 1691, also received "heart markings."

The most famous stigmatic is Padre Pio. After eight years of pain he first displayed the stigmata at the age of twenty-one, on 20 September 1918; his wounds opened up and wept a great deal of blood. For him, as for many stigmatics, his marks were painful. Of their first manifestation he wrote: "I saw before me a mysterious person . . . his hands and feet and side were dripping with blood. The vision disappeared and I became aware that my hands, feet and side were dripping blood. Imagine the agony I experienced and continue to experience almost every day. . . . I am dying of pain because of the wounds and resulting embarrassment." Padre Pio had the marks of the stigmata for fifty years. There were those who claimed they could put their fingers right through the wounds.

Padre Pio and St. Francis of Assisi have many close parallels. From an early age Padre Pio—born Francesco Forgione—wanted to join the Franciscan order, started by St. Francis. St. Francis received his stigmata after a pilgrimage to the shrine of St. Michael at Gargano in Italy; Padre Pio lived in a monastery in the small town of San Giovanni Rotondo, just a few miles from that shrine. Padre Pio's stigmata appeared just three days after he had celebrated the Feast of the Stigmata of St. Francis.

Those displaying the stigmata often have associated paranormal experiences, in particular visions and receiving channelled messages, writings and drawings. Padre Pio was frequently reported in bi-location—seen in two places at the same time.

Generally speaking, stigmatics believe the marks represent a "sign" from Jesus. Almost all stigmatics are overtly religious and have a belief in Christ. Heather Woods indicated that she believed her marks were given to her at a time when a suffering world needed a symbol of faith.

A more dispassionate analysis of the phenomenon indicates that internal beliefs and religious imagery may explain the markings. Prior to the time of St. Francis of Assisi, religious art—including depictions of Christ on the cross—were highly stylised. They were graceful, artistic, beautiful and did not show blood, wounds or suffering. Religious art changed around the thirteenth century to a more realistic image; the suffering was depicted in all its detail. This was accompanied by a change from devotion to the life of Christ, to a concentration on his suffering for all our sins. The result was greater awareness of the suffering of the crucifixion. And the claims of the stigmata soon followed.

There is "control" evidence that supports this explanation. Some Byzantine and orthodox images of Christ on the cross maintain the stylised form to the present day; and followers of these religious groups do not produce stigmatics.

No other religions exhibit the stigmata or even equivalents. This is probably because no other religion holds the same idea of sin being redeemed through the suffering of God's representative; that is a uniquely Christian belief.

It is also a historical fact that there are many more women than men who have manifested the stigmata; though the ratio is levelling out in more recent years.

The change of emphasis from devotion to the life of Christ to the suffering of Christ came about less from the established Church and more from pressure from lay groups. It was probably a reaction to the corruption of the Church at the time. St. Francis, for example, wasn't a priest; he was a lay person who set up his own monastic order.

Many unofficial religious orders were set up, often made up of women who were denied access to the mainstream Church. They led the way to concentration on the passion of the suffering of Christ; and they became the majority of stigmatics.

In more recent times even priests who have focused on the pain and suffering of Christ have displayed the stigmata. The most famous of these is of course Padre Pio, mentioned earlier.

When the Turin Shroud—whatever its authenticity—showed that the nail wounds might have been made through the wrists rather than the palms of the hands, claims of stigmatic wounds in the wrists followed. Studies of stigmata indicate that the marks conform to imagery of the suffering held by the claimant.

This would seem to suggest that claimants actually want to

display these signs of suffering; this has been shown to be true in some cases. Two years before St. Francis of Assisi reported his stigmata, one man allowed himself to be crucified and therefore bore crucifixion scars. In recent times a court prosecuted two men for crucifying a third on Hampstead Heath even though the "victim" admitted he had requested the crucifixion.

The majority of claimants seem to be displaying a psychosomatic response to their religious fervour. This is irrefutable evidence outside the realm of stigmata claims that the body can will itself to produce such marks. Dr. Magnus Huss of the Seraphim Hospital in Stockholm, Sweden, examined a girl known as Maria who was badly beaten up when she was twenty-three, after which time she would, every few weeks, produce bleeding from head, ear and eyelids. The doctor concluded that she could produce bleeding at will, from no visible wounds, when she picked arguments with other patients and reached a certain emotional state.

This ability, known as hysterical conversion, is a close cousin of a form of extreme hypochondria as exhibited by "Elizabeth," who lived in Germany in the 1920s. She could manifest the symptoms of any illness she heard about. On one occasion she went to see a slide show of the "Passion"—the crucifixion of Christ. She left feeling pains in her hands and feet. Dr. Alfred Lechler, using hypnosis, suggested that she—like Christ—had been pierced by nails in her hands and feet. Nail-like wounds appeared. Using suggestion he also induced tears of blood and bleeding wounds on her forehead. Lechler was also able to use hypnosis to heal the wounds, and later he found he could make them reappear without hypnosis.

Whether the stigmata are God-given is, of course, a matter for conviction rather than research. Research seems, however, to have identified a mechanism by which the body can—in certain extreme emotions—manifest strange markings, producing a truly extraordinary, and highly visible, mystery phenomenon.

The extraordinary stigmata case of Heather Woods of Lincoln featured in a television documentary at Easter 1994. Our book about her life, entitled *Spirit Within Her*, was published that same year.

In order to understand this phenomenon as clearly as possible, we worked with Heather at close quarters for a long period of time. The following account is not just of the stigmata, but of her personal background, which, in our view, created the passions and convictions that led to the stigmata.

At the age of nine Heather came home to find her suitcases packed; she and her sisters were uprooted from their happy home. For the rest of her childhood, Heather was moved from one institutional home to another. She endured sexual abuse, physical violence and mental cruelty at the hands of a variety of her "benefactors." She ran away over thirty times.

One aching memory of her childhood was sitting in the "best" room of the carehouse, dressed in her best clothes, waiting for a promised visit from her parents knowing that they wouldn't turn up—just like they hadn't turned up the week before. In her early years the abuse was coupled with tragedies that included her mother's breakdown, imprisonment and eventual suicide, and her own attempted "suicides," or at least cries for help. In later years she would endure the pain of a brain-damaged son, the death of a husband she loved dearly, and separation from her daughter.

By the age of forty-four, when we spoke to Heather, her body had been racked by cancers and other illness that had required many visits to hospitals and eight major operations; most of her major organs had been operated on and some even removed.

Heather's stigmata first appeared at a time when she was receiving channelled drawings and writings and experiencing visions. These came to her in trance-like states, and she believes they were "given" to her by God. The messages read like sermons; the drawings and visions were of Christ being baptised and crucified. Heather felt herself on the cross inside the body of Christ; on many occasions she felt herself with him during Biblical times. When describing her feeling that she was with Jesus at his baptism with John, she said: "It was as if I was there. I could see the water dripping from him, sparkling in the sunlight."

The appearance of the stigmata is almost always associated with visions such as these. The first stigmatic, St. Francis of Assisi, received the marks after a vision of a six-winged seraph crucified like a man. Ethel Chapman, a recent stigmatic, recalled a vivid vision of being crucified. She felt the pain and saw people jeering at her. The next morning she had stigmata markings.

Heather Woods described to us the way in which her stigmata had first manifested. It was May 1992. Having done some house decorating over the weekend she found that her palm was itching. She thought that perhaps she had been brushing too hard and had caused a blister. But the itching persisted and got worse. Both she and the friend she was with began to think there was something "weird" about it and decided that they would show it to another close friend who was also Heather's priest, Father Eric Eades. Heather described the wound: "It looked as if the top of a blister had come off. It was red raw. The white skin wasn't there. It looked just like it was raw, but it wasn't sore."

That night Heather "was given" a drawing of Christ being baptised. Heather was a channeller who received script and pictures in trance, a phenomenon described in the section on automatic writing (see pages 161–67). She refers to these words and pictures as being "given" because she believes that her religious experiences are given by God for a purpose. When she "came round" after drawing the picture she discovered that the blister-like marks had appeared on the palms and backs of both hands.

When Father Eades visited the following day, he suggested: "I think I know what it is. I think that's stigmata.... I have a feeling that something amazing is going to happen."

Heather did not know what the word "stigmata" meant; Father Eades explained to her. That night the marks got bigger, and they started to bleed for the first time. During that night Heather channelled a drawing of Christ crucified, nailed to a stake. "My hands were bleeding all the time. Thick, deep, red blood. They were not sore, just bleeding."

Heather was extremely fascinated of course. Although Father Eades left that night for a few days abroad, he asked that Heather telephone him if the stigmata developed. On Friday night, while watching television, she felt "this itching, like ants running over my foot." Father Eades had warned Heather to keep an eye on her feet. She telephoned him and he guessed immediately. "It's come to your feet, hasn't it?" he queried. Father Eades asked Heather to check the underside of her feet, but there were no markings there. Her hands were still bleeding thick, red blood. Even while they spoke on the telephone Heather's feet started to bleed also, at first with just spots of blood.

But the stigmata had not yet finished forming. On the Saturday afternoon Heather was at her sister's house, lying down in the garden. She felt that she had been bitten in the side by an insect. When Heather lifted her blouse to check they found a red mark "like a smile" on her skin.

When Father Eades returned to visit Heather he examined the marks. The marks had bled a little and caused her sock to stick to her feet. "It didn't hurt, it just had stuck," she said. The marks had now appeared on the underside of the feet also. Father Eades asked to see her side where she had told him of the mark there. Father Eades explained it in terms of Christ's wounds. "Remember that the Bible says a soldier pierced his side and that blood and water came out. Because they then thought he was dead they didn't need to break his legs, as they usually did in crucifixions. We don't know what the Roman spears were like; we're assuming it's a spear, it could have been a sword; we don't know how long the swords were, or what shape they were." He believed that the mark on Heather's side was the stigmata of the spear mark.

(Interestingly, stigmatics who have the spear mark may display it on either the left or the right side; we have interviewed stigmatics with spear marks on either side. The Bible does not say on which side Jesus was pierced, a further suggestion that the marks are manifested according to personal belief.)

Heather also made an interesting observation. She thought that the order of appearance of her three sets of wounds—hands, feet and then side—might represent the order in which they appeared on Christ's body: that perhaps he was nailed first in the hands, then in the feet and of course the spear mark came later. It does not matter if that was the case or not, the point is that Heather believed it to be probable, and it might account for the order in which she manifested the markings.

The bleeding became considerable:

> Eventually the bleeding got so bad that at night I would take my socks and shoes off and put my feet on a tea towel. I think that was the first time I noticed that the marks were weeping. Something like water was just bubbling up, running between the toes. Whatever it was, it was setting as it was running; it was just like melted sugar. It was literally just dripping off both sides, often for up to about three hours. I would feel when the bandage was wet through, then I would have to change it. And of course the marks were getting bigger every day. A lot bigger, and a lot deeper. They never at any time went right through but it was quite deep and raw. When they had finished bleeding I would bathe my feet and hands again, just to get the blood off and tidy it up. There was never a scab. You could see the rawness, and the blood just sitting there. But there was never a scab, and never any pain. They were full, raw crater-like things. Over the twenty-one weeks that I had them they got bigger, all the marks on my hands, feet and the side. They were all like open wounds, weeping and bleeding. I didn't put bandages on at night, I wanted to let the air get to them. But I would put a square bit of non-stick plaster over them.

Heather asked her doctor to visit her at home because walking was becoming painful and difficult. She could not tell him what she thought the marks were; she believed that she had been "given" the message that the marks were to be kept within her healing group and her church. "I prayed, and I was 'told' that if Dr. Bhanja [her doctor] recognised the marks as the stigmata then I was able to share with him what was going to happen over the month. But if he didn't acknowledge it I wasn't to say anything." She showed her doctor the marks. "He held my hands and looked at them; then he looked at me. He recognised it [she found out later], but apparently daren't say anything to me because he felt it would frighten me. I was waiting. I couldn't share any more with him because he hadn't recognised the marks. He gave me a few bandages and left. A few days later, when the wounds on my feet opened up, he came out to me again. This time he acknowledged what it was and I was able to share it with him."

Although at first kept within a small group there were many witnesses to Heather's stigmata who comforted and encouraged her. Her family saw the marks, of course, as did several friends. There were also many visitations from churchmen around the country. "I think what helped carry me through this is that it's not all been done behind a locked door. There have been witnesses. People have been with me when it happened, when it stopped or started again. Several people have taken photographs."

Heather was to have one last type of manifestation, a much rarer one that may in some way be related to the crown of thorns. Several stigmatics have manifested markings and scratchings on the forehead that correspond with a crown of thorns. Heather's was a very stylised version:

After the twenty-one weeks . . . things got back to normal. I was still being given writings and drawings. On the Sunday I was given in the writings that there would be a manifestation on St. Luke's Day. I was in the Order of St. Luke. St. Luke's Day was the day of prayer. We didn't know what was going to manifest, only that something would. There was a service that evening and during it a cross manifested on my forehead. Somebody said it looked like the Cross of Lorraine. It was quite deep, it looked like a burn, the sort of burn you get when you burn yourself on the iron or the cooker. It was an indentation; it didn't blister over and go red, it looked like an early scab. It was quite rough and scabby and deep. After an hour or so it started to bleed. Blood was visibly running down my nose.

Heather spoke to her doctor about the cross, and he was somewhat concerned. "It's going to be days before that heals," he told her. But in fact it was visible for only three days. "One morning I woke up and it had gone," Heather said. "The other marks had gone by then as well."

That was the end of the stigmata for 1992. But in 1993 Heather received the message, through her channelled writings, that she would again manifest the stigmata. "The message said that eighteen days before Easter the stigmata would appear, and indicated that something was going to happen on Good Friday. Using a calendar to work back eighteen days from Good Friday I realised that if it was going to happen it would be tomorrow or the next day. It actually happened in the early hours of the morning, exactly the eighteenth day before Easter. I woke up feeling a wetness in the bed. The stigmata had appeared and I had been bleeding quite a bit. The blood was all over my sheets; they had to be washed immediately it was so bad. I telephoned Father Eades to tell him it was back, and bleeding heavily."

It is generally believed that there are three mechanisms that might account for the stigmata:

- The first is not based on research but belief and is, of course, supported by stigmatics. They believe the marks are God-given, a sign from God indicating the special nature of the claimant and their religious "mission." Heather believed they were given to her as a message for the world.
- The second mechanism is the physical creation of the marks in some way. One subject, Elizabeth of Herkenrode, possibly created and certainly maintained her stigmata by banging her finger into her hand, re-living the passion and the pain of the

crucifixion every twenty-four hours. In one sense this amounts to "cheating" but not from the stigmatic's point of view; the stigmata are part of a religious experience for their subjects and physical pain and suffering are a genuine aspect of the devotion. They are doing what they believe is right. However, such a mechanism removes the stigmata from the realm of the paranormal. But most stigmatics do not mutilate themselves in this way.

- The third mechanism is the natural appearance of the marks as a psychosomatic response to religious fervour. This theory is most favoured among modern researchers. It has been tested and has parallels outside of the realms of stigmatic manifestation.

The condition is known as psychogenic purpura (spontaneous haemorrhaging with no obvious cause). It is rare, but there are several cases of people who produce on themselves the evidence of some previous trauma. One woman who had been abused during childhood manifested the spontaneous appearance of her bruise marks during psychotherapy. British psychiatrist Robert Moody reported the case of an army officer who he had treated for stress disorders and sleepwalking. During these times the officer produced the marks on his body of rope burns corresponding with injuries that had occurred while the officer had been a prisoner and had been tied up. Moody photographed these wounds, and saw them bleed. Many people who claim to have undergone "alien abductions" display marks on their bodies and bleeding from wounds they believe were inflicted by aliens. Many other people who have been in close proximity to UFOs manifest a variety of marks. Some may be attributable to the UFO, as for example the chest wounds received by Stephen Michalak in Canada. Michalak was allegedly standing close to a landed object that blasted air through a side vent, which left him bruised where it had hit him on the chest. But other wounds seem more likely to be the psychosomatic response to alleged proximity to a UFO, for example the triangular markings received by Dr. X in southern France, in 1968. Dr. X watched two UFOs flying in a valley near his home and later discovered the triangular marks (skin pigmentation), which he attributed to the encounter. Earlier we referred to Barney Hill (see pages 61–63) who manifested warts in the genital area, where he believed a device had been clamped to him during his abduction.

The phenomenon of possession, examined earlier (see pages 190–99), has produced examples of skin markings that match belief, and they are similar to stigmata. We mentioned the case of Robert Mannheim (see pages 192–94) who produced lines of suffering and even words, in scratches on his skin.

There is a difference between psychogenic purpura and stigmata, however. The army officer had once been a captive; Barney Hill believed he had been abducted by aliens; Mannheim believed himself possessed. These people manifested marks according to their own personal experiences. The stigmata are unique in that the subject receives the marks of somebody else's suffering, i.e. Christ's.

One could argue that Heather, and it seems Ethel Chapman too, may have felt that they themselves were on the cross and the marks were, therefore, of their "own" suffering. Perhaps other stigmatics felt the same. Heather said: "I found myself on the cross with our Lord. I wasn't with him as if it were the two of us; I felt myself within him, looking out."

Religious imagery, as we stated earlier, plays an important part in the type of stigmata that manifests. Heather's stigmata closely matched her own beliefs about the crucifixion and images she was familiar with from illustrated Bibles, artworks and so on. Similarly, Ethel Chapman got her marks in the form of a vision that closely related to the illustrated Bible she had been reading the night before.

The appearance of stigmata is usually associated with other experiences generally labelled "paranormal." Heather believed she had ESP, could tell the history of people she met, had premonitions, saw ghosts and spirits, channelled images and writing, had out-of-body experiences and gave healing in the form of "laying on of hands." Other stigmatics, interviewed by other researchers, have made similar claims. There have been reports that a person at a point of religious ecstasy will levitate; such a claim was made of St. Francis.

A claim made for Padre Pio was that he underwent bilocation; he was witnessed in two places at the same time. There are many "non-religious" claims of this phenomenon. Another paranormal manifestation is a perfume smell, "the odour of sanctity." A sweet smell of roses has been associated with many stigmatics, such as Padre Pio. His devotees believe they can detect his "presence" by this smell even now, years after his death.

Heather Woods worked under the spiritual guidance of Father Eric Eades, who believed he channelled healing powers from Padro Pio. Father Eric's wife, Betty, confirmed to us that she smelt that scent recently, after both Eric's and Heather's death. Ted Harrison, who has investigated many cases of stigmata, told us that Ethel Chapman and Christina Gallagher in Ireland were associating their experiences with this smell.

Heather believed that above all else her healing ministry was the most important aspect of her "mission." It was, she told us, carrying on the real work of Christ. The stigmata were, to her, a sign for others that they should see and believe in that healing ministry. Many other stigmatics have been healers, including Padre Pio, Jane Hunt in England, Berthe Mrazek in Belgium, Georgette Faniel in Montreal. This is fascinating because there is evidence from the observations of researchers, healers, and their patients, that heat is part of the healing process; heat is also associated with stigmata.

Heather Wood's stigmata generated heat. Her Aunt May said: "You could feel the heat coming from it. Even the one on her tummy, you could feel the heat there." May demonstrated to us how she reacted when she put her hand over the marks; she jerked backwards suddenly, screwing up her face. It was a gesture she could have made if she had put her hand into the flame of a candle. Heather's father, George, was at the interview and confirmed that impression. He described the heat from inches above the wounds as "hot as a match flame. Hot. Hot." He too made this same jerking, withdrawing gesture. May told us that Heather's body always generated heat. "Many a time I used to give her a hug I'd throw my arms around her and the heat that would come from her body was unbelievable."

Heat—stigmata—healing. Perhaps the connections are there for future research and experimentation, leading to a greater understanding of these processes.

There appears to be a pattern of suffering of one sort of another among stigmatics. Many seem to have gone through a period of serious illness; all seem to have suffered in some way. Heather Woods' life of suffering—her rape, physical abuse, sexual abuse, and other deprivations and traumas—when overlaid with religious belief may all have created the conditions that led to stigmata. It is a fairly consistent pattern in stigmatics.

What is perhaps important is that the individual's medical history seems to play a part in his or her experience of a wide range of paranormal claims. Many of those who believe they have been abducted by aliens have a history of illness or suffering that bears a resemblance to Heather's. Furthermore, those who perceive UFOs and have close encounter experiences also have stronger religious fervour than those who report other forms of paranormal experience. Their beliefs are often those of passionate conviction rather than reasoned analysis. In our own files, "Rohan" suffered from adverse medical histories and family separations; "Jane" experienced trauma; and there are many other such examples. Budd Hopkins reported the medical problems of "Kathie Davis," the subject of his book *Intruders*.

People seek personal development and attainment in different ways, and according to different circumstances. Many of those driven by religious zeal, including stigmatics, seek to achieve their maximum personal development in a uniquely religious way.

Research has identified a "hierarchy of needs" that all human beings seek to satisfy. When we have provided for basic needs such as food and a home, we ultimately move on to trying to satisfy higher level of needs such as personal development to "become the person we know we are capable of becoming." Deeply religious people often easily satisfy the lower needs because those needs are not of paramount importance for them. Monks, nuns, many priests, for example, live very austere lives from choice; food, a bed, a roof over their heads and a Bible have been the only possessions of some of these people, with no evident craving for more material possessions. For many of these religious people "oneness" with Christ is perhaps how they satisfy their higher needs and how they become "the person they know they are capable of becoming"; and for a few that oneness might be displayed through the stigmata.

Faced with illness, rejection, abuse and so on, people generally respond in one of two ways: they take control of their lives either by coming to terms with themselves, or by "re-creating" themselves through assertiveness training, stress management, psychotherapy and the like; or they "give up" and fall victim to their inner illness. Perhaps stigmatics have found a compromise; Christ is a figure who can be trusted with control over one's life, and those who surrender control to him and become his instrument might be regarded as neither "giving up" nor "taking control."

The stigmata, to Heather Woods, in this context, could be regarded as either a sign that Christ had recognised that desire for oneness, or it could be seen as the stigmatic's signal to the rest of the world that oneness had been achieved. The stigmata were, for Heather, a sign that she was "becoming the person she knew she was capable of becoming."

But although stigmata are a form of "damage" to the body, showing that the mind is indeed capable of hurting itself and the body that houses it, they also have a positive side that was evident for those such as Heather. In this last section of this

chapter we examine some examples of the most destructive use
that belief that can occasionally be put to.

Hexing

Michael Crichton in his book *Travels* relates the story of Mr.
Erwin who was admitted to hospital because of a spot found on
a routine chest X-ray that was thought to be cancer. Although initially agreeing to surgery, Erwin kept putting off the moment
saying he wanted time to consider. Dr. W thought that allowing
the man to vacillate in that way was wrong and confronted
Erwin: "I am Dr. W; you have cancer and I am going to take it
out!" Erwin burst into tears but then agreed to the surgery. After
the tissue was removed it was discovered that the spot was not
cancer at all, but a piece of meat that Erwin had inhaled. Erwin
was told the good news, but would not believe it. Crichton concluded: "He believed he still had cancer because Dr. W had told
him so. Two days later, Mr. Erwin crawled out of the narrow window of his room, and jumped to his death."

What created such a state of mind? In this case it seems that
Erwin allowed Dr. W to become a very powerful authority figure. The statement from Dr. W had such authority that it could
not be broken. This is not a curse of course, but it shows the
power of the authority figure. And this may be a powerful factor in the process of hexing.

The peoples of less technological cultures, such as the Australian Aborigines, have a strong belief in the power of curses.
The victim of a curse is known to suffer, and there are cases of
people dying. But is the curse a real external attack on the victim,
or does the victim do the work for those placing the curse?

The most effective curses are those placed by authority figures;
in less technological cultures this is usually the "witchdoctor."

Dr. Herbert Basedow watched the "boning" of an Australian
Aborigine and described the obvious suffering he underwent.
Boning—pointing a bone at the victim—is a powerful curse, a

sign of death. The victim saw the bone pointed at him and was immediately filled with fear, his face distorted and his cheeks lost their colour. His body shook, and he collapsed. The end result of such a curse is that the victim frets, gets increasingly weak or ill, and eventually dies.

An account of a curse being lifted discussed the opposite effects. Dr. S. M. Lambert was asked to help with an ailing missionary's assistant called Rob, in Queensland, who had been boned by a powerful Aborigine witch called Nebo. Lambert could simultaneously observe that Rob was seriously ailing, yet he could find nothing wrong with him; he had no symptoms of fever or disease. Lambert told Nebo that if the curse was not lifted, food supplies to his people would be stopped. Nebo went to Rob's sick bed and told Rob that the boning had been a mistake. Lambert noted that that same evening Rob came back to full health.

But the fact that the curse can be lifted without "magic" implies that magic is not a necessary ingredient. While working at St. Thomas' Hospital in London, Professor William Sargent was confronted by a woman who told him she had been hexed. He gave her two powerful electric shocks and told her that these had been powerful enough to beat the curse. She believed him, and she recovered. Perhaps her belief in him was the road to her recovery; if so, then perhaps her original belief in the curse was her road to illness.

Such cursing and hexing might have the ring of voodoo about it; and conjure up images of drumbeats and dancing in dark nights in graveyards. But the case of Finis P. Ernest contradicts this image. Ernest and his mother had been members of a cheerful, white, middle-class family. Ernest was a successful businessman in Oklahoma but because of family disagreements Ernest's own mother put a curse on him. When he sold their business, she told him: "Do this and something dire will happen to you." Later she exclaimed: "Something will strike you." Over a period of months Ernest suffered ill health and the best endeavours of the well-equipped Veterans Hospital in Oklahoma failed to save him. Periodically he suffered asthma attacks and convulsions. He voiced feelings of futility and hopelessness. The doctors saw that there was a connection between his attacks and his visits to his mother, and they agreed to treat him only if he stayed away from her. On 23 August 1960 he had a cheerful, positive discussion with his doctor at five o'clock in the evening. He telephoned his mother at six o'clock; she reminded him of her warning of "something dire." Before seven o'clock he was dead. Dr. Mathis, one of the doctors dealing with the case, described it as a "sophisticated version of voodoo death."

Belief surely plays some part in bringing about the effectiveness of the curse. There is a condition known as "vagal inhibition," which amounts to death from fear. When faced with fear the first response is to panic; adrenaline floods the system causing a rapid increase in the heart rate, erratic behaviour and sweating. But if the victim believes that the situation is hopeless, that death is inevitable, then a reversal of this process takes place—the vagal inhibition. The heart rate slows, perhaps to a dangerous level, breathing becomes slow, blood pressure drops. Death can be quick. The victim has died of fear of the inevitable. The connection between belief and the responses of the body is strong enough to bring about a change as dramatic as death.

8

Transmitter of Ghosts and Apparitions

In the previous chapter we looked at the mind reaching into the body to meet certain needs of the individual. But can the power of the mind reach beyond the body? The evidence is that it can indeed.

Projection of Self

One fact from the field of ghost research that surprises readers more than any other is the large number of apparitions that turn out to be of people who are alive at the time of the sighting. Because of the somewhat confusing nature of these accounts they appear in literature on ghosts, telepathy, clairvoyance, and a host of other paranormal areas. The witnesses to such apparitions either do not even realise the figure was anything other than a living person until they find out the true whereabouts of the person seen; or, more frighteningly, they assume they are seeing the crisis apparition of the person at death since ghosts are so closely associated with the dead. For the latter group the realisation that this is not the case must be a considerable relief.

These reports could indicate that a person can send a projection of him- or herself to another person who can see it. Perhaps it is an act of calling to someone, sometimes unconsciously, perhaps expressing some sort of need.

The appearance of the MP Sir Frederick Carne Rasch at a debate in the House of Commons in 1905 is a classic example of the projection of self. Rasch was at home ill at the time. His colleague Sir Gilbert Parker saw him sitting in his customary seat, wished him well but received no acknowledgement. He looked away for a moment, and when he looked back found Carne Rasch had gone. Though he tried to locate him in the lobby he failed to do so and was told no one there had seen him. However, it later transpired that two other MPs, including Sir Arthur Hayter, had also seen Carne Rasch sitting in the Commons. When later told that he had been seen in the Commons, Carne Rasch confirmed that he had been very interested in the debate he knew was being held and had been keen to be there.

In many cases—perhaps even the majority of cases—the person sighted as the apparition turns out, on later questioning, to have no knowledge of the projection and cannot think of any reason why it should have arisen. Indeed, this latter point suggests at least a possibility that some of the projections are created by the sighter for their own purposes. We would suggest that sometimes when a person receives a telepathic message from another they construct a visual representation of the person so that they can more easily understand the "delivery." A typical case of projection was reported by Mr. H. W. Hill. In the winter of 1907, Hill wrote to his close friend Mr. W. Birkbeck. Feeling unwell the following day Hill did not go into his office, spending the day in his own rooms in London. At around 3.45 p.m. Hill saw Birkbeck walk past his window towards the steps leading to his front door. "Mr. Birkbeck was a man of striking appearance, who was unlikely to be mistaken for anyone else," Hill commented later. Hill reported that he had not been aware that Birkbeck was in London but made ready to receive him. After a time it became obvious that he was not going to arrive and, presumably considering the possibility of a paranormal explanation, Hill wrote again to Birkbeck asking him what he had been thinking about at that time on that day. Birkbeck replied that he was out shooting, but told his companions that he wanted to get indoors so that he could write a reply to Hill's previous letter.

In this case we know that Hill had been thinking of Birkbeck and therefore we might consider that he "created" the apparition he saw; he might even simply have mistaken a figure for that of his friend. However, there are three factors to consider: Hill's appearance was "striking" and "unlikely to be mistaken for anyone else"; he was seen actually coming to the front steps but presumably no one knocked and asked to be admitted or Hill would have followed up with other people in the building the question of who it was; and thirdly we know that Birkbeck was thinking of communicating with his friend. It could be assumed that the apparition was Birkbeck's conscious projection to the locality where Hill was; however, at that time of that day Hill should have been in his office but was in fact at home, which Birkbeck could not have known. Even this relatively simple case shows the complexity of the subject.

Another case was the projection of a boy, Colin, seen by the mother of author Ngaio Marsh. Living in New Zealand at the time, Ngaio Marsh was teaching Colin and had become very fond of him. He lived in a nearby cottage, often visiting Marsh and bringing her flowers. One morning Marsh's mother called to Ngaio that Colin was coming up the path with some geraniums for her. She even described a new jacket he was wearing. Marsh went to the door but could not see Colin and concluded that he must have changed his mind and gone home again. The following day he did arrive and told Marsh that he had wanted to come the previous day. He had his new coat on and had picked her a bunch of geraniums, but he had been "grounded" by his nanny for being naughty.

In this case we have a clearer indication that it was Colin who originated the projection, if projection is the explanation. He intended to see Marsh but his image was seen not by Marsh but by her mother. And there is evidence of knowledge only the boy could have: the type of flowers and the new coat. Also we have a clear indication of his frustration: that he wanted to see, and was presumably dressed and ready to see, Marsh when he was prevented from doing so.

In a similar case Mrs. Marion Dansie, a patient in the Middlesex Hospital in May 1936, saw a nurse enter the room and come to her bedside. She greeted her and the nurse disappeared in front of her eyes. It was later found that the nurse was off duty that day. But an important difference in this case is that Mrs. Dansie saw the nurse enter as the door was pushed open, suggesting that the projection manipulated a physical object. We must consider the alternative that Mrs. Dansie's mind rationalised that image—assumed that the door had to be opened for her to come in and thereafter remembered it that way.

We interviewed a woman, Fleur, whose bi-location—seen by herself—suggests that physical manipulation is possible. Fleur explained: "When the children were young and we had our first house in Newbury Park I was in the playroom. I was painting, or something, at the table. I looked out of the window and what I saw really frightened me. Down in the garden I could actually see myself in the garden hanging washing out at the same time as I was here in the room. It was really quite creepy. I just couldn't understand. I did feel a bit weak. I had to sit down." It seems that both "Fleurs" were doing something physical; the one in the playroom at the table, and the one in the garden hanging out washing. It is interesting that Fleur felt "weak"; perhaps the division into two "selves" diminished her strength. We are left uncertain even which one was the "real" Fleur; but we can assume that the one doing the viewing was also the one doing the thinking and was therefore where the "essence" of the woman was present. On the other hand, the one in the garden was undertaking a relatively complex set of actions, unless the washing was part of the apparition. Or perhaps projection was not the answer in this case. Perhaps it was a timeslip—a viewing into the future or past; we can assume that Fleur periodically did hang out washing.

It is the "weakness" that suggests bi-location, if we consider the famous case of the repeater bi-locator Emelie Sagée, a teacher who in 1845 was working at a girls' school in Livonia. Several times she was seen in two places at once; sometimes both in the same room and once in the classroom and sitting in a chair outside. In the latter case she was seen by her whole class of pupils. On this occasion a pupil touched the classroom image and found it somehow insubstantial, again the suggestion of a "split" of energy. On another occasion one pupil, Antonie von Wrangel, even fainted at the shock of seeing two images of the teacher together. Sagée lost her job eventually because of the concern she caused pupils; she then admitted it was the nineteenth job in sixteen years she had lost for the same reason.

We might ask why a person should bi-locate; clearly Sagée did not find it useful and it was certainly not a career move. One hint of a reason comes from the famous report of the apparent bi-location of Queen Elizabeth I. She was in bed and either asleep or unconscious with pneumonia when one of her ladies in waiting left the chamber to quickly return to her own apartments. But in walking down the corridor she saw the queen striding up towards her. The queen does not appear to have acknowledged her. The lady quickly looked away and then back again and found the apparition gone. She hurried back to the queen's bedchamber and found the queen in bed as she had left her. Was the queen's unconscious mind roaming while she was physically immobile? She is known to have had an extraordinarily strong will, which might account for that. We might of course consider the alternative: the lady in waiting was so consumed with guilt for leaving her charge at so delicate a time that her inner turmoil became manifest as the apparition of Queen Elizabeth.

The cases we have looked at so far would be categorised as doubles, or bi-locations: but there are other, even stranger, forms of such events. The first of these is the doppelgänger, a German word for double but one usually applied to a double that replicates exactly the activities of the original and is seen by the original. Consider the simple example of "Harold" from Chicago whose story was written up by Edward Podlasky, in *Fate* (April 1966) magazine. One day in 1958 Harold suffered a migraine attack as he was sitting down to eat. Opposite him he could see an exact double of himself duplicating his every actions; the figure disappeared after the meal ended.

Religious figures, or those with religious purposes, have featured in several accounts of bi-location. There are striking bi-location accounts involving Padre Pio, who is also noted for having stigmata for fifty years. In November 1917 the chief of the Italian General Staff, General Luigi Cadorna, was contemplating suicide after disastrous defeats in Slovenia. A monk appeared at his side and told him: "Don't be so stupid!" and then disappeared just as promptly. Many years later Cadorna met Padre Pio and recognised him immediately as the monk he had seen. But it was Padre Pio who first commented: "You had a lucky escape, my friend." At the time of the sighting Padre Pio was known to be in his monastery in Foggia. When questioned about his several reported bi-locations Padre Pio only replied: "Is there any doubt about it?"

Another famous case of bi-location, or projection—as there seems to have been physical involvement, even possible teleportation—was that of Sister Mary who apparently visited the Jumano Indians in New Mexico though she never left her convent in Spain. It is alleged that between 1620 and 1631 she made 500 visits to the Americas and succeeded in converting the Jumano Indians to Christianity. Although her claims were not popular with the Catholic authorities, it was the testimony of missionaries in New Mexico that gave the claims their air of reality. During his missionary work, Father Alonzo de Benavides of the Isolita Mission in New Mexico asked both the king of Spain and the Pope who it was who had gone on ahead of him to convert the New Mexico Indians. The Indians described the person as a "lady in blue" who left them many physical objects: crosses, a chalice and rosaries. The chalice came from the Spanish convent. Their stories, and those of Sister Mary, coincided exactly.

Why should this ability to project oneself be available to people? In many cases the projection seems to have been accidental and without purpose, or arising when the purpose was not urgent or demanding. Colin, seeking to visit Ngaio Marsh, might have felt it useful to project himself—though there is no evidence he was aware of the process—but there was no demanding need such as in a crisis situation. Perhaps his projection was just accidentally triggered. In other cases some purpose is evident, such as Sister Mary's missionary work.

Another type of self-projection is known as a vardoger, a double that goes on ahead of the original. One such case is that of Erikson Gorique, a New York importer. In 1955 Gorique visited Norway for the first time. The hotel clerk greeted him like an old friend, and a business contact was certain he had met him two months previously. For it to have been precognition on the part of more than one person seems unlikely; the implication was that a projection of Gorique had preceded him.

A vardoger can be a very useful "forerunner." Student Wiers Jensen at the University of Oslo often found his meal ready for him when he got back to his boardinghouse, no matter what time he arrived, because his landlady had grown accustomed to seeing his vardoger appear prior to his "real" appearance and knew when to begin the cooking. (An alternative explanation is no less paranormal: that the landlady unconsciously knew by telepathy when Wiers had started his journey and she created the vardoger as a prop for her knowledge.)

We all of us learn to deal with new situations by the process of modelling, of envisioning a future situation so that we can rehearse ways in which we might deal with challenges and take opportunities. Perhaps the projecting of oneself, particularly in the context of the vardoger, is a form of modelling.

There is a case that suggests a tragic form of modelling, or at least some form of projection, witnessed by another. It was written up in the SPR's *Report of the Census of Hallucinations* (Vol X, p. 332) and dates from 1889. A Mrs. McAlpine was sitting by the side of a lake. Then, as she reported: "My attention was quite taken up with the extreme beauty of the scene before me. There was not a sound or movement, except the soft ripple of the water on the sand at my feet. Presently I felt a cold chill creep through me, and a curious stiffness of my limbs, as if I could not move, though wishing to do so. I felt frightened, yet chained to the spot, and as if impelled to stare at the water straight in front of me. Gradually a black cloud seemed to rise, and in the midst of it I saw a tall man, in a suit of tweed, jump into the water and sink." A week later a bank clerk, Mr. Espie, committed suicide at the spot. In his farewell letter to his wife he admitted that he had been planning the suicide for some time. Did Mr. Espie, deep in thought and obviously emotional, project an image of himself to the location as part of modelling his own suicide? It seems that Mrs. McAlpine could not have known of Mr. Espie's intentions, so any projection must have been on his part (though we might have to consider telepathy or a precognitive vision).

Projection may also be the key to precognition—if projection through time is possible. There is an intriguing case of the apparition of a witch in the Lake District that could amount to this. In 1983 the *Westmoreland Gazette* reported that a railway enthusiast had photographed the ghost of an old woman standing by a railway track. There is also a local legend that a witch predicted that "carriages without horses shall run over Loups Fell." The photographer considered that he might have photographed the witch "coming" to check on her prophecy. Perhaps she projected through time to the future—the photographer's now—and he photographed her in the act of seeing her future which she made her prediction.

A case of what could be called "double projection" arose with The Reverend Spencer Nairne and Miss Wallis in 1859. It is intriguing because it appears both parties were projecting, and at least one was projecting through time, assuming projection is the correct explanation.

The Reverend and others were shortly to travel to Norway

but spent some time in Aberdeen. On the main street, in good light, one evening, The Reverend saw, approaching him, Miss Wallis whom he had known for around twenty years; she had been a governess within his family. She was walking with another man. As they drew near, they both recognised each other and he began to speak to her. But as he did so she disappeared in front of his eyes. He could not find her anywhere. Some months later The Reverend met Miss Wallis in London. He was going to ask her what had happened when she immediately said to him: "Now I have a quarrel to settle with you, Mr. Nairne. You cut me in Aberdeen a little while ago." Nairne explained what had happened and Miss Wallis told him that in fact that was exactly what had happened to her. As she had started speaking to him he had disappeared. She had at the time been walking with her brother, and The Reverend's description of the man he had seen tallied with that of her brother. They tried to examine the date that this had happened. The Reverend had been in Aberdeen on 31 May. But Miss Wallis had not been there then; she had been there in July when The Reverend was in Norway. The fact that both saw the other disappear suggests either two projections—in which case one at least was out of time—or one complex projection and timeslip where the percipient did not notice other changes of surroundings.

So far we have considered projecting as an accidental, or involuntary, process. But there are claims of those who have deliberately sought to project. The cases of Padre Pio and Sister Mary might presumably have been deliberate, though that is not clear. However, one case, reported in *Human Personality and Its Survival of Bodily Death* by Frederick Myers, was clearly in the nature of an experiment.

The report was from S. H. B. who wrote:

On a certain Sunday evening in November, 1881 . . . I determined with the whole force of my being, that I would be present in spirit in the front bedroom on the second floor of a house situated at 22

Hogarth Road, Kensington, in which room slept two ladies of my acquaintance, viz., Miss L. S. V. and Miss E. C. V., aged respectively 25 and 11 years. I was living at this time at 23 Kildare Gardens, a distance of about three miles from Hogarth Road, and I had not mentioned in any way my intention of trying this experiment to either of the above ladies. The time of which I determined I would be there was 1 o'clock in the morning, and I also had the strong intention of making my presence perceptible.

On the following Thursday I went to see the ladies in question, and in the course of my conversation (without any allusion to the subject on my part) the elder one told me that on the previous Sunday night she had been much terrified by perceiving me standing by her bedside, and that she screamed when the apparition advanced towards her, and awoke her little sister, who saw me also.

I asked her if she was awake at the time, and she replied most decidedly in the affirmative, and upon my enquiring the time of the occurrence, she replied, about 1 o'clock in the morning.

This lady, at my request, wrote down a statement of the event and signed it.... Besides exercising my power of volition very strongly, I put forth an effort which I cannot find words to describe. I was conscious of a mysterious influence of some sort permeating in my body, and I had a distinct impression that I was exercising some force with which I had been hitherto unacquainted about which I can now at certain times set in motion at will.

Both women mentioned confirmed the sightings and that they could distinguish him clearly.

If projection can be done deliberately, how is it done?

Some thought-provoking work was done in laboratory conditions by psychiatrist Morton Schatzman who in 1980 reported on his work with a subject "Ruth." She could produce and control projections of her father, and other people, and in some cases these projections could even be seen by others. Her body responded as if actually seeing the person. During one test she claimed that she could see the figure of her daughter sitting on her lap. Neurophysiologist Peter Fenwick indicated that her brain "behaved in the same way it would have if your daughter had actually been sitting on your lap." Ruth also managed to produce an apparition of herself. She claimed: "It took about two hours of continuous trying to produce an apparition of myself. It was so hard. At first I couldn't see her but for a moment or two at a time. Finally I did learn to do it. I decided to experiment and play some games. I had the apparition sit across the room from me. I felt I was looking at someone who knew more about me than I knew about myself. I watched it closely. I tried to see if it was breathing, but I couldn't tell. The eyes fascinated me. Could I be looking through them into myself? A calm seemed to flow between us, from one to the other. It was very tiring and before long I had to take a nap."

Crisis Apparitions

Projection may also explain a phenomenon known as a crisis apparition. These are often thought to represent the ghosts of the dying, perhaps reaching out for the last time to their closest friends or relatives to say goodbye.

Here is a very straight-forward example of the genre: Professor Sir Charles Frank, a professor of physics at the University of Bristol, told the story of his wife's Finnish grandmother who woke to see her half-brother standing by her bed saying: "I have come to say goodbye." She told her husband what had happened and later discovered that her half-brother had committed suicide at the moment she had seen his apparition.

There is also the sighting of the apparition of cricketer Douglas Jardine. On 19 June 1958 a friend of Jardine's, Col D. Pritchard, was in the pavilion bar at Lords when he saw Jardine at the end of the bar. Jardine was, according to Pritchard, "most distinctive looking and impossible to mistake." Having caught each other's eye they raised a glass to each other. Soon after this, just before the start of play that day, it was announced over the loudspeaker that Jardine had died the day before, in Switzerland.

There are many accounts of crisis apparitions, and often the sighting occurs before the death is known, so there seems little doubt that some paranormal mechanism is at play here. But precisely what mechanism is open to question. Does the dying person, having left the physical body either in an OOBE or NDE or permanently in death, go to a friend or relative? Or does the dying person send only a telepathic message, and the receiver creates an image—a vision—through which to "receive" the message? Or does the dying person play no part at all: could the so-called recipient be the psychic one who picks up the death or distress and creates the whole image as a part of their experience?

In 1886 Edmund Gurney, Frederick Myers and Frank Podmore published *Phantasms of the Living*, which was an examination of apparitions and telepathy. Their tentative conclusion of the 701 recorded cases was that they represented a telepathic cry for help or recognition. Parapsychologist Professor Erlendur Haraldsson also supports this belief on the basis that people who made crisis apparitions often died violently and suddenly. He stated: "This finding gives considerable support to Myers' theory and the popular belief that the apparition of the dead person played an active role in the encounter."

On 3 January 1856 Mrs. Collier saw her son, Joseph, standing in her bedroom looking at her, although she knew he should be a thousand miles away on a riverboat. It was a frightening sight: his disfigured face and head were wrapped in a bandage. It was two weeks later that she heard he had been killed in an accident at the time she had seen him. The description given matched the image she had seen. However, one case of crisis apparition seems to suggest that the person seen had little part in generating the image, simply because the information imparted was completely wrong. It happened on 7 December 1918 when Lt.

David M'Connel was flying from Scampton in Lincolnshire to Tadcaster sixty miles to the north. He encountered fog and crashed and died just short of his destination. His watch had stopped at 3.25 p.m., presumably the time of the crash and of his death. At around that time, at Scampton, Lt James Larkin saw M'Connel standing in a doorway. He greeted Larkin with his customary "Hallo boy." Then M'Connel went on to tell Larkin that he had successfully completed the flight. "Got there all right. Had a good trip." (Which he patently had not!) One guess would be that Larkin felt something that caused him concern over his friend but that it was so unspecific he "created" the wrong message; the alternative is that M'Connel was very confused indeed.

The following case offers, if not answers, then another variation on the theme:

Armistice Day—11 November 1918—was cause for widespread celebration. Harold Owen was aboard HMS *Astraea* anchored in Table Bay but could not feel part of the high spirits. He said: "I could not enter into any spirit of gaiety. I felt horribly flat. Everything else seemed flat." It seems that he was worried about his brother Wilfred who was fighting on the Western Front. For some days Harold remained in low spirits. Then, while in his cabin, he saw Wilfred sitting in a chair though he knew it was not possible for him to be there. Although Wilfred never spoke, Harold was greatly comforted by the vision, which abruptly disappeared. But Harold was certain that he knew what it meant. "What I found impossible to explain was this self-existent awareness of mine, unrelated to any facts; I did not try. I accepted his death completely without hope and without pretence. My awareness was so profound that knowledge could not be denied," stated Harold. It later transpired that Wilfred had been killed on 4 November though news did not reach the family for some days. During those few days, however, Harold had been feeling depressed, and associated it with concern for his brother. We might consider that he had felt something that was part of, and a forerunner to, the crisis apparition.

Here is another interesting case:

While driving home to Val Di Pennes in the Tyrol on 4 May 1980, Johann Hofer was killed in a mountain tunnel by a rockfall. A witness to the incident who himself was nearly killed was able to pinpoint the time of the accident—and almost certainly the time of death—at around 11.30 p.m. Hofer had left his fiancée, Christine, and her sister at their pizzeria; they had seen him drive off at 11.05 p.m. But at 11.30 p.m. the sisters again saw Johann, in the same car in which he died, a grey Audi, drive slowly past the pizzeria and wave to them both. Hilda, the sister, clearly recognised the distinctive car markings and recognised his mannerisms as he waved; the two assumed he had not yet left town. The sisters were not the only ones to see Johann's apparition. Johann and Christine had a child who was at that time with Christine's mother. At around 11.30 p.m., and not of course knowing of Johann's death, Christine's mother persisted in feeling that someone was walking around in the bedroom; indeed, she could hear footsteps for several minutes. It was her instinct that there had been a family tragedy. Also at around the same time Johann's father thought that he heard his son's car arrive home; he recognised both the car's distinctive engine sound and the sound of a manoeuvre that was necessary to get into the house's parking space. "Knowing" that his son was now home he went back to sleep. It was in the morning, when Johann's father found that he was not home after all, that he started investigating and heard about the collapse in the tunnel. Suddenly he was sure that his son had died there. Curiously, although the tunnel collapse was over eighty yards of road, the father pinpointed to within a yard where the car was buried under the rubble. Indeed, workmen at the sight were not at that time convinced there was anybody in the rubble at all; the witness to the crash had not yet come forward. Johann's father persuaded them to excavate and they found the car with Johann's body still in it.

We might consider that the "presences" heard by Johann's father and Christine's mother could be subjective, but the sighting by Christine and her sister seems very specific. Furthermore, it has been calculated that there was no possibility that Johann could have changed his mind, driven back and waved to the pair of them, and then reached the tunnel in time for the collapse of the roof.

The uniqueness of the case is two-fold. Firstly, Johann seems to have manifested to several witnesses and not just one as if often the case with crisis apparitions—he seems to have visited three people at more or less the same time; secondly, he seems to have "taken" his distinctive car to at least two of the locations, one where it was clearly seen in good lighting conditions. Odd as that fact may seem, ghost literature is full of ghostly carriages and cars, and most ghosts are clothed, which is presumably the manifestation of inanimate objects.

If only the recipients of the messages are responsible in apparition cases, it was a remarkable coincidence that three people "created" manifestations of Johann; so much so that it seems inevitable that Johann is the common factor and must be the source of the "signal." There must have been a "transmission" from Johann to others. As to whether or not he "designed" the manifestations or whether he merely transmitted a "goodbye" message that the others picked up and perceived in their own ways, we can be less sure. The car features in two accounts. Perhaps the recipients both associated him strongly with his car, but then perhaps he associated himself personally with his car also and it was "part of him" in his mind. The footsteps in the bedroom do not suggest that he interacted with his child, which we might have thought he would, but quite what he might have been doing is also unclear; perhaps he was in communion with the child while he was pacing.

The evidence seems strong that at least some part of the crisis apparition comes from the person in distress at or near the point of death. But it does not have to be after death; even in the case of Johann, he might have lived for a few minutes during which time he "transmitted" the presences of himself. If so, we might consider that emotion is the strongest force for this ability. Johann "manifested" to his fiancée and his family, the seats of his emotion.

Another case that suggests emotion—guilt in this case—is offered by the death of Admiral Sir George Tryon. On 22 June 1893 his wife, Lady Tryon, was entertaining guests at their house in Eaton Square while the Admiral was on manoeuvres in the Mediterranean. Several guests saw the Admiral walk into the drawing room without acknowledging them and thought it rather rude, although they were surprised to see him. They did not of course know his actual circumstances at that time. At the moment of this sighting he had just died in a naval disaster of which his last words were reported as "It's all my fault."

Guardian Angels

The crisis apparition is said to be the manifestation of someone near the moment of their crisis or death. But there are also many cases of manifestations that appear at the time of crisis for the sighter. They are often referred to as guardian angels, but as we shall see there is—as often with the paranormal—a considerable overlap between these apparitions and ghosts. More to the point, there is a strong possibility that these manifestations represent mind power: an ability of the mind to call for help, construct a response and actually solve a problem.

That we refer to these "beings" as guardian angels may itself be telling us something. For some reason there is a growing acceptance of the idea that individuals have a personal guardian angel that watches over their lives and aids them in times of trouble, protects them in times of danger and guides them in times of uncertainty. This view of angels, originating largely in the USA, is far from the winged images of religious paintings. These modern angels are either unseen or look exactly like humans, but they perform benign acts. Think of the image of Clarence in the film *It's a Wonderful Life*, which was re-released to the cinema in 1998.

There are many reasons for this twentieth-century emergence of the belief in guardian angels, but one predominates. While conventional religions seem to have failed to meet many people's needs, the increase in interest in the paranormal seems to suggest that people believe in, and hanker after, more than the materialistic worldview offered by science. People need religion and all it embodies, even if they reject the formal religions or the approaches of the established Churches. The guardian angel is a concept that bridges personal needs and religion, and allows people to modify religious beliefs to suit themselves.

Sometimes their purpose seems clear enough. Air Chief Marshal Lord Dowding—a firm believer in the paranormal—believed that during the Battle of Britain angels took over flying the planes when pilots were dead or incapacitated.

Guardian angels seem to be a comfort for some, without their nature or actions being too specific. The explorer Ernest Shackleton once reported that he was accompanied by "another person" during an expedition. A companion with him also felt the same presence. In *Fate* magazine in March 1967 an article about three men who escaped from prison and were fleeing over several hundred miles comments that all three of the men felt they were accompanied by a fourth person, yet they did not discover their mutual feelings until they spoke together about it afterwards.

The fact that more than one person has similar feelings suggests something "external" to the people involved. Whether it is a protective ghost, a guardian angel or some mental projection of one or more of the group, is unclear. It needs to be more than mere imagination for it to be shared, but one powerful personality in the group may well be able to project insubstantial images to other members of the group.

In other cases the percipient of the guardian angel believes that they have been protected by specific actions. The pilot Edith Foltz-Steams, in the 1920s, believed that she was being watched over and protected. "Some 'presence' sits beside me, my 'co-pilot' as I have come to think of it. In times of great danger some unseen hand actually takes the controls and guides me to safety."

But we might find a clue as to where the angel comes from in the fact that Foltz-Steams reported several angels in her life, including her deceased father (whom she once credited with saving her from flying into a mountain) and deceased school friend (whom she credited with warning her to avoid a dangerous landing). Perhaps we are entitled to consider that she might be creating the angels from her subconscious and using them to influence her conscious mind. This is akin to channelling. Why then a variety of persona? If she was being guided by deceased spirits, presumably we can argue that a particular one happened to be "around" that day, but this seems too simplistic at best. More likely, if the channelling is from one part of her brain to another with the purpose of presenting "rational" proof to the rational side of the brain, then Ms. Foltz-Steams simply "created" the most appropriate person for the situation. A friend who would act as a neutral advisor and a father who might demand more immediate response as an authority figure.

The validity of this argument is supported by the experience of the French writer Guy de Maupassant. In 1885 he was suffering from writer's block while working on his horror story *The Horla*; then a figure entered the room. Sitting down opposite him, the figure dictated sections for use in the story. De Maupassant was concerned because someone had been able to enter his rooms without his knowing and, perhaps even more so, because the figure knew a great deal about the fiction he was writing. Then he realised who the figure was: himself. A double of himself was breaking him free of the frustration of writer's block. This case has tended to get into the literature as an example of "doubles and bi-locations" but if the figure had been of someone else, perhaps a deceased friend, might it not have been thought of as a helpful ghost? Had it been a shimmering white figure—perhaps even with wings—it would probably have been listed as an angel sighting. Writers tend to pigeon-hole these sightings according to a best guess based on description, but perhaps the process is the same whatever the appearance of the manifestation. The figure was himself; but did de Maupassant "construct" the figure in one part of his mind in order to communicate with the other? And who else could credibly advise on a work of fiction held only in the writer's mind but the writer himself? This case shows, then, the overlap between many of the areas we have looked at in this book, and how they all can possibly demonstrate mind powers.

Ms. Foltz-Steams' claims of such protective guardianship are not alone. Just as she was leading the way in the new technology of aircraft and flying, so Donald Campbell led the way in chasing the land- and water-speed records. He, too, believed that he was similarly protected by his deceased father. After a fraught and dangerous run with his Bluebird car in 1964, while waiting for the turn-around into the second run—and during a deeply frustrating bid for the world land-speed record—he had a vision of his father in the cockpit. Campbell's experience was recorded in *Bluebird and the Dead Lake* by John Pearson:

> Something did happen. It was the most incredible thing I've ever experienced. You know what happened on that first run? I nearly killed myself. I was so near going out of control that it wasn't funny, and when I was sitting in the cockpit at the end of the run I really thought I had had it. For I knew the second run would be worse, I saw no hope at all. It was then that it was so extraordinary. You know how the canopy lifts up with the windscreen in front of the cockpit? Well, I suddenly looked up into it and there was my father reflected in the windscreen as clearly as you are sitting there now. I even recognised the white shirt and flannels he used to wear. For a few seconds he just looked at me, smiling. Then he said: "Don't worry, it will be all right, boy." Then he faded away.

Campbell went on to gain the record on that second run. But

had the image come to him from his own mind, a mind that was in real turmoil? The record of that bid shows that Campbell spent months suffering from weather problems, track disintegrations, and internal politics within the team. Did he reach out for help? Again, this sighting has no clear identification: ghost of his father? angel masquerading as his father as Edith Foltz-Steams believed her guardian did? projection from his own subconscious? If the latter then it was a manifestation of mind power, a complex self-help device.

Campbell also believed that on at least two other occasions his father was with him in the cockpit of the Bluebird boat during bids for the world water-speed record. (But Campbell's guardian was not totally protective—Campbell was killed in the boat during a bid for the water-speed record in 1967.)

As we began to consider in the cases of Guy de Maupassant, Donald Campbell and Edith Foltz-Steams, there is an overlap between claims of angels and claims of ghosts. What would usually be regarded as ghost sightings in Europe seem to be more recently interpreted in the USA as guardian angel cases. Take for example Billy Graham's reference in his book *Angels: God's Secret Angels* to a claim that the image of a woman's dead daughter sought out a doctor to help the mother in a time of need. Graham asks: "Could the doctor have been called in the hour of desperate need by an angel who appeared as this woman's young daughter?" Ghost of the dead or angel taking the shape for a purpose? Let us look at a few, admittedly speculative, possibilities. If the mother constructed the form as a projection of her need and "sent it" to the doctor she might well have found it easier to create an image she could depend on, and might well have created the daughter. If the doctor "received" some kind of telepathic cry for help and constructed an image that he found easy to relate to, why construct the image of someone dead, which from his point of view would only serve to further confuse if he knew she was dead, and would serve no purpose at all if he did not know her? If an angel actually did undertake this mission, then, while it might well be advisable for the angel to appear to the mother as the daughter, why maintain that shape for the doctor? On the other hand, the fact remains that the doctor did indeed get the right message, so the mechanism, whatever it was, worked.

Ms. Polly Hayes reported an incident of ghostly protection when driving in the outside lane of the M6 motorway. She smelt her mother's perfume and believed she was being strongly urged to get into the left-hand lane, which she did. Seconds later a front tyre on her car exploded and the car veered into the hard shoulder. Polly was certain that had she not moved over prior to the tyre explosion she could well have been killed. Did her mother— who had died eight years previously—really assist her from the "other side of the veil"? Did an angel create an impression of her dead mother? Or did Polly create an elaborate theatre drama to force her, or at least strongly suggest to her own mind, to do what she knew she had to do? If so then the sequence of paranormal abilities would seem to be first a premonition or prescient vision of an incident about to happen, then a struggle within the intuitive mind as to how to convince the rational mind, and finally the construction of a "believable" scenario that would force Polly to take action.

A relevant case is reported by Kelsey Tyler, in her book *There's an Angel on Your Shoulder*. She describes it as an angel encounter— that an angel took the form of a child to get help from a passing motorist—but it would certainly fall into the category of crisis apparition given the criteria mentioned earlier. Dr. Mike Barns was driving across the Arizona desert towards Lake Tahoe when he saw a small boy standing at the side of the road. There was no sign of a vehicle anywhere. The figure, dressed in a scout uniform and wearing a red baseball cap, was waving frantically in an obvious attempt to get Barns to stop. He pulled his car over. The boy was obviously alarmed, and pleaded: "Sir, I need a ride. Right away. Please . . ." The boy got in and directed Barns along the road and then off down a small dirt track, then up a mountain road. They drove together for several miles, the boy still anxious. Near the mountaintop Barns heard the faint sounds of screaming in the distance, which alarmed him. Eventually the boy told him to stop, and he pointed over the edge of an unfenced section of the mountain road. Down in the canyon below was a yellow school bus that had crashed off the road; the sounds of the injured were now all too clear. Barns used his mobile phone to call for medical help, then left the boy by his car while he clambered down to begin applying his medical skills to help as much as he could. Barns and teams of paramedics who arrived on the scene removed the injured children to safety. The last search of the bus found only one child who had died in the crash, his neck broken. A small child in a scout uniform and a red baseball cap.

In this case Barns could not presumably have "constructed" the image from his own mind; he did not know the child. Indeed, it seems in this case that the only people who could have "created" the image were the child himself or his friends on the bus. The two cases—Barns and the mother/daughter case—seem very similar but are perhaps only superficially so, and may relate to quite different processes.

In fact the processes described in this chapter overlap more than probably any other sections of this book. Perhaps the terms used are little more than convenient pigeon holes; perhaps this chapter has been describing just one ability—projection—that can manifest in many ways.

What we can be sure of is that if these two cases happened as they have been described, they both may represent the mind's most extraordinary ability to cry for help when survival is threatened, or other needs are strong.

In the last chapter we shall examine the extraordinary evidence that the mind can do more than project images and information—it can manipulate the physical world by sheer force of will.

9

Transmitter of Power

In the preceding two chapters we have seen how the mind can transmit power to the body and beyond to create images witnessed by the world at large. But there is also evidence to suggest the mind is capable of transmitting a powerful energy that can directly affect the physical world of matter. The first evidence we shall examine is the phenomenon most people generally refer to as ghosts or hauntings.

Poltergeists: Noisy Ghosts or Unquiet Minds?

The poltergeist phenomenon has a history that is at least 2,000 years old. The poltergeist—"noisy ghost" as it is often translated from the German—is the original "thing that goes bump in the night." The translation may not be an appropriate one; noisy barely describes the wide range of phenomena that has been reported. Fires, gushes of water, strange noises and the flights of everyday objects have all been reported. And "ghost" may not be an appropriate title either: as this section will show there is good evidence that at least some poltergeists are the product of the witness's own mind.

Crumbling, dark old houses are not the exclusive domain of poltergeists. They have inhabited modern houses and tower blocks, brightly lit offices, factories and schools. Poltergeist events sometimes last for several months, persistent ones even a few years and the events are often witnessed by large numbers of people over a long period of time.

A striking case arose in Scotland in the 1960s. When we interviewed a schoolteacher who had witnessed several of the poltergeist manifestations thirty-plus years later, it was obvious that the impression left by the events was going to stay with her all her life.

Eleven-year-old Virginia Campbell had, in 1960, moved from Ireland to Sauchie, a small Scottish village, where she attended Sauchie Primary School. She had moved with her mother, leaving her father in Ireland. She was a shy girl but made friends and seemed to be settling down. Stress may be a factor in the poltergeist phenomenon. In Virginia's case, leaving her father and her home behind and, as it turned out, having to share a bedroom and even a bed with a relative, must have been traumatic and stressful.

Within a short period poltergeist activity broke out around Virginia. As the local paper reported: "Just over a week ago strange things began to happen to Virginia. Heavy pieces of furniture were seen to move when she entered a room, doors opened when she approached them and then were found difficult to shut." Hearing of the case, Dr. A. R. G. Owen, a Fellow at Trinity College, Cambridge, investigated the reports as they were happening. He was also able to talk to other people who had seen the effects. These included The Reverend T. Lund, a minister of the Church of Scotland; Dr. W. H. Nisbet, a physician; Dr. Logan, also a physician; Dr. Logan's wife, herself a physician; and Miss Margaret Stewart, a teacher at Sauchie Primary School.

Dr. Owen was to conclude: "It will be seen from the diary of the main events that the five witnesses believed themselves to have heard certain sounds and seen certain movements of objects. It is just possible in principle to suppose that one person could be the victim of illusion or hallucination. It is, however, beyond all possibility that five responsible persons should be so deceived at various occasions over a period of two weeks. Thus we must conclude that they heard actual noises and saw actual motions of real objects."

The first manifestation reported had been on 22 November, a banging noise in Virginia's house described as similar to the sound of a bouncing ball. The most common starting point for poltergeists seems to be with sounds, as if the power of the poltergeist needs to "build up." The following day there were spontaneous movements of furniture and noises around the head of the bed that Virginia slept in with her niece Margaret.

Malcolm Robinson, local investigator for Strange Phenomena Investigations and its magazine *Enigma*, reported the account of one witness:

> I was in Virginia's bedroom with a number of other individuals. I was standing close to the bed, in which Virginia was lying, she had the covers up to her chin. Suddenly I observed the covers making a "rippling movement" from the bottom of the bed up to Virginia's chin.... Seconds later, I then observed the pillow next to Virginia which had been plumped up, suddenly take what appeared to be the shape of a person's head. A clear indentation of the pillow was seen by myself and others in the room. Now during this time, strange "knockings, bangings, and scratchings, and what sounded like sawing noises" were coming from all over the room. You couldn't really pinpoint the exact source of the noise, it was coming from everywhere! Most unusual was the sound... like "a ping pong ball" constantly being bounced.

The Reverend Lund and Dr. Nisbet, who visited the house, both witnessed manifestations. An attempt to quieten the poltergeist by performing a religious service did not succeed. Religious services rarely work, and often exacerbate the problem. Virginia was sedated to try to quieten her, but it did not stop the manifestations.

When Virginia went to stay at another house in a nearby

town, Dollar, the manifestations happened there, and again they were witnessed, in this case by her doctor and others.

The manifestations were not restricted to the night or the bedroom. They followed Virginia to school where they were witnessed by her class and the teacher, Miss Stewart, whom we interviewed in 1994. The following is taken from our interview with Miss Stewart and that given to Malcolm Robinson:

> The first time I became aware of something strange was when I had given the class an essay to do. The class was quiet, and all the children had their heads down bent over their jotters busily writing away. In 1960 we still had the old school desk which had a lid top. Anyway, I looked over at Virginia, and noticed she was sitting with both hands pressed firmly down on top of her desk lid. I rose from my chair and walked over to Virginia. I was then surprised to see the desk lid rise and fall with Virginia trying her best to keep the lid shut with her hands.

However, when the child in front of Virginia got up from her place and walked towards Miss Stewart's desk, the child's desk, as Miss Stewart described it, "'rose' a few inches off the floor." Miss Stewart was aware of the possibility that children might be fooling around and immediately checked the desk, although she was fairly certain it was not trickery. She could see no sign of ropes or other ways the children could have lifted the desk.

> The most unnerving thing that I experienced in the classroom was on one occasion I was sitting behind my large oak table, Virginia was standing on the other side...with her hands clasped firmly behind her back. Suddenly a large blackboard pointer cane, which was lying flat on my table, started to "vibrate." At first it was vibrating slowly, then increased as the seconds wore on. I sat transfixed looking at this. Then the table, which was quite a heavy one, started to rise up very slowly into the air and also vibrate. I put my hands on the table and tried to push it back

down but with no success. I was quite horrified. But it did not stop there, the table continued to vibrate as it hovered a few inches off the floor. Then the table rotated ninety degrees, so that where I had moments before sat behind the long edge of the table, the table had rotated so that its narrow edge was now directly in front of my stomach. I looked up at Virginia, and saw she was quite distressed, and I remember her saying "Please Miss, I'm not doing that, honest I'm not." I calmed her down.

There were other, later manifestations witnessed by Miss Stewart and the whole class.

Over the time the poltergeist was in evidence reports included the following: levitations of fruit; spontaneous movement of small objects; and several bed movements; and even attacks, mainly the girls having their legs pinched from no obvious source.

Miss Stewart may not have known what a poltergeist was but she not only took a very positive lead in calming her class, she also recognised immediately that the manifestations seemed to relate very directly to Virginia. She told us: "I explained to the children that sometimes people are ill and don't know what's wrong with them. That doesn't necessarily mean there is anything really odd or strange. And I explained that something like that was happening to Virginia."

Miss Stewart noticed a very direct link to Virginia and one that suggests this poltergeist at least was internally generated by her rather than "attacking her" from outside. The events, she noticed, were most active over a twenty-eight-day cycle. "I didn't actually notice it to start with. It was only when I checked back, after the event, that I noticed it was following a pattern. It started off and became fairly violent. Then it plateaued and disappeared and then came back again. And it seemed to be following almost a twenty-eight-day cycle." Dr. Owen took note of that observation: "Miss Stewart took especial care to record the date, as she found it noteworthy that the time interval between this event and the earlier one was fifty-six days ... a very suggestive figure, if the phenomena are related to physiological happenings associated with a quasi-menstrual cycle occuring as a result of exceptionally rapid pubescence." In fact, for Virginia, "puberty in the full sense [had] not arrived but she [was] going through a very rapid pubescence."

Owen's assessment summarised the views of several witnesses: "The happenings seem to The Reverend Lund as being, on balance, more consistent with the functioning of a force or forces originating in Virginia than with the operation of a discarnate entity. Dr. Logan and Miss Stewart, independently of one another and of Mr. Lund, both very definitely put forward the same interpretation. On the evidence this finding is much to be preferred to any other."

So we have a well-witnessed case that seems to point to an adolescent going through many stressful changes at once: imminent menstruation; separation from her father; change of lifestyle, school and friends. And a poltergeist that manifests at the peaks of the menstrual cycle. While not fully ruling out an "entity" or "spirit" attacking Virginia, as many people believe poltergeists to be, the more likely explanation is that the poltergeist was an outward expression of Virginia's inner struggles.

A similar explanation might be offered for a quite different poltergeist that arose several years after Virginia's, in 1967, and on the other side of the world, in Miami. It was 14 January 1967 when the manager of Tropication Arts Incorporated, a novelties and souvenirs wholesalers in Miami, Florida, called the police, asking for help. His belief was that a ghost was causing havoc in his premises. Items were strangely falling from shelves, often witnessed by up to fifteen people. When the police came, they too witnessed manifestations, one getting hit by an object. As in Sauchie, the manifestations were studied by researchers as they happened. Ghost researcher Suzy Smith, William Roll, the project director of the Psychical Research

Foundation in North Carolina, and his colleague J. Gaither Pratt from the medical department of the University of Virginia all examined the case. The many witnesses and researchers, law enforcement officers and media who visited the premises all saw manifestations. Most were convinced that fraud was out of the question. On just one day alone Roll recorded twenty-eight incidents and was himself witness to thirteen of them. He was, he said, "In a position to satisfy myself that no one could have caused the occurrence by simple trickery."

A typical incident was seen by a sales representative, Larry Wolfe. "Around 12.30 on Monday I was standing by the order desk.... I heard a glass crash behind me and found a jigger had been broken. In rapid succession after that a Coke bottle crashed to the floor. Then another shot glass hit in the middle aisle... and then a shot glass fell in the third aisle. Moments later another bottle broke in aisle four and then one of those carved coconuts...landed in aisle two. Almost immediately after that an old cowbell they used to keep on the back door for delivery men to ring clanged down in that last aisle that seemed to be its favourite playground....I knew that something was happening in which humans were not involved."

Because the poltergeist seemed to target specific objects more than once, the investigators were able to set up target objects and they got positive results. Smith put a Coca-Cola bottle on a shelf and controlled the area to be sure that no one got near it; nevertheless it flew off the shelf. Roll said of the case: "It was the best chance I've ever had to observe the breakages and movements of objects by some unexplained force.... In Miami I was able to observe with my own eyes numerous instances of movement of objects and check for the possibility of fraud or accident. Neither existed."

But as in Sauchie, and as in poltergeist cases the world over, it was possible to identify one person who was the centre of the activity. A nineteen-year-old Cuban refugee, Julio Vasquez, who worked at the premises, did not like his boss. The phenomenon arose only on days when he was at work. Researchers studied him and determined that he did indeed seem to be the centre of the activity though he was not causing the manifestations by trickery or other normal means. Although Vasquez did not admit to causing the incidents he did admit that he was pleased when they happened. It turned out that there had been manifestations at his home some time earlier, and when he was taken by the investigators to their own laboratories there were manifestations there also. Vasquez was fired, and the poltergeist activity at Tropication stopped.

At the laboratory the researchers kept an even closer eye on Vasquez, yet manifestations continued. Roll said of one incident: "There was no way in which the four young men and I [those who were watching him] could see how he could have caused the incident fraudulently."

So again we have a central figure in the poltergeist event. In this case we can see that the poltergeist is doing what Vasquez either would like to do or is at least pleased is happening; it is breaking things in a premises where he does not like his boss. Vasquez's history is one of struggle and stress, factors that seem to arise in those at the centre of poltergeist activity.

Nor are such workplace-related poltergeists rare. In a case in Cardiff the first manifestations—witnessed by many people working and visiting the premises—arose when the owner was stressed by cashflow and money problems. In that instance, money was often found to have spontaneously appeared as if caused by the poltergeist. We know of at least two other cases where incidents have arisen at workplaces around one central figure who was unhappy about the work, as in Vasquez's case.

Consider the poltergeist that, in 1973, "invaded" the work premises of a small garden shop in Bromley, owned by Alf Taylor and Tony Elms. It was investigated by the SPR's Manfred Cassirer, with his colleague Pauline Runnalls. The first manifestation noted happened on 26 April 1973; Alf Taylor arrived at the shop to find Tony Elms in a state of agitation. Some kind of powder was hitting the ceiling, a jug flew off a shelf, pellets of fertiliser were flying up out of a bin against the ceiling. Even customers were being hit. The poltergeist, which seemed to be centred on Elms, was also frightening enough to the men to cause them to abandon the shop for a time. Cassirer noted: "There had been a quite disturbing incident in which Mr. Taylor had been hit on the head by a box of trowels and forks, while Mr. Elms had fared even worse and was in fact a rather frequent target of spiritual spite."

In the fertiliser there were the impressions of hands scooping up the material. On another occasion the fertiliser on a worktop formed "communications" in the shape of a date (1659). At one point the image of a skull-like face appeared in the fertiliser.

The victims of this particular poltergeist were certainly not adolescents: Elms was fifty and his colleague older. These cases, and others, suggest that the poltergeist does not just target people but is generated by them. Take for example the case of a woman reported in the book *Deliverance*, edited by Michael Perry. The poltergeist in her home destroyed one of each pair of ornaments around the house. Research showed that the woman had just had a mastectomy, the removal of one breast. The cancer was not eliminated and she had to have the second breast removed; the poltergeist continued but after that much more randomly. Eventually the woman came to terms with her illness and the changes to her body; and the poltergeist faded. There seems to be little reason to imagine that an entity would make an attack so specifically and obviously related to the woman's most urgent and stressful preoccupation of the time. It is surely more reasonable to assume that the poltergeist was the projection of her inner stresses.

It is notable that poltergeist events are frequently reported in the bedroom and in bed. This could be explained by the fact that the periods between sleep and wakefulness are probably when the "paranormal centres" of the brain are most receptive or active. But perhaps it also reflects the witness's personal involvement in the poltergeists; after all, the bed is perhaps the single most personal place in the home. In the Sauchie case there seemed to be a direct relationship between Virginia and the bed and bedroom, with many manifestations there. In a case in Amherst in Nova Scotia the witness's pillow was seen to move spontaneously and threatening writing appeared on her bedroom well. In Poona, in India, the witness's pillow moved, "gently lifted from its place at the head of my bed . . . and was placed by an invisible hand at the foot of my bed." In the case of Robert Mannheim, which is covered in more detail in the section on possession (see pages 192–94) but which started with poltergeist activity, the bed and bedcovers were disrupted over a long period of time. In 1972 in Daly City, California, a woman found a pillow pressed into her face, and her baby's crib also came under attack. There are several cases of "ghostly attacks" in beds that might or might not have a relationship to poltergeist activity.

So the bedroom might be a clue as to the personal nature of the phenomenon. And if it is that personal, we must assume it is also serving a purpose. We have argued throughout this book that if these manifestations are generated by the mind, then the mind learns to do these things because it serves a purpose. We believe purpose was evident in one case we studied over a long period of time.

In the Hertfordshire case there were no adolescents involved; just two middle-aged people living together. The couple suffered three years of poltergeist activity, which stopped only when— and exactly when—one of them died. The poltergeist activity got worse for each of them whenever only one was in the house. Arguably, the couple might have been somewhat insecure at the subconscious level; the poltergeist served to keep them closer together. Although not particularly enthused by the suggestion, the surviving partner admitted that it was a possibility.

So we can dismiss the usual suggestion that adolescents alone suffer from poltergeists; nonetheless, we can identify some possibilities that would help to explain why such a large number of adolescents are central figures in the poltergeist phenomenon.

The contributing factor, we believe, is frustration. Poltergeists seem to arise at times when people are frustrated and when there is no obvious release for that frustration, i.e. no one to blame or who can change their situation for them. Adolescents are at a point in life that is probably the most frustrating of all—not young enough to be childish, but when trying to be adult not taken seriously by adults who think of them as children; able to make their own decisions, and desiring to do so, but not legally allowed to implement them without permission of others such as parents. And at the same time the body is physically changing. It is possible that the imbalanced hormones play their part in generating these "exteriorisations"; many cases, such as the case of Virginia and the Amherst case mentioned earlier, arise around the onset of menstruation.

But of the non-adolescents we have studied, frustration is also apparent: workplace-related frustrations, lifestyle frustrations between couples, frustrations caused by unemployment.

There can be a no more personal and private aspect for an individual than their sexual drive. Researcher Nandor Fodor first suggested a connection between sex and poltergeists, which also offered an explanation for the large number of poltergeist reports among those at puberty—when sexual urges are beginning to flourish—and monks who with vows of celibacy have to channel their sexual energy elsewhere. Indeed, according to some Eastern philosophies, a vow of celibacy allows sexual energy to be channelled into a more positive, spiritual form. Some witches in the West believe that by holding back their orgasms they acquire extra power. Hereward Carrington in *The Story of Psychic Science* stated: "An energy seems to be radiated from the body . . . which induces the phenomena, when the sexual energies are blossoming into maturity within the body. It would almost seem as though these energies, instead of taking their normal course, were somehow turned into another channel, at such times, and were externalised beyond the limits of the body—producing the manifestations in question. The spontaneous outburst of these phenomena seems to be associated with the awakening of the sex-energies at that time, which finds this curious method of externalisation."

Sexual frustrations were identified very obviously in one case. It was reported to us by medium Jenny Bright, and her partner Dr. David Cross. A man living alone was hearing loud banging noises and noted the spontaneous movement of some objects. Interviews with the man uncovered the fact that he had just ended a long-term, highly passionate and active sexual relationship. It was suggested to him that these manifestations would end when he found a new partner, but that in the meantime channelling his energies through some conventional means such as sports might rid him of the poltergeist, which it did.

There are other indications of the personal nature of poltergeists in the physiological responses of some witnesses. In one case in Pontefract when the poltergeist was active the children of the family always had stomach pains. In another case in Enfield, the mother and daughter (who was the focus) often got headaches just prior to a manifestation. During the exteriorisation debate between Jung and Freud, mentioned in the following section on psychokinesis, Jung felt a pain in his diaphragm just prior to the incident. It seems likely that these are the body's signs that it is gearing up to do something, the something being the manifestation.

The conclusion is that at least some poltergeists, and some poltergeist manifestations, offer us clues as to the power of the mind because of the very nature of the manifestations and the time in the witness's life when they arise. It follows then, that poltergeists represent some of the mind's most powerful abilities—the ability to manipulate the physical world beyond the body. This is referred to in poltergeist material as Recurrent Spontaneous Psycho Kinesis (RSPK). The spontaneity of these manifestations makes them very difficult to examine in laboratory conditions, but psychokinesis (PK) has been subjected to analytical study with fascinating results. But before examining the claims of PK, we look at a strange claim of manipulation—thoughtography.

Thoughtography

It was Tomokichi Fukaria, president of Psychical Research Japan, who, in the early 1900s, coined the term "thoughtography." Fukaria saw spontaneous images appear on film when working with medium Mrs. Nagao and others. He became the first person to report on the phenomenon.

The most famous claim for thoughtography—the ability to photograph a mental impression—was made by a man named Ted Serios in 1964. He performed as part of experimental research for Dr. Jule Eisenbud in Denver, Colorado. His technique was to point a camera at his own face, concentrate on it, take a picture and see what happened. For the most part he got photographs of his own, intense face. But there were several photographs that caused a great deal of controversy. For example, one series of photographs taken in May 1965 were of a store frontage in Central City, Colorado. The photographs showed the name of the shop "The Old Gold Store." However, it had been many years since the store had used that name; its present name on its sign was "The Old Wells Fargo Express Office." In an effort to prove fraud, Eisenbud tried to find an old photograph of the store as it once was, but failed to do so. But there was even more mystery associated with Serios" mental photograph, which would have overruled any claims of fraudulence if an old photograph had been found to exist. The photographs taken by Serios showed the store front name misspelt. In his photographs it read "The Wld Gold store"; the "W" was positioned exactly where the "W" of "Wells" appeared in the modern sign.

Nor was that the only uncanny alteration. One of Serios' photographs was of an aircraft hanger belonging to the Royal

Canadian Mounted Police. But "Canadian" seems to have been misspelt as "Sainadain" and the "O" of Mounted is more like "D." And a thoughtograph of the Williams Livery Stable in Colorado, while generally accurate, actually shows different brick facing and even bricked-out windows that are not true of the real building.

Not all the images were local; Serios' thoughtographs showed scenes from Washington, Venice, London, and other places.

Unfortunately the flow of material for researchers was cut off when Serios lost his abilities. After a short period he simply was unable to produce any more thoughtographs. The fact that he had used a Polaroid camera suggested that there was no room for fraud in a darkroom—the film developed a print within the camera itself—but it also meant there was no negative for scientists to analyse.

One concern for researchers was the object Serios called a "gismo" which he held in his hand and would not let experimenters see. But when he did finally surrender it, it turned out to be an empty container. Could "faked" images have been held in the gismo? Could Serios, in full view of others, have substituted the images for those coming from the camera, or used the gismo to take the strange photographs in the first place? Controversy raged for a long time, but with Serios now literally out of the picture no further analysis could be done.

If Serios was not faking and was genuinely producing thoughtographs, a further controversy is generated within paranormal research. Those taking photographs of UFOs, ghosts and the like could arguably be making images of what they want or believe they are seeing and imprinting them on the film. It would make an already difficult area of the paranormal even more difficult to study. But it would possibly explain why some photographs of both UFOs and ghosts sent to researchers such as ourselves are accompanied by the comment: "I didn't see anything in the viewfinder when I took the picture."

Serios was not alone in producing such images, however. Another claimant was Willie Schwanholz who was examined by Professor Walter Uphoff, working in the USA in the 1980s. He used a Polaroid-type camera with the lens cap still on, which he would press to his forehead. He would move his head as he took the photograph; the resultant prints were often multiple images, as if he were taking a series of mental images on one print.

Yet another claimant was Masuaki Kiyota who produced thoughtographs under the scrutiny of scientists and television producers in Japan, though not in conditions of absolute control. For example, he could not produce images to order but could produce images when the camera was with him for a number of hours. Uphoff, who investigated the claims, believed them to be genuine, findings that were supported by film producer Alan Neuman, journalist David Tharp and Japanese scientist Professor Sasaki. Kiyota's thoughtographs produced quirks, as had Serios," but different quirks. In Kiyota's case he produced mirror-image photographs, the object seen in the upper half and duplicated and inverted in the bottom half of the frame.

Kiyota also produced moving-film images watched by Uphoff and photographer Yutaka Fakuda. In a three-minute sequence static images interspersed with black-outs showed the Tokyo Tower, several office and other blocks they thought might be from London, and the Statue of Liberty. Lastly, the image of a human face.

That a thought can be imposed on a piece of photographic paper seems outrageous, yet the evidence is there to be studied. But more generally, can thoughts and mind powers—under control—manipulate the world around us? The phenomenon of PK indicates that it can.

Psychokinesis (PK)

One extraordinary claim of the power of the human mind is its ability to move objects at a distance without physical contact. This is generally known as psychokinesis (PK).

It was Dr. Joseph Banks Rhine, most famous for his experiments into telepathy, who in the 1930s first conducted scientific experiments into PK at Duke University, North Carolina. Rhine was approached by a gambler who told him that he was capable of influencing the fall of dice on a gambling table; this triggered off Rhine's interest in the possibilities. To test the claim Rhine collected a group of volunteers and asked them to influence the fall of dice over a great many throws. If a higher number of pre-determined falls of one number could be measured, over and above that dictated by chance alone, then PK would be suggested, if not proven. Rhine believed that his experiments proved that PK was a reality, but in the years since sceptics have challenged almost every aspect of his work, claiming that it was not statistically sound, not properly supervised and so on.

In the 1970s physics professor John Hasted of Birkbeck College in London University conducted experiments into PK. He also reported positive outcomes in his experiments. One test subject, teenager Nicholas Williams, is said to have bent keys while at a distance from them and "rippled" aluminium sheeting. In some cases Hasted and Nicholas were together outside the room when the rippling was presumably taking place (judged by the fact that the metal was rippled on their return). Sceptics have argued that proof was not forthcoming simply because Hasted never witnessed the changes himself. Hasted set up another experiment asking PK test subjects to "scrunch" paperclips in a glass ball. It could be successfully accomplished only when there was a small hole in the ball, which led to the challenge that it must be fraudulent, despite the fact that the scrunching effect could not be duplicated in a normal way by pushing implements through the hole.

Both PK and poltergeist researchers have noticed that when evidence, even compelling evidence, is forthcoming it always falls a little short of absolute proof. There is always some room for doubt. It is as if an intelligence behind the process refuses to offer cast-iron proof but seeks to leave room for doubt. If we as-

sume, as in this case, that the intelligence behind the phenomenon is the human mind then why should it seek to leave that
"room for doubt"? We suggest that there is a natural "limiting
mechanism" in the human mind that prevents it from creating
effects that it would itself find too overwhelming for its own belief systems. The state of mind of the test subjects is also important, as in so many claims of the paranormal. Hasted found that
if he was empathetic towards the claims of a subject, if he believed in the subject's abilities and worked with the subject
rather than challenging him or her, the positive results were
more marked. It seemed that Hasted's own attitude helped to re-
inforce and strengthen the abilities of the subject. Empirical science does not like that kind of reasoning, but then history is
replete with the wrong scientific assumptions. Perhaps in the future science will be able to understand what mechanism in the
human mind alters the outcome of such experiments and why.

Work on PK has been conducted by many researchers, from
amateur enthusiasts to scientific institutions. During 1997
there were several breakthroughs that strongly suggest that PK
is a reality.

In November 1997 the Telegraph Group of newspapers reported on the claims of proof for the existence of PK. Since the
early 1980s Professor Robert Jahn and colleagues working at the
Princeton Engineering Anomalies Research Project (PEAR) were
undertaking large-scale testing to determine whether or not individuals could affect—by power of the mind—the output of a
random-event generator. Over 100 people took part in the experimentation, which PEAR's website states involves "millions of
trials." The equipment could produce either a one or a zero at
random; over a long period of time the output should be an equal
number of each. The purpose set for the test subjects was to affect—using their minds—the output of the equipment to create a
statistically significant bias. The team calculated that statistically significant bias arising by accident would not occur more
than once in 1,000 billion times.

The results were significant. Six out of nine different sets of experiments demonstrated statistically significant evidence for PK. Professor Jahn commented: "We believe that we now have pretty incontrovertible evidence for this phenomenon." He went on to add, of the population sample: "These effects seem to be broadly spread among human operators—it seems to be a common ability." The subjects affected several different pieces of equipment, all confirmed to be in working order prior to the experimentation. As a "control" the test subjects were asked to affect random-event generators whose functioning was based on fixed mathematical formulas—they should not have been able to do so; the output should not be subject to psychic influence—and indeed there were no measurable effects. This suggests that the experimental procedures were being correctly conducted and that the results were "real" and valid evidence of the phenomenon. "We would now lay claim to have the largest datasets and the most systematic experiments ever performed," Professor Jahn commented.

Even sceptics who normally reject such results in spite of the evidence were put to task by these experiments. Professor Stephen Donnelly of Salford University, and the deputy editor of *UK Skeptic* stated: "I have a lot more problems with these results as a sceptic."

One criticism that is often voiced by sceptics is that there is not enough testing and an insufficient range of subjects for the results to be significant. In this case such criticism would hardly be reasonable, but one sceptic took up a completely opposite stance to defend his position. Chris French, head of psychology at Goldsmiths' College, London, commented: "There's also a worry that with the huge number of trials needed, conventional statistical theory starts to break down."

Jahn and his colleagues regarded the proof as now in place and were determined to move on to establish the nature, rather than the existence, of the phenomenon. "We don't see much point in continuing the collection of yet more data. We're setting up experiments to get a better comprehension of these phenomena."

The Society for Research on Rapport and Telekinesis (SOR-RAT) had conducted a most exceptional series of tests in the 1960s and 1970s. The group, formed by Professor John Gneise-nau Neihardt, consisted largely of psychics. The testing was done within a framework of a seance-like atmosphere and re-sulted in many claims of almost "inspired poltergeistery." The whole group witnessed rappings, levitations, a planchette that "hopped like a frog," and more. They conducted experiments in sealed glass boxes and claimed successes with a wide range of results including the appearance of spontaneous writing, the suggestion of apports and disapports (in effect the teleportation of an object from within the box to the outside of the box) and un-connected rings becoming linked together.

They conducted spoon-bending experiments within a sealed glass bottle. The spoon was hung inside the sealed bottle and the group willed the spoon to bend, stroking the bottle. During one such attempt the spoon handle twisted and the bowl flattened until it jammed in the bottle.

"One of modern science's greatest puzzles" is the title of-fered to Nina Kulagina, a Russian housewife who demon-strated PK many times, first in the 1960s. She was tested by psychologist L. L. Vasiliev at The Institute for Brain Research in Leningrad. She could move objects apparently by force of will, and without contact, when they were under glass. Some of her work was filmed. Most famously she was able to separate the white and yolk of an egg; this was also filmed. Medical moni-tors attached to Kulagina during the experiments recorded that she lost weight and that her pulse and blood sugar responses were consistent with the responses that would usually be recorded by a person under stress.

Kulagina inspired a second famous PK experimenter, Felicia Parise. In 1971 Parise watched film of Kulagina's PK experiments and decided to try to reproduce them. She seemed unable to control the responses but there were spontaneous movements of objects, items flying off shelves around her for example, which suggested some random force was being generated from her. She seemed to be concerned about the randomness and gave up the experiments. It must be pointed out that Kulagina had also suffered from these random "bursts" though they did not dissuade her from continuing. These claims are reminiscent of the famous argument between Freud and Jung. Jung became angry during a heated debate with Freud and there was an explosive sound from a bookcase. Jung had reported feeling a change come over his body and he was of course in a moment of stress. Jung announced: "There, that is an example of a so called catalytic exteriorisation phenomenon." Freud was dismissive and the argument continued; then it happened again.

The *Daily Mail* of 17 May and 25 July 1996 reported the successes of Dr. Les Kirkup, a physicist working at the University of Technology in Sydney, Australia, who has invented a device that operates machinery by brainwaves. Three electrodes are secured to the head, and the brainwave output is amplified half a million times. This degree of power can operate household items such as televisions and video recorders. In demonstrations he was able to turn on a light, start up a toy and drive a model car on a track. According to one description, Kirkup "closed his eyes and relaxed, raising the voltage from his brain waves from 0.9 to 3.5. The desk-lamp across the room clicked on. As he opened his eyes, the voltage dropped and the light switched off."

Although this performance is not PK—the connections from the electrodes are sent by wires to the amplifier and that in turn sends an infra-red signal to the device—the fact is that the origination of the movement in the device comes from brainwaves on the part of the subject. The scientists have identified what they call a "mind switch" that exists when the brain moves from alpha waves (in relaxation) to theta waves (which occur when a person is more deeply asleep). Understanding "mind switch" will perhaps lead both to the understanding of PK and to its proper use.

Ashley Craig, a health science professor working in Australia, made the point: "What we have done is to identify signals within the brain which we believe everyone can control and devise some novel technology to pick and analyse those signals. Once analysed, those signals can be made to activate any device such as a household appliance."

We have noted that the "switch" is at the point of drowsiness and that many paranormal phenomena are said to occur during the transition from sleep to wakefulness and vice versa. Perhaps these periods are when the brain is most susceptible to paranormal perceptions and abilities. The fact that this is also when hallucinatory images are most common suggests that it is a time when its creative abilities come to the fore, and we have argued throughout this book that it is the creative part of the brain that is the key to the paranormal abilities.

Conclusion

The production of paranormal physical phenomena is a kind of skill which appears to be subject to the laws of learning; simple procedures have to be followed. As with professional skills... success is achieved by learning, example, practice, aptitude and experience. A step-by-step advance from simple and more plausible paranormal tasks is indicated. Belief and expectancy then snowball.

C. Brookes Smith and D. Hunt
Journal of the Society for Physical Research (Vol 47, 1973)

In this book we have examined claims that seem to indicate that the human mind is capable of extraordinary feats. But why should this be so? The most probable explanation is that these faculties developed in primitive humans, like any other ability or attribute, to enhance our chances of survival. Let us summarise the evidence in the light of this theory.

When dreaming, we occasionally get a glimpse of the paranormal. In the dream state the mind is functioning without the interference of the conscious mind. In fact, the conscious mind seems to be a barrier to using many of the mind powers; perhaps dreams are the first clue that there is more to the mind than is evident in our everyday lives. In lucid dreams some control over the dream can be achieved, and with practice perhaps our conscious mind could tap into the subconscious part of the mind and learn and develop from this contact.

Multiple Personality Syndrome is a clear indication that the conscious mind is not always aware of what is happening in other parts of the brain. MPS also shows the mind has the ability to control automatic body responses.

Some evidence from damaged minds—savants for example—shows that the mind is capable of working in quite exceptional ways when it does not "know the rules" or when it seeks to ignore them. There is no reason to believe that "normal" people cannot also access those abilities; the problem is that we have not yet found out how. Either savants have developed methods that other people have not developed, or they have an inherent approach that others have forgotten. But the fact remains that savants access their memories and perhaps other mind powers in ways that are different to those used by the majority of people.

Hypnosis seems to offer some insight into how the mind works; it produces an altered state that has similarity to the meditative state achieved by fakirs and athletes in "the zone." These altered states, again, suggest that we could use our minds in more efficient and effective ways.

We put forward the suggestion that the recent phenomenon of alien abduction may be evidence that the mind is seeking to develop itself or re-gain these natural psychic skills. We believe that these experiences—whatever their source—create conditions that experiencers generally find either deeply fascinating or very frightening, thereby pushing the mind to its limits and causing the right brain to open up. The brain "switches on" its most efficient powers in order to deal with the strangeness of the experience. Once activated, these right-brain abilities such as artistic talent remain active if the person seeks to develop them. The evidence from abduction research supports that those experiencers who take a positive attitude to their "abduction," and are aided by like-minded researchers, go on to develop spiritual and artistic qualities or acquire psychic abilities to dowse, to channel or to heal. Their "journeys" of personal development are similar to both near-death experiences and shamanic journeys, leading us to conclude that they are related experiences, or at least drawn from the same well. The manifestation of an alien technology may be no more than a modern translation of an age-old phenomenon. And like near-death experiences and shamanic journeys it is an experience that develops mind powers and talents.

Channellers, dowsers, mediums and the like all seem to have extraordinary ways of accessing information from the world at large or, possibly, information stored in their own unconscious. By letting go of their rational, calculating mind they seem to engage a "fast-track through memory," and perhaps a wider reach as well. Any aid to faster memory access must be a valuable aid to survival.

For most people "blasts" of psychic perception are a shock, and rarely occur. It fascinates them but they seldom learn to control it. Perhaps it was not always that way: perhaps humans were once in touch with those abilities for many everyday uses. Clearly this would have been a benefit to survival. To heal the body and to resist pain would have given our early ancestors the powers they needed to compete in a harsh environment, where individuals might have frequently found themselves cut off from tribal support. But these abilities would also have their disadvantages. A sick mind can create a sick body. If stigmata are evidence that the body can be physically affected by conviction and belief, does it not follow that a stressed and troubled mind can create cancers or ulcers?

In the near-death experience (NDE) we see the so-called life review. Before being offered the choice to go on into death or return, the person is "treated" to a review of his or her life. The life review sounds awfully like "my life flashed before me" reported by people who seemed to be facing certain death but lived to tell the tale. Can there be a survivalist explanation for this phenomenon? Could it be that the conscious mind in dire circumstances reviews the data in the unconscious very rapidly, trying to find any information that might help? A mind in desperation would "pull the stops out" and use otherwise atrophied abilities. This would suggest a practical, and non-paranormal, reason for the life review part of the experience, but it would not, on the other hand, mean that an inherent faculty could not come into play at other critical times, such as NDE. In short, the NDE might be a time when abilities to channel and access the memory more efficiently than usual come into play. If we could discover how to make it happen at will, we would have a powerful ability to hand.

This applies to all psychic skills. The ability to project the "self" to other locations, or to bi-locate, has obvious benefits for survival. Many who have had this experience were able to call for help in a psychic way—sometimes appearing as a "ghost." The information-gathering potential of the out-of-body experience is now appreciated by security services around the world. "Knowledge is power" and always has been, even for our ancestors.

It may be that our mind powers are self-regulating. In PK we see evidence that people can affect the material world by the force of their will, but the changes are minute. In RSPK, in poltergeist phenomena, we see enormous power unleashed. If this could be controlled how useful it might be; it would never matter if you lost the remote control to the television, or wanted to pass a book to someone. But conversely, it would be a force to fear in the wrong hands, or in this case perhaps we should say "in the wrong minds." Life would start to look like the dark side of a Stephen King thriller! Perhaps it is just as well that there is no evidence (yet!) that that sort of power can be controlled or learned.

Although we might have had or developed these physic abilities as a primitive animal, it seems we have lost them in the modern world. Like unused muscles, they show signs of lack of exercise. The rare manifestations are probably, at best, only a reminder of talents we once could bring to bear on the world around us. Why should we have lost such useful talents? Perhaps, by adapting the world to meet our needs, we have in the process reduced our need for the survival benefits associated with paranormal abilities.

We suggest that people have lost touch with these innate capabilities because they have chosen to depend on rationalism and technology. If that is true, then it poses one further question. Why should we—particularly in the West—have started to seek to re-gain use of these paranormal facilities?

This recent fascination for the paranormal gained momentum in the late 1960s. This probably came about for two reasons: first, the experimental use of hallucinogenic drugs may have awakened inherent abilities, or memories of abilities, and created a craving for those deeper perceptions; second, humankind had started to become its own predator, which rekindled our survival instincts. Since the late 1950s there has been a deep-seated fear of nuclear holocaust, which has greatly influenced recent generations; for instance, the peace movements arose from the 1960s' "Ban the Bomb" marches. In short, we may be feeling that the world is getting out of our control, and faced with new threats to our existence, we are calling on all our reserves for survival. If we expand the scope of our perceptions, we increase our chances of survival; for example, if we can "get in touch" with the natural planetary energies that we believe we have lost empathy for, then we might treat the planet more gently—the cornerstone of many "green" concepts. Since this is typical of the message channelled from, in particular, aliens, either the messengers share our concerns or the channellers are getting in touch with something within themselves.

In summary, the powers and mysteries of the mind reviewed in this book have, we believe, a common origin as a survival mechanism. As we became a technological species, our dependence on artificial devices numbed our capacity to use these natural talents. Indeed, there is a feeling in technological societies that we are fast becoming nothing more than extensions of our own machines. But inbred qualities take a long time to disappear completely; we believe that the so-called paranormal often represents "blasts" of accidental release of those powers under conditions of altered state, stress, meditation and so on. Experiments have confirmed the reality of certain of those qualities—telepathy and PK, for example—but in weak doses. Phenomena not usually regarded as mind powers—the appearance of ghosts, disruptions caused by poltergeists—may also be the power emissions from the mind breaking free spontaneously.

Although most people accept with gratitude the advantages that scientific and technological progress has offered, there has been a growing feeling in recent decades that science and technology are moving too fast for our own good. We believe that this fear has stimulated both an interest in the paranormal and an active quest to re-gain those abilities so that we can live in harmony with our environment.

The quest is not to confront science, nor to challenge it, for science is both inevitable and valuable. The challenge is to develop the individual at the same pace as science and technology, and to reconcile the best of the new with the best of the old.

Bibliography, References and Recommended Reading

Allen, Thomas, *Possessed*, Doubleday, 1993

Bernstein, Morey, *The Search for Bridey Murphy*, Bantam, 1990

Blackmore, Susan, *Dying To Live*, Grafton, 1993

Carrington, Hereward, *The Story of Psychic Science*, Rider, 1930

Cassirer, Manfred, *The Persecution of Mr. Tony Elms (The Bromley Poltergeist)*, privately published, 1993

Cassirer, Manfred, *Medium on Trial*, PN Publishing, 1996

Chopra, Deepak, M.D., *Quantum Healing*, Bantam, 1989

Clark, Arthur C., *World of Strange Powers*, Collins, 1989

Crichton, Michael, *Travels*, Pan Books, 1988

Dennett, Daniel C., *Consciousness Explained*, Penguin, 1991

Evans, Hilary, *Visions, Apparitions, Alien Visitors, A Comparative Study of the Entity Enigma*, Aquarian Press, 1984

Evans, Hilary, *Gods, Spirits, Cosmic Guardians*, Aquarian Press, 1987

Fairley, John & Welfare, Simon, *Arthur C. Clarke's World of Strange Powers*, Collins, 1990

Fenimore, Angie, *Beyond Darkness: My Near-Death Journey to Hell and Back*, Simon & Schuster, 1995

Fenwick, Peter & Fenwick, Elizabeth, *The Truth in the Light, An Investigation of Over 300 Near Death Experiences*, Headline, 1995

Frank, Gerald, *The Boston Strangler*, Handbooks Ltd, 1996

Fuller, John G., *The Ghost of Flight 401*, Souvenir Press, 1978

Fuller, John G., *The Interrupted Journey: Two Lost Hours Aboard a Flying Saucer*, Souvenir Press, 1980

Graham, Billy, *Angels: God's Secret Agents*, Hodder & Stoughton, 1995

Gregory, Richard L., (ed.) *The Oxford Companion to the Mind*, Oxford University Press, 1987

Gurney, Edmund, Myers, Frederick W. H., & Podmore, Frank, *Phantasms of The Living*, Kegan, Paul, Trench, Trubner & Co, 1918

Harrison, Ted, *Stigmata*, HarperCollins, 1994

Hickson, Charles & Mendez, William, *UFO Contact at Pascagoula*, privately published, 1983

Hopkins, Budd, *Missing Time*, Ballantine, 1981

Hopkins, Budd, *Intruders*, Random House, 1987

Hopkins, Budd, *Witnessed*, Simon & Schuster, 1996

Huxley, Aldous, *The Devils of Loudun*, Penguin Books, 1973

Kalweit, Holger, *Shamans, Healers and Medicine Men*, Shambhala, 1992

Karle, Hellmut, *The Filthy Lie*, Hamish Hamilton, 1992

Moody, J.R.M.D., Raymond A., *Life After Life*, Phantom Books, 1976

Morehouse, David, *Psychic Warrior*, Michael Joseph, 1996

Morse, Dr. Melvin with Perry, Paul, *Transformed by The Light*, Piatkus, 1993

Myers, Frederick W. H., *Human Personality and Its Survival of Bodily Death*, Longmans, Green and Co, 1927

Ornstein, Robert, *The Evolution of Consciousness*, Prentice Hall, 1991

Ostrander, Sheila & Schroeder, Lynn, *Psychic Discoveries: The Iron Curtain Lifted*, Souvenir Press, 1997

Pearson, John, *Bluebird and the Dead Lake*, Fontana, 1965

Perry, Michael (ed.), *Deliverance*, SPCK, 1987

Playfair, Guy Lyon, *This House Is Haunted*, Souvenir Press, 1980

Rhine, J. B., *The Reach of the Mind*, William Sloane Associates Inc, 1947

Richards, John Thomas, *SORRAT, A History of The Neihardt Psycho-Kinesis Experiments 1961–1981*, The Scarecrow Press, 1982

Ring, Kenneth, Ph.D., *The Omega Project*, William Morrow, 1992

Robbins, Tony, *Unlimited Power*, Fawcett, 1987

Rogo, D. Scott, *Life After Death*, Geld Publishing, 1986

St. Clair, David, *Child Possessed*, Corgi Books, 1982

Schnabel, Jim, *Remote Viewers: The Secret History of America's Psychic Spies*, Dell Publishing, 1997

Solomon, Grant, *Psychic Surgeon*, Thorsons, 1997

Spencer, John, *Gifts of the Gods?*, Virgin, 1994

Spencer, John and Anne, *Spirit Within Her*, Boxtree, 1994

Spencer, John and Anne, *Alien Contact*, Orion, 1997

Spencer, John and Anne, *Poltergeist Phenomenon*, Headline, 1997

Stephenson, Ian, M.D., *Twenty Cases Suggestive of Reincarnation*, The University Press of Virginia, 1974

Treffert, Darrold A., *Extraordinary People*, Black Swan, 1990

Tyler, Kelsey, *There's an Angel on Your Shoulder, Angel Encounters in Everyday Life*, Berkeley Books, New York, 1994

Wilson, Colin (ed.), *The Mammoth Book of the Supernatural*, Robinson, 1991

Wilson, Colin, *The Psychic Detectives*, Pan Books, 1984

About the Authors

John and Anne Spencer have been active researchers of the parnormal for over twenty years. John is Chairman of the British UFO Research Association and they are both members of several international organizations on the paranormal. They are at the forefront of experimental work and research into many unsolved mysteries. Both John and Anne have lectured to paranormal groups around the world, and they regularly appear in the media. They have an extensive list of publications in the UK.

About the Authors

Also available from TV Books:
these other books in

The True-Life Encounter Series

Alien Contact by John and Anne Spencer

Has Earth already been visited by beings from elsewhere? Have alien beings made contact with people of Earth? John and Anne Spencer, active researchers of the paranormal for over twenty years, examine the evidence.

320 pages; ISBN 1–57500–023-7; US $12.95, Canada $19.00.

Unexplained Natural Phenomena by Keith Tutt

In an era of conservative-minded science, how do we explain inexplicable natural phenomena such as ball lightning and sightings of the Loch Ness monster? Keith Tutt, an award-winning documentarian, looks into these strange occurences.

304 pages; ISBN 1–57500–024-5; US $12.95, Canada $19.00.

UFO Sightings by Alan Baker

Every year, people all over the world report seeing unusual objects in the sky. What are these unidentified flying objects? Alan Baker, author of the *Encyclopedia of Alien Encounters*, offers explanations.

304 pages; ISBN 1–57500–022-9; US $12.95, Canada $19.00.

Ghosts and Spirits by Alan Baker

Even today, in our wired, technological world, life after death and the presence of undefined spirits consumes our interest. Alan Baker brings us an encyclopedic discussion of ghosts and spirits through the ages in this comprehensive volume.

304 pages; ISBN 1–57500–027-X; US $12.95, Canada $19.00.

Mysteries and Magic by John and Anne Spencer

From the beginning of time, we have been obsessed with magic, witchcraft, the unexplained. John and Anne Spencer take us on a comprehensive tour of magic and mysteries throught the ages.

304 pages; ISBN 1–57500–030-X; US $12.95, Canada $19.00.

Available wherever books are sold, or call 1-800-331-3761.